HOW TO START AND FINISH STRONG
COLLEGE PREP
VOLUME 1

A MOSTLY SCRIPTURE APPROACH

Thomas Witzig

Jesus said, "I will show you what someone is like who comes to me, hears my words, and acts on them: He is like a man building a house, who dug deep and laid the foundation on the rock. When the flood came, the river crashed against that house and couldn't shake it, because it was well built." - Luke 6:47-48 CSB

"For no one can lay any other foundation than what has been laid down. That foundation is Jesus Christ." - 1 Corinthians 3:11 CSB

With deep appreciation to my wife Diane for her support and dedicated to our grandsons Graham and Peter that they may build their lives on a solid spiritual foundation.

Note: The series **How to Start and Finish Strong** has two volumes:

College Prep Volume 1 – A Mostly Scripture Approach
College Prep Volume 2 – Key Strategies for Spiritual Growth

There are corresponding eBook versions with all Bible verses fully expanded. The Appendix is the same in both Volumes.

HOW TO START AND FINISH STRONG
COLLEGE PREP
VOLUME 1

A MOSTLY SCRIPTURE APPROACH

THOMAS WITZIG

College Prep Volume 1 – A Mostly Scriptural Approach by Thomas Witzig

Copyright © 2024 by Thomas Witzig
All Rights Reserved.
ISBN: 978-1-59755-782-5

Published by: ADVANTAGE BOOKS™, Longwood, FL. www.advbookstore.com

All Rights Reserved. This book and parts thereof may not be reproduced in any form, stored in a retrieval system or transmitted in any form by any means (electronic, mechanical, photocopy, recording or otherwise) without prior written permission of the author, except as provided by United States of America copyright law.

Scripture quotations marked CSB have been taken from The Christian Standard Bible®, copyright©. 2017 by Holman Bible Publishers. Used by permission. Christian Standard Bible® and CSB® are federally registered trademarks of Holman Bible Publishers.

Scriptures marked NIV are taken from The Holy Bible, New International Version ®. Copyright© 1973, 1978, 1984, 2011 by Biblica, Inc.™. Used by permission of Zondervan.

Scriptures marked ESV are taken from The Holy Bible, English Standard Version® Copyright© 2001 by Crossway, a publishing ministry of Good News Publishers. Used by permission.

Scripture quotations marked (NLT) are taken from The Holy Bible, New Living Translation, copyright ©1996, 2004, 2015 by Tyndale House Foundation. Used by permission of Tyndale House Publishers, Carol Stream, Illinois 60188. All rights reserved.

Scriptures marked KJV are taken from The Holy Bible King James Version and are public domain.

Library of Congress Catalog Number: 2024937349

Name:	Witzig, Thomas Author
Title:	*College Prep Volume 1 – A Mostly Scriptural Approach*
	Thomas Witzig
	Advantage Books, 2024
Identifiers:	ISBN Paperback: 9781597557825
	ISBN eBook: 9781597557986
Subjects:	RELIGION: Christian Life – Inspirational
	RELIGION: Christian Life – Spiritual Growth

First Printing: November 2024
24 25 26 27 28 29 30   10 9 8 7 6 5 4 3 2 1

Table of Contents

FOREWORD 7

1: WHAT IS THE BIBLE AND WHY IS IT OUR SOURCE OF TRUTH? 11

2: THE NATURE AND ATTRIBUTES OF GOD THE FATHER 23

3: WHO IS JESUS AND WHAT IS HE LIKE? IS JESUS GOD? 45

4: WHO IS THE HOLY SPIRIT AND WHAT ARE HIS FUNCTIONS? 89

5: WHAT IS TRUTH? - A BIBLICAL VIEW 111

6: THE TEN COMMANDMENTS - A CONCISE OVERVIEW 129

7: PRAYER – WHAT IS IT? WHY IS IT IMPORTANT? HOW TO DO IT? 139

8: GENESIS 1-11 INTERPRETING CURRENT ISSUES WITH A BIBLICAL WORLDVIEW 165

EPILOGUE 253

APPENDIX 255

Thomas Witzig

Foreword

As students complete high school and prepare for college, trade school or a first job they must make many key decisions. These issues are important at any time in life but especially in the late teen years and early 20's where these choices will impact the course of the rest of their life and their level of spiritual maturity. What truths will guide them? Will they be able to defend them when they leave home, family, and friends and enter the world on their own?

As I was writing this book a new research building was going up outside the parking deck at my workplace. Over many months I watched the detailed efforts to construct the foundation of this massive building. Wiring and pipes of all types were carefully laid deep in the ground and then covered with tons of sand and concrete. Now the building is rising quickly above ground, and that foundation is completely covered and invisible. But I know what is under there and how difficult it would be to ever change it. *Like this building, a solid spiritual foundation is vital to life, and it needs to be built on Biblical truth* **(Figure 1)**.

Thomas Witzig

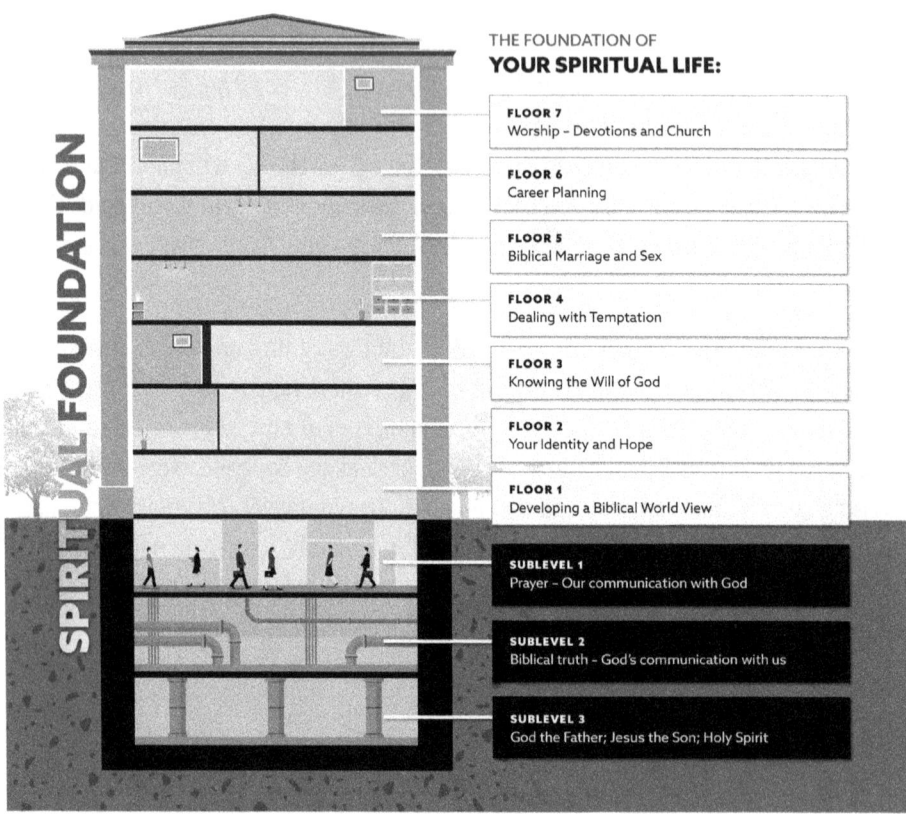

Figure 1: The sublevel of any building is unseen after the building is erected but it determines how the building will hold up to the storms that will come. Likewise, your spiritual life is built on a foundation of understanding God the Father, God the Son Jesus, and God the Holy Spirit. God communicates truth through His Word the Bible. We communicate with God by reading His Book and praying. We then build our spiritual life on this solid foundation so that we can face the crises in life and finish strong.

In this book, the Bible is the main text (hence the title *Mostly Scripture*). Dr. Martyn Lloyd-Jones, a well-known English preacher of the twentieth century said, "There is nothing more important in the Christian life than the way in which we approach the Bible, and the way in which we read it. It is our textbook, it is our only source, it is our only authority. We know nothing about God and about the Christian life in a true sense apart from the Bible." All of the problems we will experience in life have already been addressed in the Bible so that we can be prepared. There are other books with advice on these topics, but it is important that we are grounded on what God, our Creator and Designer, has to say. In this book, the Bible is the source document for all the topics, and it never goes out of date! The bolded headings are meant to highlight the nuggets of truth in the Bible passages. The frequent questions aim to stimulate the reader to apply the Biblical concepts to their own life and guide the discussion with others if the book is being used in a small group. Do not avoid these as they are intended as real-world current examples of what the Bible is talking about.

Volume 1 contains 8 chapters that will establish the foundation on which to build your spiritual life. Before studying Genesis 1-11 in Chapter 8, we need to understand some foundational concepts. What is the Bible and why do we use it as our source of truth? Who is the God of the Bible? Who is Jesus? Who is the Holy Spirit? What are their characteristics? Why do I need prayer to communicate with them? To be a Christian is to know and understand who Jesus Christ is. You cannot be a Christian without Christ – it's impossible. We will learn all of this from the Bible.

Before starting, how does your physical age compare with your spiritual age? They often do not correlate with each other. Using the diagram in **Figure 2** where do you place yourself? You cannot change your physical age, but you can grow spiritually. Your spiritual growth is a continuum from your first day of life as a Christian until you die.

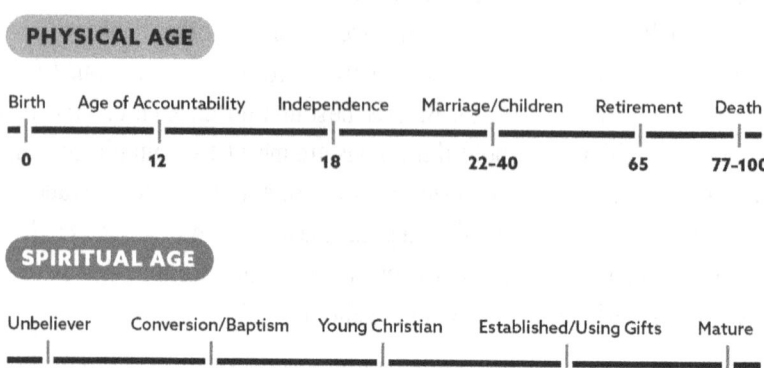

Figure 2: Mark your physical and spiritual ages before and after you finish the course. The goal is to grow spiritually.

This book is designed for those who are followers of Jesus Christ (Christians or Christ-followers, believers). If you are not sure about that decision, then first read the **Appendix** which shows you the way to believe in Jesus as your personal sacrifice for sin and become a Christ-follower. If you are already a Christ-follower, then jump right into Chapter 1!

1

What is the Bible and Why is it Our Source of Truth?

The Word of God, the Bible, is the primary way that God communicates with us and is the most powerful book you will ever read. Although written over 2,000 years ago, the principles still remain relevant today. However, the truths need to be read and applied to each of us personally in each generation. The purpose of the Bible is to be our guidebook for living and to tell us how to receive forgiveness for our sins and attain the promise of eternal life. It also gives us power to live a victorious life in this rather dark world. Jesus reminds us of our need for knowing the Bible in Mark 12:24, "Jesus replied, 'Your mistake is that you don't know the Scriptures, and you don't know the power of God.'" - Mark 12:24 NLT.

• ***The Bible is a collection of individual books***. The Bible (derived from the Greek word *biblia* or books), consists of 66 "books" sometimes referred to as letters (**Figure 3**). These books were written over a period of some 1200 years from 1100 B.C. to 100 AD. by multiple authors. In most cases we know who the writer was. The Old Testament contains the old covenant that God made with Israel, the people group that would eventually bring the Messiah Jesus into the world. "Now if you will carefully listen to me and keep my covenant, you will be my own possession out of all the peoples, although the whole earth is mine, and you will be my kingdom of priests and my holy nation.' These are the words that you are to say to the Israelites." - Exodus 19:5-6 CSB. The New Testament describes the eyewitness accounts of the coming of the Messiah Jesus. Jesus established the new covenant with His blood sacrifice for our sins. He was the ultimate sacrifice, the only one we now need to claim, to absolve of us our sins and obtain eternal life in Heaven. Jesus Himself said this: "In the same way he also took the cup after supper and said, 'This cup is the *new covenant in my blood*, which is poured out *for you*.'" - Luke 22:20 CSB. The authors of the Bible were inspired by the Holy Spirit to do the writing. This is why Old Testament authors could write about Jesus even though He was not coming to this earth for thousands of years.

Figure 3: The 66 books of the Bible. The first 5 books of the Old Testament are called the Pentateuch or Torah and were completed about 400 BC. The other books were written later – Historical and Prophetical around 200 B.C; the Poetical books about 100 BC. The New Testament books were all completed by 100 A.D.

OLD TESTAMENT - 39 BOOKS

LAW – 5
- GENESIS
- EXODUS
- LEVITICUS
- NUMBERS
- DEUTERONOMY

POETRY – 5
- JOB
- PSALMS
- PROVERBS
- ECCLESIASTES
- SONG OF SOLOMON

MAJOR PROPHETS – 5
- ISAIAH
- JEREMIAH
- LAMENTATIONS
- EZEKIEL
- DANIEL

HISTORY – 12
- JOSHUA
- JUDGES
- RUTH
- 1 SAMUEL
- 2 SAMUEL
- 1 KINGS
- 2 KINGS
- 1 CHRONICLES
- 2 CHRONICLES
- EZRA
- NEHEMIAH
- ESTHER

MINOR PROPHETS – 12
- HOSEA
- JOEL
- AMOS
- ORADIAH
- JONAH
- MICAH
- NAHUM
- HABAKKUK
- ZEPHANIAH
- HAGGAI
- ZECHARIAH
- MALACHI

1: What is the Bible and Why is it Our Source of Truth?

NEW TESTAMENT - 27 BOOKS

GOSPELS - 4
- MATTHEW
- MARK
- LUKE
- JOHN

PAUL'S LETTERS TO FRIENDS - 4
- 1 TIMOTHY
- 2 TIMOTHY
- TITUS
- PHILEMON

HISTORY - 1
- ACTS

PAUL'S LETTERS TO CHURCHES - 9
- ROMANS
- 1 CORINTHIANS
- 2 CORINTHIANS
- GALATIANS
- EPHESIANS
- PHILIPPIANS
- COLOSSIANS
- 1 THESSALONIANS
- 2 THESSALONIANS

GENERAL LETTERS - 9
- HEBREWS
- JAMES
- 1 PETER
- 2 PETER
- 1 JOHN
- 2 JOHN
- 3 JOHN
- JUDE
- REVELATION

The original text of the Bible did not have chapters and verses. The chapter divisions commonly used today were developed by Stephen Langton, an Archbishop of Canterbury. Langton put the modern chapter divisions into place in around A.D. 1227. The Wycliffe English Bible of 1382 was the first Bible to use this chapter pattern. Since the Wycliffe Bible, nearly all Bible translations have followed Langton's chapter divisions. https://www.gotquestions.org/divided-Bible-chapters-verses.html, accessed November 25, 2022.

The Hebrew Old Testament was divided into verses by a Jewish rabbi by the name of Nathan in A.D. 1448. Robert Estienne, who was also known as Stephanus, was the first to divide the New Testament into standard numbered verses in 1555. Stephanus essentially used Nathan's verse divisions for the Old Testament. Since that time, beginning with the Geneva Bible, the chapter and verse divisions employed by Stephanus have been accepted into nearly all of the Bible versions. Additional information regarding the history of the Bible and the different versions is beyond the scope of this book. A concise overview can be found in *A Handbook of the Christian Faith* by John Schwarz Bethany House, 2004.

• ***The Bible was inspired by the Holy Spirit***. The Bible is inspired by God and no matter what stage of life you are in or your cultural group or gender, the Bible will speak truth to you. The Bible is like a kaleidoscope— by reading it regularly and listening to what it is saying, it will speak differently as you experience life events. It never gets old and has no expiration date. This is the only Book that you can and will read many times over and over and it will never grow old.

Tips for reading the Bible.

• ***You need to actually read it***! The truths of the Bible will not jump from the desk, or the computer screen into your brain without actually reading or listening to it! Although you will likely read the Bible on a computer or phone, I recommend you own at least 1 print version of the Bible so that you can see, feel, and get the big picture as to how the Bible and its books, chapters, and verses fit together. This is more difficult to grasp with an electronic version. Also, a print Bible is nice when you are "off the grid", the power goes off, or perhaps you live in an area of the world where your phone is monitored by others. If you need a print Bible and cannot afford one, please request one from the author at telmer@duck.com. Read at least 10 minutes a day or have it read to you while walking or riding.

• ***Read with a purpose, not just for knowledge***. When reading the Bible, read for application. Ask yourself, "What is the Bible saying to me about what is going on in my life right now?"

• ***Pray before you read.*** Ask God, "reveal to me from the Bible, the help I need to handle the situation(s) I am going to face in my life today".

Why read the Bible?

• ***The Bible is an instruction book.***

"For whatever was written in the past was written for our instruction, so that we may have hope through endurance and through the encouragement from the Scriptures." - Romans 15:4 CSB

- ***It is the Word of the God of the Universe — we want to know what He says.***
"For the word of God is full of living power. It is sharper than the sharpest knife, cutting deep into our innermost thoughts and desires. It exposes us for what we really are." Hebrews 4:12, NLT.

- ***It is truth, and we can trust it.***
"For the word of the LORD is right, and all his work is trustworthy." - Psalm 33:4 CSB

- ***It cannot be held back.***
"And because I preach this Good News, I am suffering and have been chained like a criminal. But the word of God cannot be chained." 2 Timothy 2:9, NLT.

- ***It is permanent and relevant.*** Permanent means it never gets old. Relevant means it is for all ages and all cultures. The application of Biblical truth always needs to be individualized to each person and generation.
"Heaven and earth will disappear, but my words will remain forever." Luke 21:33, NLT.

"As the prophet says, 'People are like grass that dies away; their beauty fades as quickly as the beauty of wildflowers. The grass withers, and the flowers fall away. But the word of the Lord will last forever.' And that word is the Good News that was preached to you." 1 Peter 1:24, 25, NLT.

- ***It reveals the path for us. If we follow our own way, we get into trouble as the Israelites did.***

"Your word is a lamp for my feet and a light for my path." Psalm 119:105, NLT.

"You are not to do as we are doing here today; *everyone is doing whatever seems right in his own sigh*t." - Deuteronomy 12:8 CSB

Questions:

1. Why is the Bible "timeless"? How is the Bible different than a scientific publication?

2. What do we mean when we say that Biblical truths are "principle-based"? How does that affect their ability to be "timeless?"

3. Is the Bible reliable?

4. What is a metaphor? Why is it important to understand metaphorical writing?

Questions with suggested answers:

1. Why is the Bible "timeless"? How is the Bible different than a scientific publication?

Answer: Any field of science is continuously advancing. In the medical world that I work in the treatments and diagnostic tests change often. For example, if you were interested in knowing how to evaluate and treat a patient with new, untreated Hodgkin Lymphoma and read a publication from the 1970's you would read about doing a lymphangiogram and a staging abdominal operation. Today, neither technique is used – instead we have the PET/CT scan. The Bible however teaches us through foundational principles that will never go out of date and can be applied to all people groups.

2. What do we mean when we say that Biblical truths are "principle-based"? How does that affect their ability to be "timeless"?

Answer: Concepts (Biblical or otherwise) are timeless. The concepts of how to question and examine a patient and the concepts of gentleness and compassion are indeed timeless, but the technical side changes. Although I have written many scientific papers that have been published, few if any will be referenced or quoted 10 years from now. The Bible is different because it is written by God, and the principles (such as the Ten Commandments) are timeless. I often joke with my pastor friends that they can pull out a sermon they preached 30 years ago, quickly update the examples, and use it again. The same cannot be said of technical writing.

3. Is the Bible reliable?

Answer: Yes, for two main reasons – firstly, the authors were inspired by God the Holy Spirit. "Above all, you must understand that no prophecy in Scripture ever came from the prophets themselves or because they wanted to prophesy. It was the Holy Spirit who moved the prophets to speak from God." 2 Peter 1:20, 21, NLT.

Paul said to Timothy – "All Scripture is inspired by God and is profitable for teaching, for rebuking, for correcting, for training in righteousness," - 2 Timothy 3:16 CSB. Peter said that King David wrote under the guidance of the Holy Spirit - "You said through the Holy Spirit, by the mouth of our father David your servant: Why do the

Gentiles rage and the peoples plot futile things?" - Acts 4:25 CSB. Secondly, many of the authors were eyewitnesses to what they wrote.

Luke writes at the beginning of his recorded gospel, "Many have undertaken to compile a narrative about the events that have been fulfilled among us, *just as the original eyewitnesses and servants of the word handed them down to us.* It also seemed good to me, since I have carefully investigated everything from the very first, to write to you in an orderly sequence, most honorable Theophilus, *so that you may know the certainty of the things about which you have been instructed."* - Luke 1:1-4 CSB

Peter also was an eyewitness to history and clearly tells us that his writing was factual. "For we did not follow cleverly contrived myths when we made known to you the power and coming of our Lord Jesus Christ; instead, we were eyewitnesses of his majesty. For he received honor and glory from God the Father when the voice came to him from the Majestic Glory, saying 'This is my beloved Son, with whom I am well-pleased! " We ourselves heard this voice when it came from heaven while we were with him on the holy mountain.'" - 2 Peter 1:16-18 CSB. The "holy mountain" is in reference to the mount of transfiguration experience Peter personally had with Jesus (see Matthew 17).

John writes also as an eyewitness. "What was from the beginning, *what we have heard, what we have seen with our eyes*, what we have observed and have touched with our hands, concerning the word of life -- that life was revealed, and *we have seen it and we testify and declare to you* the eternal life that was with the Father and was revealed to us -- what we have seen and heard we also declare to you, so that you may also have fellowship with us; and indeed our fellowship is with the Father and with his Son Jesus Christ." - 1 John 1:1-3 CSB

4. What is a metaphor? Why is it important to understand metaphorical writing?

Answer: According to Webster's Dictionary:

https://www.merriam-webster.com/dictionary/metaphor a metaphor is "a figure of speech in which a word or phrase literally denoting one kind of object or idea is used in place of another to suggest a likeness or analogy between them (as in drowning in money)." Metaphors are very common in the Scriptures and important to understand. Read Psalm 19 below and identify the metaphors regarding the physical world we live in. "The heavens declare the glory of God, and the expanse proclaims the work of his hands. Day after day they pour out speech; night after night they communicate knowledge. There is no speech; there are no words; their voice is not heard. Their message has gone out to the whole earth, and their words to the ends of the world. In the heavens he has pitched a tent for the sun. It is like a bridegroom coming from his home; it rejoices like an athlete running a course. It rises from one end of the heavens and circles to their other end; nothing is hidden from its heat. The instruction of the LORD is perfect, renewing one's life; the testimony of the LORD is trustworthy, making the inexperienced wise. The precepts of the LORD are right, making the heart glad; the command of the LORD is radiant, making the eyes light up. The fear of the LORD is pure, enduring forever; the ordinances of the LORD are reliable and altogether righteous. They are more desirable than gold -- than an abundance of pure gold; and sweeter than honey dripping from a honeycomb. In addition, your servant is warned by them, and in keeping them there is an abundant reward. Who perceives his unintentional sins? Cleanse me from my hidden faults. Moreover, keep your servant from willful sins; do not let them rule me. Then I will be blameless and cleansed from blatant rebellion. May the words of my mouth and the meditation of my heart be acceptable to you, LORD, my rock and my Redeemer." - Psalm 19:1-14 CSB

More reasons to read the Bible.

• It is "God's Word" written by the Trinity through revelation to human writers.
"Above all, you must understand that no prophecy in Scripture ever came from the prophets themselves or because they wanted to prophesy. It was the Holy Spirit who moved the prophets to speak from God." 2 Peter 1:20, 21, NLT.

• The Bible is a complete revelation—nothing needs to be added or subtracted.
Revelation 22:18, 19.

• Reading the Bible is associated with strength and with the living not the dead.
1 John 2:14.

• Knowledge of God is a "multiplier" of grace and peace.
"May grace and peace be multiplied to you through the knowledge of God and of Jesus our Lord." - 2 Peter 1:2 CSB

• The Word of God is strong like a fire. It is better than a dream.
Jeremiah 23:28-29

- **Reading the Bible always produces fruit.**
"It is the same with my word. I send it out, and it always produces fruit. It will accomplish all I want it to, and it will prosper everywhere I send it." Isaiah 55:11, NLT.

- **Reading the Bible reminds us of what we need to do. All of us need "wake-up calls".** 2 Peter 3:1-2.

- **When we preach and teach, we do it using arguments from Scripture.**
"As usual, Paul went into the synagogue, and on three Sabbath days *reasoned with them from the Scriptures*, explaining and proving that it was necessary for the Messiah to suffer and rise from the dead: This Jesus I am proclaiming to you is the Messiah." - Acts 17:2-3 CSB

"Now a Jew named Apollos, a native Alexandrian, an eloquent man w*ho was competent in the use of the Scriptures,* arrived in Ephesus." - Acts 18:24 CSB

Questions:

1. Why is reading the Bible necessary your entire life?

2. Why do I need a print version of the Bible? I don't want to carry that around.

3. Which version should I read?

4. What if I have trouble understanding what I am reading?

5. Do I need to read the Old Testament too?

Questions with suggested answers:

1. Why is reading the Bible necessary your entire life?

Answer: People usually read a book, even a really good book, only once. The Bible is different because some verses will be more pertinent in the different phases of your life. It is also written for all generations and people groups (as long as it is available in various languages). God speaks to you through the Bible; therefore, you have to read it often. Give God a chance to speak truth into your life, it will be well worth it. We also have to be reminded as we forget. Peter said, "Dear friends, this is now the second letter I have written to you; in both letters, I want to stir up your sincere understanding by way of reminder, so that you recall the words previously spoken by the holy prophets and the command of our Lord and Savior given through your apostles." - 2 Peter 3:1-2 CSB. Lastly, we need to know the Bible so that we can detect false teaching. Peter again says, "Above all, be aware of this: Scoffers will come in the last days scoffing and following their own evil desires." - 2 Peter 3:3 CSB

2. Why do I need a print version of the Bible? I don't want to carry that around.

Answer: The Bible is now readily accessible on our phones and computers via the internet. It is very convenient to be able to read it anywhere or listen to it during a walk or your commute. However, you need at least one print copy of the Bible in your personal library. The reasoning here is for you to understand how the Books of the Bible are organized and fit together. Also, it is likely there will come a time when accessing the Bible on the internet will be banned or monitored. Having that print copy is vital.

3. Which version should I read?

Answer: Read a version that is an accurate translation of the original writings and is readable for you in your language of preference ('mother tongue'). Go to the internet site "Blue Letter Bible https://www.blueletterbible.org or Bible Gateway https://www.biblegateway.com where you can display the Bible text in multiple versions and select the one you find is easiest for you to understand. Most of the versions quoted in this book are from the Christian Standard Bible (CSB), the New Living Translation (NLT) and the New International Version (NIV). Other excellent translations are the English Standard Version (ESV), King James Version (KJV, also known as the Authorized), and the New American Standard Bible 2020 (NASB20). The Message and The New Living Bible are paraphrases and are also easily readable. If you use the *Blue Letter Bible* app on the internet you can read the verse in question on all these versions at once using the Tools tab, followed by the Bible tab (**Figure 4**). Reading the same verse in several translations will help explain the meaning.

1: What is the Bible and Why is it Our Source of Truth?

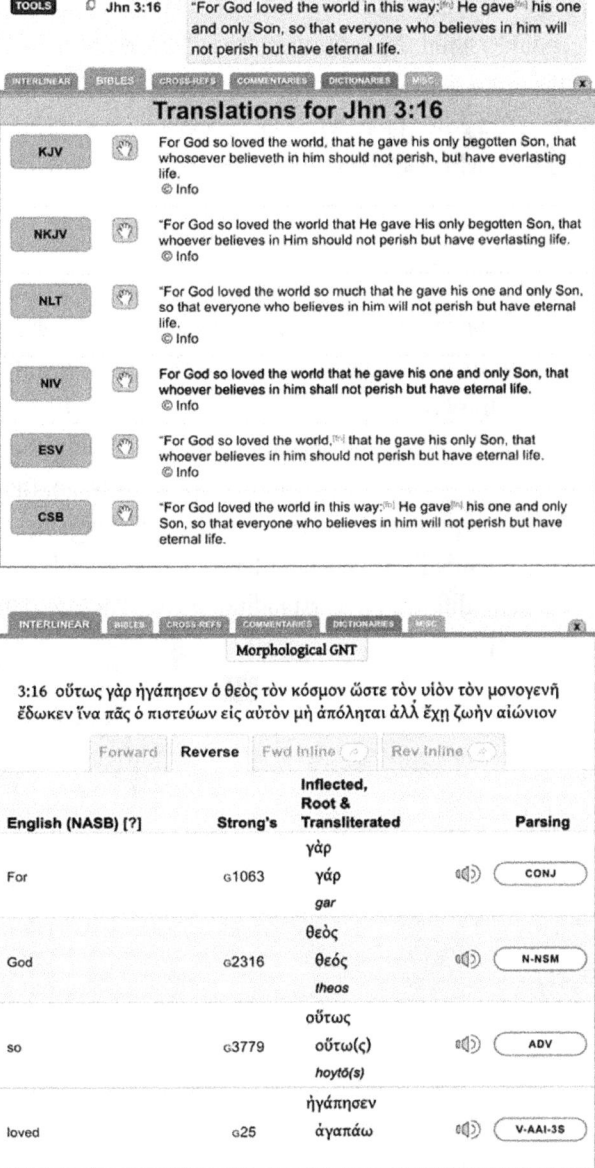

Figure 4: Screenshots from *Blue Letter Bible* app demonstrating the ease to display a verse in multiple translations. The interlinear tab allows one to see and learn about the original language and its meaning. It also provides immediate access to multiple commentaries.

4. What if I have trouble understanding what I am reading?

Answer: In order to understand the Scriptures, it is often necessary to understand the original language the text was written in and the historical setting. This is where going to church and listening to a gifted preacher, being in a small group, using a commentary or study guide can really help. Make sure that what you are reading is from a reliable source.

5. Do I need to read the Old Testament too?

Answer: Yes, the Old Testament (OT) is necessary to understand the New Testament (NT). For example, Jesus quotes frequently from the OT. Jesus is the fulfillment of the prophecies of the OT. Many of the stories of the OT point to Jesus. Jesus clearly said this - "Don't think that I came to abolish the Law or the Prophets. I did not come to abolish but to fulfill. For truly I tell you, until heaven and earth pass away, not the smallest letter or one stroke of a letter will pass away from the law until all things are accomplished." - Matthew 5:17-18 CSB. Jesus fulfilled the punishment for sin when He dies on the cross for our sins. You will have difficulty understanding the NT Book of Hebrews without some knowledge of the OT.

2

The Nature and Attributes of God the Father

God is your Heavenly Father.

In the New Testament, Jesus as He is teaching the disciples about prayer, makes a revolutionary statement by addressing God as Father. In the Old Testament, individuals did not address God in this personal way. However, once Jesus comes, He addresses God as His Father throughout the Gospels. The Greek word translated "Father" in the New Testament is "*pater*" and the Aramaic word is "*abba*". They are endearing terms, and we could say in English "Dearest Father".

• *Jesus establishes the concept that we pray to God as our Heavenly Father.* Notice this in the Disciples Prayer and His Great High Priestly Prayer of John 17.

"After this manner therefore pray ye: *Our Father which art in heaven*, Hallowed be thy name." - Matthew 6:9 KJV

"These words spake Jesus, and lifted up his eyes to heaven, and said, *Father, the hour* is come; glorify thy Son, that thy Son also may glorify thee:" - John 17:1 KJV

"And he said, Abba, Father, all things are possible unto thee; take away this cup from me: nevertheless not what I will, but what thou wilt." - Mark 14:36 KJV

• *If God is our Heavenly Father, then that makes us God's adopted children!*
"But to all who did receive him, he gave them the right to be children of God, to those who believe in his name," - John 1:12 CSB

"For ye have not received the spirit of bondage again to fear; but ye have received the Spirit of adoption, whereby we cry, Abba, Father." - Romans 8:15 KJV

"And because ye are sons, God hath sent forth the Spirit of his Son into your hearts, crying, Abba, Father." - Galatians 4:6 KJV

So, if God is our Father, it is very important for us to understand God and His nature.

Moses said, "And now, Israel, what does the LORD your God ask of you except to fear the LORD your God by walking in all his ways, to love him, and to worship the LORD your God with all your heart and all your soul?" - Deuteronomy 10:12 CSB.

If you are indeed committed to do what this verse says – to trust, love, worship and walk with the God of the Bible, then it is necessary to know Him, His characteristics, and attributes. Why? So, that you understand whether to trust and believe in Him, how to worship Him and what to expect. Understanding what the Bible says about God will enable you to correct the many misconceptions people and the media have about Him.

The Old Testament was translated into English from the original Hebrew. In the English, the word "Lord" can be written as lord, Lord, or LORD. There are different Hebrew words behind these English words. The Hebrew name the writer used for God tells us something about Him and the intent of the writer. When "lord" is used, it is referring to someone like your boss. Today we might say "Sir" or "Ma'am" but in old English (like in the movies or on the Downton Abbey series) we hear people address their superiors as "my lord". When the Bible uses 'Lord' it refers to God and when it is in 'all caps (LORD) then it means Yahweh or Jehovah God. Below is a succinct summary of the names of God which in turn shed light on His nature and attributes. *As you read the list, meditate on the great God that you serve.*

The Names for God tell us about His nature.
• ***Yahweh = LORD, Jehovah***, the proper name of the one true God; self-existent One. This comes from the Hebrew letters Yud, Hay, Vav, Hay = YHWH. To pronounce the word, the Jews added vowels to make "Yahweh". It is the most common Hebrew word used for God and appears 6,519 times in the Bible.

"Trust ye in the LORD for ever: for in the LORD JEHOVAH is everlasting strength:" - Isaiah 26:4 KJV

"That men may know that thou, whose name alone is JEHOVAH, art the most high over all the earth."
- Psalm 83:18 KJV

• *Adon or Adonai = Lord or Master*. Adonai occurs 434 times and is often translated Jehovah. Thus, in English if we read Jehovah, we would not know without further study whether it was Yahweh or Adonai. The Jews often used Adonai instead of Yahweh because they were afraid of inadvertently taking the name of the Lord in vain as warned against in the Ten Commandments (Commandment 3).

"Thou shalt not take the name of the LORD thy God in vain; for the LORD will not hold him guiltless that taketh his name in vain." - Exodus 20:7 KJV

• *El Shaddai = Lord God Almighty = the all-sufficient One; the One that sustains us.*
El is another word for God and when it is paired with a second word (in this case Shaddai) it expands the meaning about the character and functions of God. El Shaddai is used only 7 times. Gen 17:1 is one example.

"When Abram was ninety-nine years old, the LORD appeared to him, saying, 'I am God Almighty. Live in my presence and be blameless.'" - Genesis 17:1 CSB In this verse LORD is Yahweh/Jehovah and God Almighty is El Shaddai. This name is easy to remember if you recall the popular Christian song by that name written by Michael Card and John Thompson and recorded by Michael Card on his 1981 album, Legacy. Amy Grant later recorded it. Listen to the song (or sing it yourself) and you will remember El Shaddai much easier.

• *El Elyon = the Most High God, the Most Exalted God*. Used 28 times in the Bible.
"I call to God Most High, to God who fulfills his purpose for me." - Psalm 57:2 CSB

• *Jehovah-Raah = The Lord is my Shepherd*. Used by David in the 23rd Psalm and three other times. Rô'eh from which Raah derived, means "shepherd" in Hebrew.

"The LORD is my shepherd; I have what I need." - Psalm 23:1 CSB

• *Jehovah nissi = the Lord my banner, the Lord my miracle*. Used only once.
"And Moses built an altar and named it, 'The LORD Is My Banner.'" - Exodus 17:15 CSB

- ***Jehovah-rapha = The Lord who heals.***

"He said, 'If you will carefully obey the LORD your God, do what is right in his sight, pay attention to his commands, and keep all his statutes, I will not inflict any illnesses on you that I inflicted on the Egyptians. For I am the LORD who heals you.'" - Exodus 15:26 CSB

- ***Jehovah Sabaoth = the Lord of Hosts or Armies.*** Used over 285 times.

"Restore us, *O LORD God of hosts*! Let your face shine, that we may be saved!" - Psalm 80:19 ESV

- ***Jehovah Shalom = the Lord is peace.***

"So Gideon built an altar to the LORD there and called it The LORD Is Peace. It is still in Ophrah of the Abiezrites today." - Judges 6:24 CSB

- ***Jehovah Jireh = the Lord will provide.***

"And Abraham named that place The LORD Will Provide, so today it is said: 'It will be provided on the LORD's mountain.'" - Genesis 22:14 CSB

This is the only verse that uses Jehovah Jireh but the song by Don Moen (on YouTube) made it popular. Listen to it when you need encouragement. God indeed will provide.

- ***Elohim = God.*** As opposed to the words above for Lord/LORD, Elohim is the word translated over 2000 times in the OT as God.

"In the beginning God (Elohim) created the heavens and the earth." - Genesis 1:1 CSB

"God (Elohim) replied to Moses, 'I AM WHO I AM. This is what you are to say to the Israelites: I AM has sent me to you.'" - Exodus 3:14 CSB

- ***Theos = Greek for God or god.*** In the New Testament, theos is the Greek word often translated God. It is a masculine noun which is why God is our Father not our mother. Depending on the context it could be written God (1320 times) or rarely god (13 times).

"This is the message we have heard from him and declare to you: God is light, and there is absolutely no darkness in him." - 1 John 1:5 CSB

- ***Most High God or God Most High.*** This description of God the Father occurs 53 times beginning with Genesis 14:18 – Luke 8:28.

"When the Most High gave the nations their inheritance and divided the human race, he set the boundaries of the peoples according to the number of the people of Israel." - Deuteronomy 32:8 CSB
Psalm 47:2

"Now listen: You will conceive and give birth to a son, and you will name him Jesus. He will be great and will be called the Son of the Most High, and the Lord God will give him the throne of his father David. He will reign over the house of Jacob forever, and his kingdom will have no end." - Luke 1:31-33 CSB

• ***God is the "only God" – that is why Christianity is "monotheistic"***. God makes it very clear that He is the only God. Our God that we serve is the only one spelled with a capital G, and He has no competitors. This truth is in both the Old and the New Testament. If you remember only one passage let it be Isaiah 45:5-6.

"This is what the LORD, the King of Israel and its Redeemer, the LORD of Armies, says: I am the first and I am the last. There is no God but me." - Isaiah 44:6 CSB

"I am the LORD, and there is no other; there is no God but me. I will strengthen you, though you do not know me, so that all may know from the rising of the sun to its setting that there is no one but me. I am the LORD, and there is no other." - Isaiah 45:5-6 CSB

"Listen, Israel: The LORD our God, the LORD is one." - Deuteronomy 6:4 CSB

• ***In the New Testament Paul confirms this***. The "One God" principle applies to both Jews and Gentiles—that's all of us!

"So now, what about it? Should we eat meat that has been sacrificed to idols? Well, we all know that an idol is not really a god and that there is only one God and no other." 1 Corinthians 8:4, NLT.

"There is only one God, and there is only one way of being accepted by him. He makes people right with himself only by faith, whether they are Jews or Gentiles." Romans 3:30, NLT.

• ***Jesus said that being monotheistic is very important.***
"One of the scribes approached. When he heard them debating and saw that Jesus answered them well, he asked him, 'Which command is the most important of all?' Jesus answered, 'The most important is Listen, O Israel! *The Lord our God, the Lord is one.*

Love the Lord your God with all your heart, with all your soul, with all your mind, and with all your strength. The second is, Love your neighbor as yourself. There is no other command greater than these.'" - Mark 12:28-31 CSB

Questions:

1. Why did Paul in writing to the Greek city of Corinth (the book of Corinthians) specifically focus on idols and gods?

2. Does knowing that there is only One God make it easier or harder for you?

3. What other major religions are monotheistic?

4. Is the God of Judaism the same as the God we believe in?

5. Is the God of Islam the same as the God we believe in?

6. What does it mean in Exodus 3:14 when God says "I AM WHO I AM"? Why is understanding God this way important?

7. After reading about God's nature and how do view God as one of His children? How do you now view God the Father?

Questions with suggested answers:

1. Why did Paul in writing to the Greek city of Corinth (the book of Corinthians) specifically focus on idols and gods?

Answer: Corinth is about an hour's drive from Athens, Greece. The Athenians for centuries had worshipped a whole host of gods and had temples to the gods. Paul responded to this in his famous Mars Hill (Areopagus) address in Athens. The Areopagus is right next to the famous Parthenon. "Paul stood in the middle of the Areopagus and said: 'People of Athens! I see that you are extremely religious in every respect. For as I was passing through and observing the objects of your worship, I even found an altar on which was inscribed: To an Unknown God. Therefore, what you worship in ignorance, this I proclaim to you. The God who made the world and everything in it -- he is Lord of heaven and earth -- does not live in shrines made by hands.\'" - Acts 17:22-24 CSB. Someday make it a point to visit Athens and the Areopagus where Paul spoke. This passage will come to life as you observe exactly why Paul taught this way. He was using their worship of idols to point out the importance of worshipping the only God instead. Today in the United States idols are less obvious but still there – the idols of money, success, beauty, fame, and sex.

2. Does knowing that there is only One God make it easier or harder for you?

Answer: Easier. When there is only "One Way" you cannot go the wrong way (unless you totally ignore the directions)! There are many difficult decisions in life. Often there are multiple choices and the way unclear. However, in this decision God has not left us any other choice – He is the only God and there is no other.

3. What other major religions are monotheistic?

Answer: Judaism and Islam.

4. Is the God of Judaism the same as the God we believe in?

Answer: Yes, because they base their concept of God on the Pentateuch (the first five books of Moses). They do have difficulty on believing that Jesus was God and the Messiah.

5. Is the God of Islam the same as the God we believe in?

Answer: It is a difficult question and one that you will hear differing opinions. Both religions believe in "One God". The Christian view is based on the Bible; the Islamic one is based on the Koran. In discussing this with a Muslim they will agree with you on there being "one God". A more difficult question is, when a Muslim prays to Allah is the person praying to the same God as Jehovah/Yahweh? We likely will not know the answer to this until heaven.

6. What does it mean in Exodus 3:14 when God says, "I AM WHO I AM"? Why is understanding God this way important?

Answer: Our God is self-sufficient and does not depend on us or circumstances. He said this to Moses in the story of the burning bush that was not consumed. "God replied to Moses, "I AM WHO I AM. This is what you are to say to the Israelites: I AM has sent me to you." - Exodus 3:14 CSB. The Hebrew words for the phrase are hâyâh ăsher hâyâh which means "to be". According to https://www.gotquestions.org/I-AM-WHO-I-AM-Exodus-3-14.html "when used as a stand-alone description, *I AM* is the ultimate statement of self-sufficiency, self-existence, and immediate presence. God's existence is not contingent upon anyone else. His plans are not contingent upon any circumstances. He promises that He will be what He will be; that is, He will be the eternally constant God. He stands, ever-present and unchangeable, completely sufficient in Himself to do what He wills to do and to accomplish what He wills to accomplish." Accessed February 19, 2024. The New Testament link to this verse occurs in John 8:58 CSB "Jesus said to them, 'Truly I tell you, before Abraham was, I am'. Here Jesus also claims 'I AM' to the Pharisees. He was explaining that He is God and was always present in Heaven. He is pre-existent, like God the Father.

7. After reading about God's nature, how do you now view God the Father?

Answer: We have no control in life over who our earthly father is and how he treats you. However, we do need to clearly understand that our Heavenly Father is unchanging and has adopted us a His children. We are to view God the Father like Jesus did – as His "Dearest Father". Read again the Lord's Prayer in Matthew 6:9-13 and remember we start the prayer by saying "Our Father which art in Heaven, hallowed be thy name." This view of God is vital to your relationship with Him. As author R. Kent Hughes said in his commentary on the Sermon on the Mount, "So the idea that God is our Father, our Abba, is not only a sign of our spiritual health and of the authenticity of our faith, it is one of the most healing doctrines in all of Scripture."

What is God like? In addition to what we learn from His Names, 3 key words succinctly describe God– Omniscient (all knowing), Omnipresent (present everywhere at the same time), and Omnipotent (all powerful).

- ***Omniscient - God knows everything including the future.***

"And the Father who knows all hearts knows what the Spirit is saying, for the Spirit pleads for us believers in harmony with God's own will." - Romans 8:27 NLT
Isaiah 44:6-7

- ***Omnipresent – God is everywhere even in the dark moments.***

"Where can I go to escape your Spirit? Where can I flee from your presence? If I go up to heaven, you are there; if I make my bed in Sheol, you are there. If I live at the eastern horizon or settle at the western limits, even there your hand will lead me; your right hand will hold on to me. If I say, 'Surely the darkness will hide me, and the light around me will be night -- even the darkness is not dark to you. The night shines like the day; darkness and light are alike to you.'" - Psalm 139:7-12 CSB

2: The Nature and Attributes of God the Father

"Am I a God who is only near" -- this is the LORD's declaration – "and not a God who is far away? Can a person hide in secret places where I cannot see him?" -- the LORD's declaration. "Do I not fill the heavens and the earth? " -- the LORD's declaration." - Jeremiah 23:23-24 CSB

• **Omnipotent - all powerful; independent; does whatever He wishes; no limits.**
"The God who made the world and everything in it" -- he is Lord of heaven and earth – "does not live in shrines made by hands. Neither is he served by human hands, as though he needed anything, since he himself gives everyone life and breath and all things." - Acts 17:24-25 CSB

"Then the LORD said to Moses, 'Is there any limit to my power? Now you will see whether or not my word comes true!'" Numbers 11:23, NLT.

"Our God is in heaven and does whatever he pleases." - Psalm 115:3 CSB

• **Living - God is alive and well.**
"The LORD lives -- blessed be my rock! The God of my salvation is exalted." - Psalm 18:46 CSB
Hebrews 10:31

• **God lives in Heaven not in a church or temple**. The earthly temple was made to honor God not as His actual abode.
"This is what the LORD says: Heaven is my throne, and earth is my footstool. Where could you possibly build a house for me? And where would my resting place be?" - Isaiah 66:1 CSB

Questions:

1. Why is it important to believe in a God that is living?

2. In Exodus 20 God gives Moses the Ten Commandments. The first three relate to the nature of God. "Do not have other gods besides me. Do not make an idol for yourself, whether in the shape of anything in the heavens above or on the earth below or in the waters under the earth. ... but showing faithful love to a thousand generations of those who love me and keep my commands. Do not misuse the name of the LORD your God, because the LORD will not leave anyone unpunished who misuses his name." - Exodus 20:3-4, 6-7 CSB. Why do these commandments "make sense" in light of what you read

about the nature of God? Do you find it easier and important to honor those commandments in light of God's nature?

3. What are the implications of "He is the God who made the world and everything in it. Since he is Lord of heaven and earth, he doesn't live in man-made temples," Acts 17:24, NLT.

Questions with suggested answers:

1. Why is it important to believe in a God that is living?

Answer: Having *a living God* is critical to your faith. Why would you spend time worshipping something that could not act on your behalf? For example, the Greeks in times past believed in mythical gods and built temples to them. If you go to Athens Greece, you cannot miss seeing the Parthenon Temple on top of the Acropolis. It is indeed a remarkable structure, but it is built to a mythical god – it's all made up! The statues are missing heads or have had to be restored. They cannot do anything for us.

2. In Exodus 20 God gives Moses the Ten Commandments. Why do these commandments "make sense" in light of what you read about the nature of God? Do you find it easier and important to honor those commandments in light of God's nature?

Answer: Once we understand the true nature of God and His power, we will never dishonor Him or take Him lightly or make fun of Him. If you are still not convinced of this, then read the verses again!

3. What are the implications of "He is the God who made the world and everything in it. Since he is Lord of heaven and earth, he doesn't live in man-made temples," Acts 17:24, NLT.

Answer: Although it is ideal and important to go to church on Sunday to worship and hear God's Word preached, we should not think of God as only being there. In some religions it is important to "go to the temple" but as noted above God is omnipresent and thus, He does not only live in a building.

God as the Creator of the universe and nations.

• *Creation - Genesis 2:4 is the first passage to use the Hebrew Yahweh/Jehovah. Notice that LORD is in all-caps to indicate this.*

"These are the records of the heavens and the earth, concerning their creation. At the time that the LORD God made the earth and the heavens," - Genesis 2:4 CSB

God of the resurrection. Who else can resurrect a dead person?
Romans 4:17

God of nature – He maintains power and control over nature.
Matthew 8:24-27

The steadfast God – He cannot be manipulated or controlled.
Isaiah 45:9-12, Isaiah 44:8, Psalm 18:2, Psalm 18:31

Unseen – we do not know what He looks like. He has never been seen.
1 John 4:12, Deuteronomy 4:15-16

Holy – God is holy and only He is holy. Holy means separation from all sin.

"Lord, who will not fear and glorify your name? For you alone are holy. All the nations will come and worship before you because your righteous acts have been revealed." - Revelation 15:4 CSB
Isaiah 6:3, NLT, Isaiah 8:13 NLT

Loving - God is loving; and His love is unfailing.
Psalm 33:22, Psalm 52:8, 1 Kings 10:9 CSB, Joel 2:13, 2 Corinthians 13:11, 13, Ephesians 3:19

"Dear friends, *let us love one another*, because *love is from God*, and everyone who loves has been born of God and knows God. ... God's love was revealed among us in this way: *God sent his one and only Son into the world so that we might live through him*. Love consists in this: not that we loved God, but that *he loved us and sent his Son* to be the atoning sacrifice for our sins. ... No one has ever seen God. If we love one another, God remains in us and his love is made complete in us. ... And we have come to know and to believe the love that God has for us. *God is love, and the one who remains in love remains in God, and God remains in him.*" - 1 John 4:7, 9-10, 12, 16 CSB.

God is righteous and He imparts that righteousness to us through Jesus.
2 Peter 1:1

"More than that, I also consider everything to be a loss in view of the surpassing value of knowing Christ Jesus my Lord. Because of him I have suffered the loss of all things and consider them as dung, so that I may gain Christ and be found in him, not having a righteousness of my own from the law, but one that is through faith in Christ -- the righteousness from God based on faith." - Philippians 3:8-9 CSB
Psalm 89:14, Isaiah 6:1-5

God is always Light. Darkness is a characteristic of the devil.

"This is the message he has given us to announce to you: God is light and there is no darkness in him at all." 1 John 1:5, NLT.
Psalm 104:1-2, Isaiah 60:19, John 8:12

Despite His power, God is also very personal, not abstract.

• *Intimate, personal conversation between Moses and God.*
"The LORD replied, 'I will personally go with you, Moses, and I will give you rest--everything will be fine for you.'" - Exodus 33:14 NLT
Genesis 15:5-8 CSB

God is like a Shepherd; Jacob (Israel) said He is "my Shepherd".

"Then he blessed Joseph and said, 'May the God before whom my grandfather Abraham and my father, Isaac, walked--the God who has been my shepherd all my life, to this very day, the Angel who has redeemed me from all harm--may he bless these boys. May they preserve my name and the names of Abraham and Isaac. And may their descendants multiply greatly throughout the earth.'" - Genesis 48:15-16 NLT

"[A Psalm of David.] The LORD is my shepherd; I shall not want." - Psalm 23:1 KJV

God is loyal to us because we are special.
Psalm 94:14, NLT.

Question with suggested answer:

Why does David describe God as a shepherd?

Answer: David, the Psalmist, gives us a great word picture of a key attribute of God—that of a Shepherd in the 23rd Psalm. We see from these verses also that despite God being "awesome" and "big" and "holy," He is also personal. Jacob, Moses, and David, all mention their close relationship with God. As Francis Schaeffer the great Christian author and lecturer of the 20th century would often say "He is the infinite personal God". All these people above went through really hard times. The will of God was often unclear for them. But they felt close to God and realized that He was personally shepherding them. When suffering strikes, we need a Shepherd and God will be there for us just like He was for the patriarchs.

God of the Impossible. Sometimes God's promises do seem impossible and that is because we cannot see the future like God can.

"Jesus looked at them and said, 'With man this is impossible, but with God all things are possible.'"
- Matthew 19:26 CSB

"The LORD of Armies says this: 'Though it may seem impossible to the remnant of this people in those days, should it also seem impossible to me?' -- this is the declaration of the LORD of Armies." - Zechariah 8:6 CSB

Understanding - there is nothing in your life that He does not understand.

"How great is our Lord! His power is absolute! His understanding is beyond comprehension!" - Psalm 147:5 NLT

He is for us. He works things out for good (synergy).

"And we know that God causes everything to work together for the good of those who love God and are called according to his purpose for them." Romans 8:28, NLT.

"What can we say about such wonderful things as these? If God is for us, who can ever be against us?" Romans 8:31, NLT.

The God who forgives. He is able to forgive sin.

"But if we confess our sins to him, he is faithful and just to forgive us and to cleanse us from every wrong." 1 John 1:9, NLT.

All-seeing - He sees the heart and what you truly are.

"People may think they are doing what is right, but the LORD examines the heart." Proverbs 21:2, NLT.

Kind - God is so kind that He provided for our salvation.

"He is so rich in kindness that he purchased our freedom through the blood of his Son, and our sins are forgiven." Ephesians 1:7, NLT.
1 Peter 5:10, Exodus 33:19

Compassionate

• *David says He has always been that way.*
"Remember, LORD, your compassion and your faithful love, for they have existed from antiquity."
- Psalm 25:6 CSB
Exodus 34:6, Psalm 34:18

• *Jonah described God as gracious, compassionate, and forgiving.*
"So he complained to the LORD about it: 'Didn't I say before I left home that you would do this, LORD? That is why I ran away to Tarshish! I knew that you were a gracious and compassionate God, slow to get angry and filled with unfailing love. I knew how easily you could cancel your plans for destroying these people.'" Jonah 4:2, NLT.

Merciful – God is full of great mercy.
Psalm 89:1, NLT.

"Blessed be the God and Father of our Lord Jesus Christ. Because of his great mercy he has given us new birth into a living hope through the resurrection of Jesus Christ from the dead" - 1 Peter 1:3 CSB

Angry at sin and its effects. God is deity but He does have emotions. He is slow to anger but He does get angry, and His anger is righteous because it is directed to sin. We sometimes refer to this as the "wrath of God".

"For God's wrath is revealed from heaven against all godlessness and unrighteousness of people who by their unrighteousness suppress the truth." - Romans 1:18 CSB

• *Without the righteousness of God applied to us through faith we are subject to the wrath of God because of our sin.*

"The one who believes in the Son has eternal life, but the one who rejects the Son will not see life; instead, the wrath of God remains on him." - John 3:36 CSB

- ***God expressed disappointment, grief, and regret over the sin of humans.***
"When the LORD saw that human wickedness was widespread on the earth and that every inclination of the human mind was nothing but evil all the time, the LORD regretted that he had made man on the earth, and he was deeply grieved. Then the LORD said, "I will wipe mankind, whom I created, off the face of the earth, together with the animals, creatures that crawl, and birds of the sky -- for I regret that I made them." - Genesis 6:5-7 CSB

- ***God was angry with Moses because of his sin. It cost Moses the chance to physically enter the Promised Land.***
"The LORD was angry with me on your account. He swore that I would not cross the Jordan and enter the good land the LORD your God is giving you as an inheritance." I won't be crossing the Jordan because I am going to die in this land. But you are about to cross over and take possession of this good land." - Deuteronomy 4:21-22 CSB

- ***God's anger is slow but righteous and effective. He gets angry over sin.***
"The LORD is slow to get angry, but his power is great, and he never lets the guilty go unpunished. He displays his power in the whirlwind and the storm. The billowing clouds are the dust beneath his feet." Nahum 1:3, NLT.

"But if our unrighteousness highlights God's righteousness, what are we to say? I am using a human argument: Is God unrighteous to inflict wrath? Absolutely not! Otherwise, how will God judge the world?" - Romans 3:5-6 CSB

- ***His anger against sin will be shown to full extent at the time of judgment.***
"One of the four living creatures gave the seven angels seven golden bowls filled with the wrath of God who lives forever and ever." - Revelation 15:7 CSB

"Then I heard a loud voice from the temple saying to the seven angels, 'Go and pour out the seven bowls of God's wrath on the earth.'" - Revelation 16:1 CSB

- ***He is a God of restraint with the use of His anger.***
"I will delay my anger for the sake of my name, and I will restrain myself for your benefit and for my praise, so that you will not be destroyed." - Isaiah 48:9 CSB

- ***He is to be respected and feared (reverential trust).***

"And now, Israel, what does the LORD your God ask of you except to fear the LORD your God by walking in all his ways, to love him, and to worship the LORD your God with all your heart and all your soul?" - Deuteronomy 10:12 CSB

"And you -- you are to be feared. When you are angry, who can stand before you? From heaven you pronounced judgment. The earth feared and grew quiet" - Psalm 76:7-8 CSB

"Uzziah sought God during the days of Zechariah, who taught him to fear God. And as long as the king sought guidance from the LORD, God gave him success." - 2 Chronicles 26:5 NLT

Benevolent - He is a God of good deeds—we are to talk about these.

"Declare his glory among the nations, his wondrous works among all peoples. For the LORD is great and is highly praised; he is feared above all gods." - Psalm 96:3-4 CSB

Generous – He gives from His endless riches.

"Tell those who are rich in this world not to be proud and not to trust in their money, which will soon be gone. But their trust should be in the living God, who richly gives us all we need for our enjoyment." 1 Timothy 6:17, NLT.
Luke 12:32

Reliable - He is always with us; never fails us; never forsakes us.

"Stay away from the love of money; be satisfied with what you have. For God has said, *'I will never fail you. I will never forsake you'*" Hebrews 13:5, NLT.
1 Peter 4:19

Questions:

1. What does it mean in Deuteronomy 10:12 that we are to "fear God"?

2. We all want to think of God as loving. Why do people get upset when they read that God gets angry with sin? What is entailed in the "wrath of God".

Questions with suggested answers:

1. What does it mean in Deuteronomy 10:12 that we are to "fear God"?

Answer: Read the verse again carefully. "And now, Israel, what does the LORD your God ask of you except to fear the LORD your God by walking in all his ways, to love him, and to worship the LORD your God with all your heart and all your soul?" - Deuteronomy 10:12 CSB. The Hebrew word *yārē'* is translated fear and indeed it can be meant to be afraid. But the more important meaning is that of "reverence, reverential trust" or to "stand in awe of". If we indeed trust and respect God then we will A) walk in His ways (not ours); B) love Him; C) worship Him and D) do all of these with our whole heart and soul i.e., with vigor.

2. We all want to think of God as loving. Why do people get upset when they read that God gets angry with sin? What is entailed in the "wrath of God".

Answer: God gets angry over sin and disobedience. Ray Ortlund Jr in his commentary on Isaiah explains this in medical terms which I can relate to. "What is the wrath of God? His wrath is his active, resolute opposition to all evil. His delight is spontaneous and intrinsic to his being, but *his wrath is provoked by the defiance of his creatures*. His love will never make peace with our evil. What we must understand is that God's wrath is perfect, no less perfect than 'the riches of his kindness and forbearance and patience (Romans 2:4). His wrath is not moody vindictiveness; *it is the solemn determination of a doctor cutting away the cancer that's killing his patient*. And for God, the anger is personal, not detached and clinical. This Doctor hates the cancer, because he loves the carriers of the disease and he will rid the universe of all their afflictions. He has already scheduled 'the day of wrath when God's righteous judgment will be revealed' (Romans 2:5)." Ortlund, Raymond C., Jr. Isaiah: God Saves Sinners. Preaching the Word series. Wheaton, Il.: Crossway Books, 2005.

Watchful - the God of Protection; God is the ultimate security system.

"The LORD is watching everywhere, keeping his eye on both the evil and the good." Proverbs 15:3, NLT.

"For you are my hiding place; you protect me from trouble. You surround me with songs of victory. Interlude" Psalm 32:7, NLT.

Jude 1:24-25, Psalm 18:2

Hopeful - He is a God of hope.
Psalm 33:22, NLT.

"Now may the God of hope fill you with all joy and peace as you believe so that you may overflow with hope by the power of the Holy Spirit." - Romans 15:13 CSB

Peaceful - He is a God of peace.

"And now, may the God of peace, who brought again from the dead our Lord Jesus," Hebrews 13:20, NLT.

A God who rescues and enjoys rescuing people.

- *Those in distress*

"In my distress, I prayed to the LORD, and the LORD answered me and rescued me." Psalm 118:5, NLT.
2 Peter 2:7-9

- *The weak and helpless.*

"I will praise him from the bottom of my heart: 'LORD, who can compare with you? Who else rescues the weak and helpless from the strong? Who else protects the poor and needy from those who want to rob them?'" Psalm 35:10, NLT.

- *His servants*

"But give great joy to those who have stood with me in my defense. Let them continually say, 'Great is the LORD, who enjoys helping his servant.'" Psalm 35:27, NLT.

God of miracles; God of wonders; God of redemption.

"God, your way is holy. What god is great like God? You are the God who works wonders; you revealed your strength among the peoples." - Psalm 77:13-14 CSB

Reliable - a promise-keeper. God never lies to us.

"God is not a man, so he does not lie. He is not human, so he does not change his mind. Has he ever spoken and failed to act? Has he ever promised and not carried it through?" - Numbers 23:19 NLT

Truthful.

"I have not spoken in secret, somewhere in a land of darkness. I did not say to the descendants of Jacob: Seek me in a wasteland. I am the LORD, who speaks righteously, who declares what is right." - Isaiah 45:19 CSB

Independent - God Himself needs nothing from us; He has no needs. He will supply for your needs (but not necessarily your wants).

"And human hands can't serve his needs—for he has no needs. He himself gives life and breath to everything, and he satisfies every need there is." Acts 17:25, NLT.

Complex - God has a deep mind that is unfathomable to us.

"Oh, the depth of the riches both of the wisdom and of the knowledge of God! How unsearchable his judgments and untraceable his ways! For who has known the mind of the Lord? Or who has been his counselor? And who has ever given to God, that he should be repaid? For from him and through him and to him are all things. To him be the glory forever. Amen." - Romans 11:33-36 CSB

Teacher - God is our leader and teacher.

"This is what the LORD, your Redeemer, the Holy One of Israel says: I am the LORD your God, who teaches you for your benefit, who leads you in the way you should go." - Isaiah 48:17 CSB

Just - A God who loves justice.

• *Faithful and just regarding sin; He forgives if we ask Him*
"But if we confess our sins to him, he is faithful and just to forgive us and to cleanse us from every wrong." 1 John 1:9, NLT.
Psalm 7:17, Psalm 11:7

"Hate evil and love good; establish justice in the city gate. Perhaps the LORD, the God of Armies, will be gracious to the remnant of Joseph." - Amos 5:15 CSB

"But let justice flow like water, and righteousness, like an unfailing stream." - Amos 5:24 CSB

- ***His justice requires punishment that sometimes falls on the descendants of the one that sinned.***

"He passed in front of Moses, and said, 'I am the LORD, I am the LORD, the merciful and gracious God. I am slow to anger and rich in unfailing love and faithfulness. I show this unfailing love to many thousands by forgiving every kind of sin and rebellion. Even so, I do not leave sin unpunished, but I punish the children for the sins of their parents to the third and fourth generations.' Moses immediately fell to the ground and worshiped." Exodus 34:6-8, NLT.

1 Kings 21:29

- ***He is jealous in a good way; unwilling to share His glory because He is the only God.***

He acts in His best interests and will not let His glory be taken from Him.

"The pronouncement concerning Nineveh. The book of the vision of Nahum the Elkoshite. The LORD is a jealous and avenging God; the LORD takes vengeance and is fierce in wrath. The LORD takes vengeance against his foes; he is furious with his enemies. The LORD is slow to anger but great in power; the LORD will never leave the guilty unpunished. His path is in the whirlwind and storm, and clouds are the dust beneath his feet." - Nahum 1:1-3 CSB

Isaiah 48:11

A God of endurance and encouragement.

"Now may the God who gives endurance and encouragement grant you to live in harmony with one another, according to Christ Jesus, so that you may glorify the God and Father of our Lord Jesus Christ with one mind and one voice." - Romans 15:5-6 CSB

Unchanging - God not age like we do. This quote is repeated in Hebrews 1:10.

"Long ago you established the earth, and the heavens are the work of your hands. They will perish, but you will endure; all of them will wear out like clothing. You will change them like a garment, and they will pass away. But you are the same, and your years will never end." - Psalm 102:25-27 CSB

Eternal – always was and always will be.

"'I am the Alpha and the Omega,' says the Lord God, 'the one who is, who was, and who is to come, the Almighty.'" - Revelation 1:8 CSB

2: The Nature and Attributes of God the Father

Awesome – we have a 'great and awesome God' on your side.

"Don't be terrified of them, for the LORD your God, a great and awesome God, is among you." - Deuteronomy 7:21 CSB

Summary Statements about God Isaiah 40 and Psalm 33.

There are two chapters in the Bible that really give us a great picture of what God is like. They are Isaiah 40 and Psalm 33 written by Isaiah and David, respectively. You will recognize Isaiah 40:12-14 as words in the beautiful worship song *Behold Our God* put together by Stephen Altrogge and Ryan, Jon, and Megan Baird (Sovereign Grace Music). This song has been successful because it is *Scripture put to music* and it is very glorifying to God. Go play it right now as part of your worship to God. Read them now in your Bible.

Questions:

1. If God is all-powerful why does He allow war?

2. How has your view of God changed by reading these verses?

3. What does God look like? Do you ever see pictures of God on the wall or in museums?

Questions with suggested answers:

1. If God is all-powerful why does He allow war?

Answer: Re-read Romans 11:33-36 CSB above about the complexity of God. Also remember that God is just, and He will mete out justice. It does not always come when we want it to, but it does come. When God brings justice suffering is usually involved as it is in war. Indeed, it is helpful to remember that the causes of suffering in the world are many but one of them is God's judgement. A good example of this is contained in Isaiah 10 where the prophet clearly tells us that God used the Assyrians in the 700's BC to exert judgement (war) on the Israelite Northern Kingdom and then God turned around and judged the Assyrians ("But when the Lord finishes all his work against Mount Zion and Jerusalem, he will say, 'I will punish the king of Assyria for his arrogant acts and the proud look in his eyes.'" – Isaiah 10:12 CSB)! "God's sovereignty and man's responsibility are always in perfect balance in the Word of God. Even though we are not able to reconcile these paradoxical facts, we can believe both because the Bible teaches both. God is sovereign in His universe; and at the same time man is fully accountable to

43

God for all his acts." Martin, Alfred. *Christ in Isaiah*. Moody Manna series. Chicago: Moody Bible Institute, 1968.

2. How has your view of God changed by reading these verses?

Answer: Discuss with your classmates or friends or small group. Once you appreciate the nature of God it should be sobering to you, and you should want to honor and worship Him. You certainly will want to never disobey Him or the third Commandment "Do not misuse the name of the LORD your God, because the LORD will not leave anyone unpunished who misuses his name." – Exodus 20:7 CSB

3. What does God look like? Do you ever see pictures of God on the wall or in museums?

Answer: "No one has ever seen God. The one and only Son, who is himself God and is at the Father's side –he has revealed him." – John 1:18 CSB. We see pictures of the earthly Jesus because many people saw Him during His 33 years on the earth.

3

Who is Jesus and What is He Like? Is Jesus God?

Introduction: A Christian by definition is a "Christ follower" or a "follower of Jesus Christ" meaning that the person follows the teachings of Jesus. If your faith is based on Jesus and you are going to trust Him to get you through this life and into Heaven, you had better know all you can about Him. The Bible tells us a lot about Jesus both in the Old Testament and by the writers of the New Testament who were eyewitnesses to Jesus. Jesus was not a created being like the angels and all of us. Before the creation of the world, Jesus existed with God in Heaven as God the Son and a member of the Trinity. We have sparse data on that phase of Jesus. Then He was sent to earth where He took on human flesh as the Son of Man to be the perfect sacrifice for our sin. This is the main story of the Bible. Presently, Jesus is Head of the Church and is back in Heaven interceding for us and our prayers. In the future, He will return to rescue Christ-followers from this earth and take us back to Heaven to ever be with Him forever.

Jesus is a controversial figure, primarily because He stated that He is the only way to Heaven, and many do not like that. However, the Christian faith is based on facts – that Jesus died as the ultimate blood sacrifice for sins of humankind, was resurrected on the third day, interacted with people for 40 days, then ascended back to Heaven where He lives to intercede for us. Most people will tolerate a conversation about God and even prayers in public to God but when Jesus is brought into the conversation it can get tense. Jesus is the central figure in the story of the Bible from start to finish. After Adam and Eve sinned in Genesis, death entered the world, and Satan needed to be dealt with. The only way to accomplish this was for God to send Jesus to die for us and save us from eternal death. This victory of God over Satan is predicted in Genesis. Jesus identifies Himself as God in the flesh and clearly states that He is the "only way to eternity in Heaven". Providing only "one Way" makes the route to Heaven straightforward. As you read this chapter do it slowly and meditate on all the facts about Jesus and what He means to you. If you want to be inspired about Jesus and who He is, watch this famous 3-minute clip by Pastor Dr. S.M. Lockridge on "Jesus – Do You Know Him?" https://www.youtube.com/watch?v=ZKsN-AeqJP0&t=0s

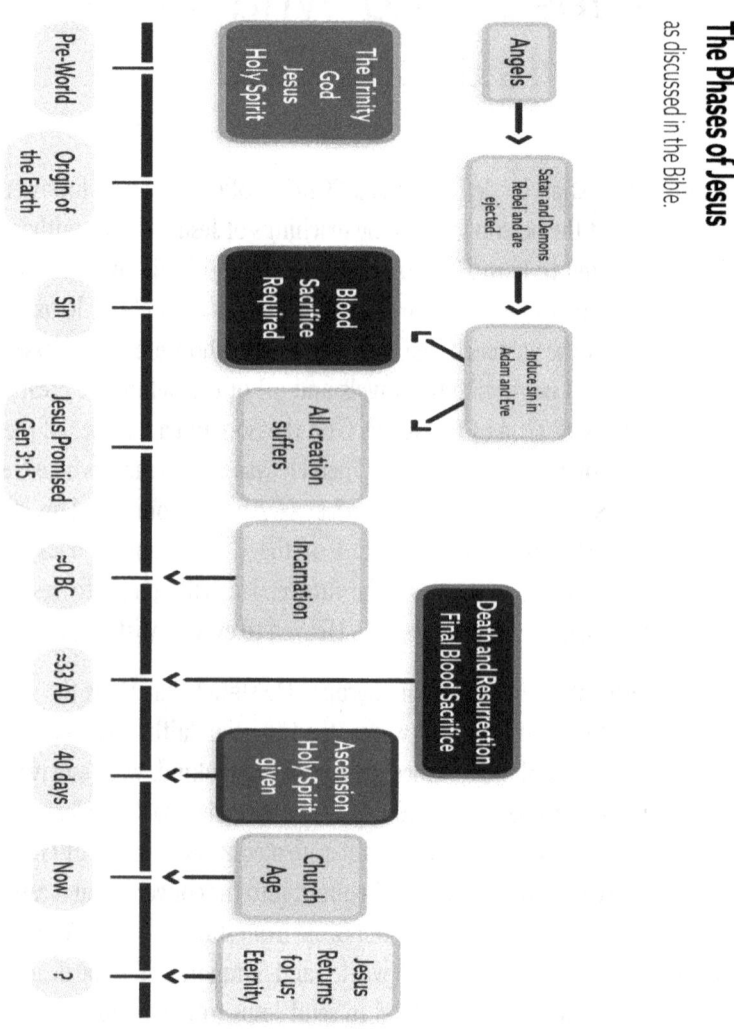

Figure 5: A timeline of the phases of Jesus as described in the Bible.

Phase 1 – Jesus, as Son of God, was in Heaven before the world was created.

Jesus is part of the Trinity and is God the Son. Jesus was pre-existent which means He was always there and had no beginning like we humans do. Jesus birth that is celebrated at Christmas was not His beginning; it was only the beginning of His time on this earth. 1 John 1:1-2 CSB

Genesis 1:1-2 CSB

- *Jesus was called "the Word", "God" and "light" by John.*
"In the beginning was the Word, and the Word was with God, and the Word was God. He was with God in the beginning. All things were created through him, and apart from him not one thing was created that has been created. In him was life, and that life was the light of men. That light shines in the darkness, and yet the darkness did not overcome it." – John 1:1-5 CSB

- *Jesus said He is the "I Am"– pre-existent before the world began.* Jesus clearly tells us this in John 17 where He shared glory with God the Father. They were unified in purpose. They love each other.
"Your father Abraham rejoiced to see my day; he saw it and was glad. The Jews replied, 'You aren't fifty years old yet, and you've seen Abraham?' *Jesus said to them, 'Truly I tell you, before Abraham was, I am.'*" – John 8:56-58 CSB

"This is eternal life: that they may know you, the only true God, and the one you have sent – Jesus Christ. I have glorified you on the earth by completing the work you gave me to do. '*Now, Father, glorify me in your presence with that glory I had with you before the world existed.*'" – John 17:3-5 CSB

"I have given them the glory you have given me, so that they may be one as *we are one*." John 17:22-23 CSB

- *Jesus tells his disciples that "I was there when Satan was cast out of Heaven"*. This confirms that Jesus is eternal and was present in Heaven before the world was even created.

"The seventy-two returned with joy, saying, 'Lord, even the demons submit to us in your name.' He said to them, 'I watched Satan fall from heaven like lightning.'" – Luke 10:17-18 CSB

- ***Jesus is the Creator —He was part of the Trinity and pre-existed before the world began***. He now sits, His work finished, at the right hand of God in heaven.

"Long ago God spoke to the fathers by the prophets at different times and in different ways. In these last days, he has spoken to us by his Son. God has appointed him heir of all things and made the universe through him. The Son is the radiance of God's glory and the exact expression of his nature, sustaining all things by his powerful word. After making purification for sins, he sat down at the right hand of the Majesty on high." – Hebrews 1:1-3 CSB

"He is the image of the invisible God, the firstborn over all creation. For everything was created by him, in heaven and on earth, the visible and the invisible, whether thrones or dominions or rulers or authorities – all things have been created through him and for him. He is before all things, and by him all things hold together." – Colossians 1:15-17 CSB

- ***Jesus is predicted to be the solution of sin and to win the battle of Satan vs God***. This event occurred while Jesus was in Heaven before the world was created.

"So the LORD God said to the serpent: Because you have done this, you are cursed more than any livestock and more than any wild animal. You will move on your belly and eat dust all the days of your life. I will put hostility between you and the woman, and between your offspring and her offspring. He will strike your head, and you will strike his heel." – Genesis 3:14-15 CSB
1 John 3:8

- ***The plan to send Jesus was indeed a plan developed before the world began***.

"Fellow Israelites, listen to these words: This Jesus of Nazareth was a man attested to you by God with miracles, wonders, and signs that God did among you through him, just as you yourselves know. Though he was delivered up according to God's determined plan and foreknowledge, you used lawless people to nail him to a cross and kill him. God raised him up, ending the pains of death, because it was not possible for him to be held by death." – Acts 2:22-24 CSB

Phase 2: Jesus predicted as the Messiah in the Old Testament.

The result of the sin of the created angel Satan (he rebels and is ejected from heaven before the earth is created) and the sin of Adam and Eve (yielding to the temptation of Satan in the Garden of Eden), death enters the world. God tells Satan that He will ultimately lose this cosmic battle in Genesis 3:14-15. By design, God requires a blood sacrifice for sin. Why, we are never told but this emphasizes the seriousness of sin as a blood sacrifice results in death of the animal. Jesus, God's Son, was perfect in Heaven. He was sent to earth to be the ultimate sacrifice for all sin – yours and mine. Jesus thus is the predicted Messiah. We call Him "Immanuel" because He indeed was "God with us" or "God in the flesh". He was a perfect representation of God. Although we have never seen God the Father nor God the Holy Spirit, those living in the first century did see God in the flesh (Jesus). They wrote about Jesus and what He did as eyewitnesses to history.

• ***The earthly Jesus comes from the line of Abram (Abraham)***. Starting in Genesis 12 the story in the Bible focuses on this family that will eventuate in the birth of Jesus. The genealogy of Jesus is recorded in Matthew 1 and Luke 3.
Genesis 12:1 CSB

"An account of the genealogy of Jesus Christ, the Son of David, the Son of Abraham" – Matthew 1:1 CSB

"As he began his ministry, Jesus was about thirty years old and was thought to be the son of Joseph, son of Heli, " – Luke 3:23 CSB

• ***Jesus is the "root of Jesse the father of David" predicted by Isaiah 11:10 CSB***
"And Jesse fathered King David. David fathered Solomon by Uriah's wife, ... So all the generations from Abraham to David were fourteen generations; and from David until the exile to Babylon, fourteen generations; and from the exile to Babylon until the Christ, fourteen generations." – Matthew 1:6, 17 CSB

• ***Isaiah the great prophet predicted the glory of King Jesus in this great vision***. We know this vision in Isaiah is Jesus by John 12:41. This is a good example of how one part of Scripture explains another part.
"In the year King Uzziah died, I saw the Lord. He was sitting on a lofty throne, and the train of his robe filled the Temple." Isaiah 6:1, NLT.

"Isaiah was referring to Jesus when he made this prediction, because he was given a vision of the Messiah's glory." John 12:41, NLT.

• ***As Messiah, Jesus is our sin-bearer as predicted by Isaiah in Isaiah 53***.
It is difficult to understand this Old Testament passage about Jesus unless you are a follower of Jesus and have the Holy Spirit as your guide. Read Isaiah 53:1-12.

- ***Jesus was sent from Heaven to earth by God the Father to be our sin-bearer; to rescue us from sin.***

"And we have seen and we testify that the Father has sent his Son as the world's Savior."
– 1 John 4:14 CSB

Philippians 2:5-8

Questions:

1. Was Jesus created like the angels and Satan?

2. What is the importance of understanding the Old Testament predictions of Jesus and the incarnation?

Questions with suggested answers:

1. Was Jesus created like the angels and Satan?

Answer: No, Jesus always was and has no beginning. We know this from the passages that say that Jesus was the Creator, that He was with God the Father before the world. Jesus clearly says this Himself when He prayed to God while on earth. "I have glorified you on the earth by completing the work you gave me to do. Now, Father, glorify me in your presence with that glory I had with you before the world existed." - John 17:4-5 CSB

2. What is the importance of understanding the Old Testament predictions of Jesus?

Answer: You cannot understand the Christmas story and its songs without the Old Testament background. It is also important to realize that Jesus is God the Son, was present in Heaven with God and the Holy Spirit forever. He was not created – He was and is God. God the Father sent Him as predicted in Genesis 3 to be our sacrifice for sin and to conquer Satan. He temporarily gave up His rightful position in Heaven as God to go to earth, live a sinless life, be our sacrifice for our sin and return to Heaven. This is the what Paul is talking about in Philippians 2:5-8. To do this God had to introduce Jesus in the flesh as Son of Man into the world. God needed a family for Jesus, so He used the descendants of Abraham, the Hebrews (Israelites) as that family. This family story starts in Genesis 12.

3: Who is Jesus and What is He Like? Is Jesus God?

Phase 3: The birth of Jesus – His entry to our world to accomplish the mission of saving us from our sins.

In this section we learn the meaning of Christmas and the terms – "the annunciation" "the virgin birth" and "the incarnation". This will help understand the songs we sing at Christmas and the plays that are presented.

• ***Jesus is predicted by the Old Testament prophet Isaiah to be born of a virgin – this is the "virgin birth" we celebrate at Christmas.***
"Therefore, the Lord himself will give you a sign: See, the virgin will conceive, have a son, and name him Immanuel." - Isaiah 7:14, Isaiah 9:6

• ***God names Him Jesus; He was not named by Mary and Joseph. The birth announcement comes through the angel Gabriel to Mary and is called "the annunciation". In the 6th month refers to the 6th month of Elizabeth's pregnancy with John the Baptist (see Luke 1:5-25).***
"In the sixth month, the angel Gabriel was sent by God to a town in Galilee called Nazareth, to a virgin engaged to a man named Joseph, of the house of David. The virgin's name was Mary. And the angel came to her and said, 'Greetings, favored woman! The Lord is with you.'" - Luke 1:26-28 CSB

• ***The angel announced that He would be a boy, and His name was to be Jesus.***
"But she was deeply troubled by this statement, wondering what kind of greeting this could be. Then the angel told her: "Do not be afraid, Mary, for you have found favor with God. Now listen: You will conceive and give birth to a son, and you will name him Jesus." - Luke 1:29-31 CSB

• ***Gabriel clearly explains that this Jesus is the Messiah and His kingdom is eternal.***
"He will be great and will be called the Son of the Most High, and the Lord God will give him the throne of his father David." He will reign over the house of Jacob forever, and his kingdom will have no end." - Luke 1:32-33 CSB

• ***Mary questions how this can happen without sexual relations with Joseph.*** Gabriel explains that the pregnancy was by the Holy Spirit.
Mary asked the angel, "How can this be, since I have not had sexual relations with a man?" The angel replied to her: "The Holy Spirit will come upon you, and the power of the Most High will overshadow you. Therefore, the holy one to be born will be called

the Son of God. And consider your relative Elizabeth -- even she has conceived a son in her old age, and this is the sixth month for her who was called childless. For nothing will be impossible with God." "I am the Lord's servant," said Mary. "May it be done to me according to your word." Then the angel left her. - Luke 1:34-38 CSB

- ***His name Immanuel, "God with us" is a perfect description of Jesus.*** Jesus indeed was God and when He came to earth in the flesh as a baby to his surrogate parents Mary and Joseph, He was God with us for a short time (about 33 years). The Christmas story is about Jesus taking on humanity in the form of a human and coming to earth to save us. Matthew 1 quoted below clearly states that Jesus was implanted into the uterus (womb) of Mary by the Holy Spirit before they had any sexual intercourse (thus we refer to Mary as a surrogate mother to Jesus).

"The birth of Jesus Christ came about this way: After his mother Mary had been engaged to Joseph, it was discovered before they came together that she was pregnant from the Holy Spirit. So her husband Joseph, being a righteous man, and not wanting to disgrace her publicly, decided to divorce her secretly. But after he had considered these things, an angel of the Lord appeared to him in a dream, saying, 'Joseph, son of David, don't be afraid to take Mary as your wife, because what has been conceived in her is from the Holy Spirit. She will give birth to a son, and you are to name him Jesus, because he will save his people from their sins.' Now all this took place to fulfill what was spoken by the Lord through the prophet: See, the virgin will become pregnant and give birth to a son, and they will name him Immanuel, which is translated God is with us." - Matthew 1:18-23 CSB

- ***This miracle is called the incarnation (God in the flesh).***

"The Word became flesh and dwelt among us. We observed his glory, the glory as the one and only Son from the Father, full of grace and truth." - John 1:14 CSB

- ***Jesus was born of humble parents and the birth announcement came to lowly shepherds. Notice what the angel said – the Messiah has come. The shepherds respond by going and seeing for themselves. There were multiple eyewitnesses to this story.***

"In the same region, shepherds were staying out in the fields and keeping watch at night over their flock. Then an angel of the Lord stood before them, and the glory of the Lord shone around them, and they were terrified. But the angel said to them, 'Don't be afraid, for look, I proclaim to you good news of great joy that will be for all the people: Today

3: Who is Jesus and What is He Like? Is Jesus God?

in the city of David a Savior was born for you, who is the Messiah, the Lord." This will be the sign for you: You will find a baby wrapped tightly in cloth and lying in a manger.' Suddenly there was a multitude of the heavenly host with the angel, praising God and saying: 'Glory to God in the highest heaven, and peace on earth to people he favors!' When the angels had left them and returned to heaven, the shepherds said to one another, 'Let's go straight to Bethlehem and see what has happened, which the Lord has made known to us.' They hurried off and found both Mary and Joseph, and the baby who was lying in the manger. After seeing them, they reported the message they were told about this child, and all who heard it were amazed at what the shepherds said to them. But Mary was treasuring up all these things in her heart and meditating on them. The shepherds returned, glorifying and praising God for all the things they had seen and heard, which were just as they had been told." - Luke 2:8-20 CSB

Questions:

1. Why was Mary "deeply troubled" when the Angel Gabriel tells her what is to come?

2. Jesus was clearly born of a virgin – why is this important?

3. Read Luke 1:5-25 about the birth of John the Baptist. Why is his birth important and what does it add to the story?

4. Why did God place baby Jesus into the hands of common people?

5. What is the "immaculate conception"?

Questions with suggested answers:

1. Why was Mary "deeply troubled" when the Angel Gabriel tells her what is to come?

Answer: First of all, people are not used to personal visits by angels! Secondly, she was a virgin and understood completely how babies came about – they were the result of sexual intercourse between a man and a woman, and she had never had that since she was engaged to Joseph but not married. Thirdly, she was beginning to grasp the potential embarrassment of being pregnant before marriage.

2. Jesus was clearly born of a virgin – why is this important?

Answer: He was God in the flesh. Mary was a wonderful and godly woman, but she was not God and Jesus had to be perfect. If He had born to a woman who was already married and had children, we would be forever doubting His deity – many would simply say He was another child of Joseph and Mary and thus not a "perfect sacrifice" for the sins of all humans.

3. Read Luke 1:5-25 about the birth of John the Baptist. Why is his birth important and what does it add to the story?

Answer: John the Baptist was the natural son of Elizabeth and Zachariah. They had been childless and were now old, so his birth was also somewhat of a miracle. Secondly, John the Baptist's birth and life was also predicted in the Old Testament in Isaiah 40 – "A voice of one crying out: Prepare the way of the LORD in the wilderness; make a straight highway for our God in the desert. Every valley will be lifted up, and every mountain and hill will be leveled; the uneven ground will become smooth and the rough places, a plain. And the glory of the LORD will appear, and all humanity together will see it, for the mouth of the LORD has spoken." - Isaiah 40:3-5 CSB. That this is in reference to John the Baptist is confirmed by Luke (3:4-6). Thirdly, birth of John is 6 months ahead of Jesus and the angel Gabriel announces both. He is one of the people in the Bible who was said to have the Holy Spirit while still *in utero* (in the womb). This is amazing. He has a unique purpose in the Jesus story and dies a martyr before Jesus is crucified.

4. Why did God place baby Jesus into the hands of common people?

Answer: Well, they may not have been rich, but they did fit perfectly in the predicted lineage of Jesus (see the genealogies of Jesus in Matthew 1 and Luke 3). God loves to surprise us, and He revealed the birth via the angels to Elizabeth and Zechariah and to the lowly shepherds and later to the wise men. The fact that Jesus comes into the world through common people gives us assurance that He is for "all people" not just royalty.

5. What is the "immaculate conception"?

Answer: The term does not refer to the conception of Jesus as many understand. Rather, it refers to a Roman Catholic belief that Mary herself was divine and sinless. In brief, according to Patrick Gray, a Professor of Religious Studies at Rhodes College in Memphis TN, writing in the Wall Street Journal December 22, 2022, "the Immaculate Conception deals with the birth of Mary herself. Pope Pius IX formally defined the doctrine in 1854, stating that Mary, "in the first instance of her conception, by a singular privilege and grace granted by God, in view of the merits of Jesus Christ . . . was preserved exempt from all stain of original sin." The Catholic Church celebrates it as a feast day on Dec. 8."

When Mary the mother of Jesus understood she had been selected to bear Jesus through the Holy Spirit she praised God. She referred to God as "her Savior" indicating that she was mortal and needed to be saved too." And Mary said: "My soul praises the greatness of the Lord, and my spirit rejoices in God my Savior, because he has looked with favor on the humble condition of his servant. Surely, from now on all generations will call me blessed," - Luke 1:46-48 CSB. It is very appropriate to honor Mary, to call her the Virgin Mary, to recognize her devotion to Jesus and her fulfillment of the mission assigned to her. She indeed was a virgin at the time of Jesus' birth, but she was not a virgin forever and had other children later. The Bible names four half-brothers of Jesus: James, Joseph, Simon, and Judas (Matthew 13:55) and also unnamed half-sisters (Matthew 13:55–56). She was not deity like God, Jesus, or the Holy Spirit thus we do not worship her as such. An excellent more extensive answer can be found at https://www.gotquestions.org/virgin-Mary.html.

Phase 4: The early life of Jesus on this earth – birth to age 30. We do not know much about this phase of His life. There is the birth, the day 8 circumcision, the dedication around day 40, the visit to the Temple at age 12 and then nothing until age 30. Why the wait? You can ask Him when you get to Heaven! The meticulous writers of the Gospel were not around to see this part of His life but certainly many people did see him grow up. Mary could have informed them but for some reason this phase was not important to the mission of Jesus and thus is not recorded. He did have to grow up in order to complete the mission. One would not have expected a child doing the miracles and teachings that a 30-year-old would do. Here is what we do know.

- ***8 days old: He was circumcised and named on day 8.*** He was dedicated 33 days later following the custom of the Jews (Leviticus 12:1-4).

"Then an angel of the Lord stood before them, and the glory of the Lord shone around them, and they were terrified. ...'Today in the city of David a Savior was born for you, who is the Messiah, the Lord.' ... When the eight days were completed for his circumcision, he was named Jesus -- the name given by the angel before he was conceived. And when the days of their purification according to the law of Moses were finished, they brought him up to Jerusalem to present him to the Lord (just as it is written in the law of the Lord, Every firstborn male will be dedicated to the Lord) and to offer a sacrifice (according to what is stated in the law of the Lord, a pair of turtledoves or two young pigeons)." - Luke 2:9, 11, 21-24 CSB

• *Simeon confirms to Joseph and Mary that Jesus indeed was the Messiah. This scene in the temple recorded by Luke includes the testimony of Simeon and Anna. Both have brief but significant roles in the history of Jesus.*

"There was a man in Jerusalem whose name was Simeon. This man was righteous and devout, looking forward to Israel's consolation, and the Holy Spirit was on him. It had been revealed to him by the Holy Spirit that he would not see death before he saw the Lord's Messiah. Guided by the Spirit, he entered the temple. When the parents brought in the child Jesus to perform for him what was customary under the law," - Luke 2:25-27 CSB

• *Simeon's prayer. The mission and destiny of Jesus were clear – He was for "all people" Jews and Gentiles.*

"Simeon took him up in his arms, praised God, and said, Now, Master, you can dismiss your servant in peace, as you promised. For my eyes have seen your salvation. You have prepared it in the presence of all peoples -- a light for revelation to the Gentiles and glory to your people Israel." - Luke 2:28-32 CSB

Luke 2:33-35 CSB

• *Anna the prophetess also provided witness to the fact that Jesus was the Messiah who would redeem the people.*

"There was also a prophetess, Anna, a daughter of Phanuel, of the tribe of Asher. She was well along in years, having lived with her husband seven years after her marriage, and was a widow for eighty-four years. She did not leave the temple, serving God night and day with fasting and prayers. At that very moment, she came up and began to thank God and to speak about him to all who were looking forward to the redemption of Jerusalem." - Luke 2:36-38 CSB

• *We have no photos of Jesus.* The Bible says He did not look much different than other boys. In his early years He appeared ordinary.

"He grew up before him like a young plant and like a root out of dry ground. He didn't have an impressive form or majesty that we should look at him, no appearance that we should desire him." - Isaiah 53:2 CSB

3: Who is Jesus and What is He Like? Is Jesus God?

- ***He grew up in Nazareth, grew strong spiritually and physically – these are descriptors of His humanity. People liked Him.***

"When they had completed everything according to the law of the Lord, they returned to Galilee, to their own town of Nazareth. The boy grew up and became strong, filled with wisdom, and God's grace was on him." - Luke 2:39-40 CSB

"And Jesus increased in wisdom and stature, and in favor with God and with people." - Luke 2:52 CSB

- ***Age 12: He was intelligent as recognized by the Pharisees.*** This story gives us a glimpse of the young Jesus. He was intelligent beyond his age, and He knew who He was and His mission. He was a good listener and learned the strategy of asking questions. He was also satisfied with not explaining everything to even His parents.
Luke 2:41-50, Luke 2:51-52

- ***He was a carpenter – this verse tells us His early occupation and that He grew up in a family with brothers and sisters. Later, people had a hard time reconciling this picture of Him as "the boy next door" with His being the Messiah.***

"'Isn't this the carpenter, the son of Mary, and the brother of James, Joses, Judas, and Simon? And aren't his sisters here with us?' *So they were offended by him.*'" - Mark 6:3 CSB

Questions:

1. Summarize the key points in the earthly life of Jesus from after His birth to the age of 30 when He begins His 3-year earthly public ministry.

2. How do we know that Jesus came for all people groups?

Questions with suggested answers:

1. Summarize the key points in the earthly life of Jesus from after His birth to the age of 30 when He begins His 3-year earthly public ministry.

Answer: There is the circumcision on Day 8 and his dedication in the Temple 33 days later (about day 40) when we learn the confirmatory statements of Simeon and Anna. At age 12 we get a glimpse of His superb intellect as He reasons and debates with the Pharisees in the Temple. He grew up in Nazareth and worked as a carpenter with His earthly father Joseph. They taught Him about God, and they were faithful in going to the Passover each year which provided religious education. He had siblings. The siblings and neighbors did not consider Him God. *Thus, Jesus grows up experiencing family, friends, worship, and work like most people did in His town and culture.* That is why He is so effective as our Savior – He understands us and our temptations. If He would have been a supernatural kid (in school and sports etc.) He would not be able to claim an understanding of the rest of us. Therefore, he had to be like his brothers and sisters in every way, so that he could become a merciful and faithful high priest in matters pertaining to God, to make atonement for the sins of the people. For since he himself has suffered when he was tempted, he is able to help those who are tempted. - Hebrews 2:17-18 CSB

2. How do we know that Jesus came for all people groups?

Answer: The Bible is "History – His Story" the story from start to finish. It is about Jesus because the world needed a Savior after the Fall in Genesis. God uses the Israelites to bring Jesus into the world, but salvation is for all of us. We know this because Simeon, a Jew, stated in the Jewish temple when he saw and held baby Jesus, "Simeon took him up in his arms, praised God, and said, Now, Master, you can dismiss your servant in peace, as you promised. For my eyes have seen your salvation. *You have prepared it in the presence of all peoples -- a light for revelation to the Gentiles and glory to your people Israel.*" - Luke 2:28-32 CSB

Phase 5: The 3-year earthly ministry of Jesus.

At this point Jesus is now 30 years old. He is a mature man who has grown up in a family with siblings, worshiped in the Temple with His Jewish friends, and experienced the influence of the Roman rulers. He has done all of this without people noticing anything extraordinary about Him. This will now dramatically change as He works to fulfill His specific aims that He was sent to earth for. What were these Specific Aims?

Aim 1: Establish that Jesus was God (His deity) in the flesh - the incarnation.

Aim 2: Prove that He was the Messiah - the One predicted in the Old Testament to come and save people from their sins.

Aim 3: Develop and mentor the disciples and other team members to carry on the ministry of the Church after He departs this earth.

3: Who is Jesus and What is He Like? Is Jesus God?

Aim 4: Live a sinless life of perfection.

Aim 5: Die by crucifixion (bloodshed) as the perfect sacrifice for the sins of all people. This was His main mission as discussed in John 17.

Aim 6: Be physically resurrected in the body (a dramatic miracle) and prove it for 40 days.

Aim 7: Ascend back to Heaven and send the Holy Spirit to direct the Church.

These Aims were perfectly choreographed, and all were accomplished.

- **How did Jesus accomplish these aims? What was His plan?**

Jesus said He was God the Son (Son of God). Christ-followers put their trust in Jesus because they are confident that He always was and is God. We often refer to this characteristic as "Christ's Deity" or the "Deity of Christ". This is a critical statement to prove because many will say that Jesus was "just a good man" or "an excellent teacher". The Bible clearly states that Jesus Himself knew who He was and that He was equal to God and was God in the flesh. God the Father and God the Holy Spirit testified to this fact also. Besides simply saying that He was God, Jesus also demonstrated it by His many miracles that were directly witnessed and recorded by the Apostles. Lastly, His ability to be resurrected from the dead is the biggest miracle of all.

- **John said Jesus is indeed God the Son. John tells us that when he wrote "Word", he meant Jesus. No one has ever seen God the Father, but many people saw God the Son.**

"In the beginning was the Word, and the Word was with God, and the Word was God."
- John 1:1 CSB

"No one has ever seen God. But his only Son, who is himself God, is near to the Father's heart; he has told us about him." John 1:18, NLT.
Revelation 19:11-13

- **How did Jesus see Himself? He said He was God!**

"When Jesus came to the region of Caesarea Philippi, he asked his disciples, 'Who do people say that the Son of Man is?' They replied, 'Some say John the Baptist; others, Elijah; still others, Jeremiah or one of the prophets.' 'But you,' he asked them, 'who do you say that I am?' Simon Peter answered, 'You are the Messiah, the Son of the living

God.' Jesus responded, 'Blessed are you, Simon son of Jonah, because flesh and blood did not reveal this to you, but my Father in heaven.'" - Matthew 16:13-17 CSB

• The Jewish leaders realized what He was saying – that He was God and it irritated them to the point that they executed Him. They totally missed it.
"This is why the Jews began trying all the more to kill him: Not only was he breaking the Sabbath, but he was even calling God his own Father, making himself equal to God." - John 5:18 CSB

• Jesus said, "Do you see me? If you do, then you are actually seeing God!"
"Jesus shouted to the crowds, 'If you trust me, you are really trusting God who sent me. *For when you see me, you are seeing the one who sent me.* I have come as a light to shine in this dark world, so that all who put their trust in me will no longer remain in the darkness.'" John 12:44-46, NLT.
John 14:9

"The Son reflects God's own glory, *and everything about him represents God exactly*. He sustains the universe by the mighty power of his command. After he died to cleanse us from the stain of sin, he sat down in the place of honor at the right hand of the majestic God of heaven." Hebrews 1:3, NLT.

• The Holy Spirit recognized Jesus as God as told by John the Baptist. The Holy Spirit was with Jesus in Heaven and on earth as predicted by Isaiah.
"I didn't know he was the one, but when God sent me to baptize with water, he told me, 'When you see the Holy Spirit descending and resting upon someone, he is the one you are looking for. He is the one who baptizes with the Holy Spirit.' I saw this happen to Jesus, so I testify that he is the Son of God."- John 1:33, 34, NLT.
Isaiah 11:2

• Apostles Paul and Peter clearly stated that Jesus was God.
"Concerning his Son, Jesus Christ our Lord, who was a descendant of David according to the flesh and was appointed to be the powerful Son of God according to the Spirit of holiness by the resurrection of the dead." - Romans 1:3-4 CSB
Romans 9:5, 2 Peter 1:1

3: Who is Jesus and What is He Like? Is Jesus God?

- ***He demonstrated qualities of God—He acted God-like—He could read our minds.***
"Jesus knew within himself that his disciples were complaining, so he said to them, 'Does this offend you?'" John 6:61, NLT.

- ***He was Omniscient; He accurately predicted His own future regarding His earthly death for our sins and resurrection 3 days later.***
"For I, the Son of Man, must suffer many terrible things," he said. "I will be rejected by the leaders, the leading priests, and the teachers of religious law. I will be killed, but three days later I will be raised from the dead." Luke 9:22, NLT.

- ***He accepted worship; never refused it. This supports the Deity of Christ.***
"The eleven disciples traveled to Galilee, to the mountain where Jesus had directed them. When they saw him, they worshiped, but some doubted." - Matthew 28:16-17 CSB

- ***He said He is the only way to Heaven.***
"Therefore I told you that you will die in your sins. For if you do not believe that I am he, you will die in your sins." - John 8:24 CSB

- ***He has total authority in heaven and on earth. No human, even a great human, would ever dare make such a statement.***
"Jesus came near and said to them, 'All authority has been given to me in heaven and on earth.'" - Matthew 28:18 CSB

- ***Jesus is the "Only Sovereign" (further evidence of monotheism); King of Kings; Lord of lords. He is also 'The Immortal One"; Jesus is forever.***
"I direct you in the presence of God, who gives life to all things, and of Christ Jesus, who testified the good confession before Pontius Pilate, that you keep the commandment without fault or reproach until the appearing of our Lord Jesus Christ, which He will bring about at the proper time--He who is the blessed and only Sovereign, the King of kings and Lord of lords, who alone possesses immortality and dwells in unapproachable light, whom no one has seen or can see. To Him be honor and eternal dominion! Amen."
- 1 Timothy 6:13-16 NASB
Revelation 17:14, Revelation 19:15, 16

- ***The demons believe that Jesus is God.***
"You believe that God is one. Good! Even the demons believe – and they shudder." - James 2:19 CSB
Matthew 8:28-33

- ***Jesus is God. This fact is established by His resurrection after dying on the cross.***
"The Good News is about his Son. In his earthly life he was born into King David's family line, and *he was shown to be the Son of God when he was raised from the dead by the power of the Holy Spirit.* He is Jesus Christ our Lord. Through Christ, God has given us the privilege and authority as apostles to tell Gentiles everywhere what God has done for them, so that they will believe and obey him, bringing glory to his name." - Romans 1:3-5 NLT

There are many gods but only one Jesus and only one God. This truth is key to the Christian faith and is clear from the many writers of Scripture quoted above. Time spent worshipping Jesus is worth it because He is indeed the Living God. Prayers that are offered to Him are heard; we do not pray to some dead idol, nor are we meditating on or to some mystical being. Our lives were bought with a heavy price by the death of Jesus and His resurrection makes Him worth worshipping.

Questions:

1. Why is it important for Jesus to be who He really said He is? What does it matter?

2. Explain the terms we often hear in Christmas songs, Christmas sermons – virgin birth, incarnation, annunciation, Messiah, and Immanuel.

3. The phrase "King of Kings and Lord of Lords" is a key part of Handel's Messiah. Where did Handel get that phrase?

Questions with suggested answers:

1. Why is it important for Jesus to be who He really said He is? What does it matter?

Answer: The key purpose for Jesus coming to earth was to be the 'perfect sacrifice' and thus die for our sin. If He was just a man, and fallible like all the rest of us, then He would not have fulfilled the ultimate sacrifice role, and we would die in our sin.

2. Explain the terms we often hear in Christmas songs, Christmas sermons - "virgin birth", incarnation and Messiah. Why is Christmas important? Contrast Christmas with Easter. Why do we give gifts at Christmas? How does Satan take away the meaning of Christmas?

Answer: The virgin birth refers to the fact that Mary became pregnant with Jesus in a miraculous way by the Holy Spirit without sexual intercourse with Joseph with whom she was engaged. This was necessary so that Jesus could claim He was "God in the flesh" not a normal human born of human egg and sperm. How this happened we are told no more than "by the Holy Spirit". It makes no scientific sense; we will have to wait until Heaven to ask how it was done. But the Bible clearly makes the point that Mary was a virgin and that is the way we see her today – the Virgin Mary. She went on to marry Joseph and they had children. She was a wonderful, godly, faithful woman for which we honor her for. However, we are never told to worship her. The term "incarnation" means "in the flesh" with carne meaning "flesh or meat". Jesus is "God in the flesh" or "God with skin on". This made Jesus more believable to people because they could see and talk with Him and worship Him. Christmas is important because it celebrates the incarnation event. We give gifts based on the wise men who brought gifts to Jesus as a baby. Satan has made Christmas into a commercial holiday by taking the gift-giving to extreme and the who Santa Claus story. It's important to "keep Christ in Christmas".

3. The phrase "King of Kings and Lord of Lords" is a key part of Handel's Messiah. Where did Handel get that phrase?

Answer: 1 Timothy 6:13-16 NASB20; Revelation 17:14 CSB; Revelation 19:15, 16, NLT.

Jesus said He was the Messiah. The writers of the Old Testament looked forward to the fulfillment of Genesis 3:15 - the coming of the Messiah who would provide the ultimate blood sacrifice to atone once and for all for our sins. This was the Messiah that was promised. But the date of the appearance of the Messiah and whom it was remained unknown. That is why Jesus establishes not only the fact that He is God in the flesh but also that indeed He is the one that was predicted – He is the Messiah and look for no other.

- *The angel in the birth announcement of Jesus to the shepherds said in effect that the Messiah has come. This is why the angels, and the shepherds are part of every Christmas play.*

"Then an angel of the Lord stood before them, and the glory of the Lord shone around them, and they were terrified. ...Today in the city of David a Savior was born for you, who is the Messiah, the Lord." - Luke 2:9, 11 CSB

- *Jesus was the Messiah that the Jews were looking for – He clearly said so.*

"I tell you this beforehand, so that when it happens you will believe that I AM the Messiah." - John 13:19 NLT

- **Jesus told the Pharisees He was the Messiah. They went ballistic!**

"But Jesus kept silent. The high priest said to him, 'I charge you under oath by the living God: Tell us if you are the Messiah, the Son of God.' 'You have said it,' Jesus told him. 'But I tell you, in the future you will see the Son of Man seated at the right hand of Power and coming on the clouds of heaven.' Then the high priest tore his robes and said, 'He has blasphemed! Why do we still need witnesses? See, now you've heard the blasphemy.'"
- Matthew 26:63-65 CSB

- **Jesus did numerous miracles to prove He was the Messiah. The verses that describe these miracles are too numerous to recite here (see Days 377-386 of Mostly Scripture qd.). John also said there were many more not recorded.**

"While he was in Jerusalem during the Passover Festival, many believed in his name when they saw the signs he was doing." - John 2:23 CSB

"Jesus performed many other signs in the presence of his disciples that are not written in this book. But these are written so that you may believe that Jesus is the Messiah, the Son of God, and that by believing you may have life in his name." - John 20:30-31 CSB

- **Even the Pharisees acknowledged His miracles.**

"Then the leading priests and Pharisees called the high council together. 'What are we going to do?' they asked each other. 'This man certainly performs many miraculous signs.'" - John 11:47 NLT

- **Peter said these miracles attested to Jesus' Deity and being the Messiah.**

"Fellow Israelites, listen to these words: This Jesus of Nazareth was a man attested to you by God with miracles, wonders, and signs that God did among you through him, just as you yourselves know." - Acts 2:22 CSB

- **Peter was convinced Jesus was the Messiah.**

"Therefore let all the house of Israel know with certainty that *God has made this Jesus, whom you crucified, both Lord and Messiah*." - Acts 2:36 CSB
Acts 5:42

"Simon Peter answered, '*You are the Messiah*, the Son of the living God'" Matthew 16:16, NLT.
Acts 3:20."

3: Who is Jesus and What is He Like? Is Jesus God?

• *Apollos, the great debater, said "The Messiah you are looking for is Jesus".*
Acts 18:27, 28

• *Martha believed He was the Messiah.*
John 11:21, 27

• *The people of Samaria studied Him and concluded He was the Messiah.*
John 4:40-42

• *Philip was convinced and preached all over that Jesus was the Messiah.*
Acts 8:5

• *Paul was convinced after his road to Damascus miraculous conversion.*
"Immediately he began proclaiming Jesus in the synagogues: 'He is the Son of God.' ... But Saul grew stronger and kept confounding the Jews who lived in Damascus by proving that Jesus is the Messiah." Acts 9:20, 22 CSB
Acts 17:2-3, Acts 18:5

• *Even the Devil believes that Jesus was the Messiah and is subservient to Jesus.*
"Some were possessed by demons; and the demons came out at his command, shouting, 'You are the Son of God.' *But because they knew he was the Messiah*, he stopped them and told them to be silent." Luke 4:41, NLT.
Luke 4:33-36

Questions:

1. Apollos was known as a great orator and debater. What does it say in Acts 18 about the source of information he used?

2. Read Isaiah 6 again. How do we know that Isaiah was talking about Jesus?

3. What were the predicted qualities of the Messiah in the Old Testament in Isaiah 53?

4. How did Jesus indeed fulfill those requirements?

Questions with suggested answers:

1. Apollos was known as a great orator and debater. What does it say in Acts 18 about the source of information he used?

Answer: "Now a Jew named Apollos, a native Alexandrian, *an eloquent man who was competent in the use of the Scriptures*, arrived in Ephesus. He had been instructed in the way of the Lord; and being fervent in spirit, *he was speaking and teaching accurately about Jesus,* although he knew only John's baptism. ... For he vigorously refuted the Jews in public, *demonstrating through the Scriptures* that Jesus is the Messiah." - Acts 18:24-25, 28 CSB

Apollos used the Bible as his source book to prove that Jesus was God. We should always examine the Bible when first addressing a question that comes up. What does the Bible say? Many times, you will have your answer. The Bible is time tested and since it is from God it is reliable.

2. Read Isaiah 6 again. How do we know that Isaiah was talking about Jesus?

Answer: We know because of what the Apostle John wrote in John 12:41. It says that the vision was about Jesus. This is a good example of how we say "Scripture explains Scripture". In other words, sometimes a New Testament passage will explain or expand upon an Old Testament one.

The Isaiah 6 text gives us a word picture of the power and majestic Jesus. In this passage we don't see the "gentle and serene" Jesus. He is that, but it is also important to understand His power and majesty. When you follow Jesus, you are following God and we need to be respectful. One of the best songs about Isaiah 6 is "I Saw the Lord" by Dallas Holm. You can listen to it on YouTube and you will be inspired.

3. What were the predicted qualities of the Messiah in the Old Testament in Isaiah 53?

Answer: Jesus was not recognized as the Messiah when He was young. He did not appear particularly remarkable in appearance. His suffering initially was interpreted that He was very human and indeed He did suffer pain and crucifixion as a human. His knowledge was evident when He was very young as He was able to discuss weighty matters with the Pharisees as a boy. His preaching, miracles and of course the resurrection and ascension were phenomenal and proof of His God nature.

4. How did Jesus indeed fulfill those requirements?

Answer: That is the story of the Gospels – it's all recorded to provide proof of the predictions in Isaiah 53. Read John 17 – Jesus prayer to God as He was nearing the

3: Who is Jesus and What is He Like? Is Jesus God?

completion of His work as Messiah. These verses tell us that Jesus was pre-existent in Heaven with God before the world began. The prayer indicates that Jesus was sent on a specific mission and that He would return to Heaven.

Was Jesus also human? What does the Bible say about His humanity?

As demonstrated above, Jesus clearly was God and the predicted Messiah. By taking on flesh, He thus had human physiology. The people living at that time saw Him in the flesh for 33 years and witnessed both His God nature and human nature.

• *When Jesus agreed to come to earth in the incarnation, He temporarily took on flesh. He, as God, came from Heaven to take on human 'carne' (meat or flesh). In order to become a bodily sacrifice for our sins He had to have a body and thus He had to become human to die a physical death.*

"The Word became flesh and dwelt among us. We observed his glory, the glory as the one and only Son from the Father, full of grace and truth." - John 1:14 CSB

• *This humanity was demonstrated by His recognition as part of the family of Joseph and Mary. Growing up He did not look any different than the other children. This caused irritation in the people when Jesus said He was the Messiah.*
John 6:42, Mark 6:3

• *He needed physical protection as a child.*
Matthew 2:13-14

• *The disciples recognized both His humanity and His deity.*
Acts 2:22-24

• *Luke shows His need for sleep while also showing His God-qualities in controlling nature. This was a miracle.*
Luke 8:22-25

• *He experienced hunger, thirst, and pain.*
"Then Jesus was led up by the Spirit into the wilderness to be tempted by the devil. After he had fasted forty days and forty nights, he was hungry." - Matthew 4:1-2 CSB John 19:28, Matthew 27:26-31

- **He had emotions.**

"I have told you these things so that my joy may be in you and your joy may be complete." - John 15:11 CSB

"Taking along Peter and the two sons of Zebedee, he began to be sorrowful and troubled. He said to them, 'I am deeply grieved to the point of death. Remain here and stay awake with me.'" - Matthew 26:37-38 CSB
Mark 3:5

"Jesus wept." - John 11:35 CSB

- *He experienced physical death – He died as a result of the crucifixion.*

"From noon until three in the afternoon darkness came over the whole land. About three in the afternoon Jesus cried out with a loud voice, 'Eli, Eli, lema sabachthani?' That is, 'My God, my God, why have you abandoned me?' ... But Jesus cried out again with a loud voice and gave up his spirit. ... So Joseph took the body, wrapped it in clean, fine linen, and placed it in his new tomb, which he had cut into the rock. He left after rolling a great stone against the entrance of the tomb." - Matthew 27:45-46, 50, 59-60 CSB

"When they came to Jesus, they did not break his legs since they saw that he was already dead. But one of the soldiers pierced his side with a spear, and at once blood and water came out." - John 19:33-34 CSB

Jesus needed to defeat Satan, the Devil, to fulfill the prediction in Genesis 3:15.

When Jesus came to earth it represented another opportunity for Satan to try and block the Messiah. He first attempted to do that through Herod when he ordered the execution of all the baby boys. Jesus was taken to Egypt and escaped. Then early in His earthly ministry Satan tries to tempt Jesus to take the easy way out and abandon the mission. Jesus deflects the temptation by using the Word of God. Jesus goes all the way to the Cross for us and completes the mission.

- *He was tempted to do evil, but He did not yield to the temptation.*
Luke 4:1-13

- *Perfection: despite living as a human, He lived a perfect, sinless life so that He could be the perfect sacrifice.*

3: Who is Jesus and What is He Like? Is Jesus God?

"For you were called to this, because Christ also suffered for you, leaving you an example, that you should follow in his steps. *He did not commit sin, and no deceit was found in his mouth;* when he was insulted, he did not insult in return; when he suffered, he did not threaten but entrusted himself to the one who judges justly." - 1 Peter 2:21-23 CSB

• *Righteous* – *when we believe in Jesus, God miraculously imparts His righteousness to us and we are saved, i.e., we "become right in His sight".*
"He made the one who did not know sin to be sin for us, so that in him we might become the righteousness of God." - 2 Corinthians 5:21 CSB

"More than that, I also consider everything to be a loss in view of the surpassing value of knowing Christ Jesus my Lord. Because of him I have suffered the loss of all things and consider them as dung, so that I may gain Christ and be found in him, not having a righteousness of my own from the law, but one that is through faith in Christ -- *the righteousness from God based on faith*." - Philippians 3:8-9 CSB

Jesus builds His team during His 3-year earthly ministry and the team then worked to build the Church after His resurrection.

• *Picking the team members.*
"As he was walking along the Sea of Galilee, he saw two brothers, Simon (who is called Peter), and his brother Andrew. They were casting a net into the sea -- for they were fishermen. 'Follow me,' he told them, 'and I will make you fish for people.' Immediately they left their nets and followed him. Going on from there, he saw two other brothers, James the son of Zebedee, and his brother John. They were in a boat with Zebedee their father, preparing their nets, and he called them. Immediately they left the boat and their father and followed him." - Matthew 4:18-22 CSB

• *Team training – Jesus' ministry was a mix of teaching, preaching, miracles and all the while building and mentoring His disciples. The disciples were eyewitnesses, and it was "on the job" training. Jesus was a great teacher.*
"Now Jesus began to go all over Galilee, teaching in their synagogues, preaching the good news of the kingdom, and healing every disease and sickness among the people." - Matthew 4:23 CSB

Matthew 22:33 CSB

"So they sent their disciples to him, along with the Herodians." 'Teacher,' they said, 'we know that you are truthful and teach truthfully the way of God. You don't care what anyone thinks nor do you show partiality.'" - Matthew 22:16 CSB

"Some of the scribes answered, 'Teacher, you have spoken well.'" - Luke 20:39 CSB
John 13:13 CSB

- *Miracles validated Jesus as the Messiah and taught the disciples how to trust the Holy Spirit to give them the power to do the miracles we see in the Book of Acts.*

Phase 7: The death and resurrection of Jesus – what did it accomplish?

Jesus in His humanity died as a blood sacrifice for our sins. It is understandable that God would require some payment (atonement) for the sins we commit; however, it is difficult to comprehend why He decided on a blood sacrifice. The need for blood goes way back to Genesis where God shed blood of animals to provide the skins to cover Adam and Eve after they sinned the first time. He also clearly showed the need for an animal sacrifice in the story of Cain and Abel (Genesis 4). Then the requirement for blood sacrifices in the Jewish temple for many years sets up the need for the final (and ultimate) sacrifice that Jesus provided. All along only the best cleanest animals were used for sacrifice. Jesus was the perfect sacrifice because He was perfect and sinless.

Jesus did die – this is important to provide validity for the resurrection. He died on a wooden cross using a Roman execution method called crucifixion.

- *Jesus told His disciples His mission was to fulfill the Law. He did that on the Cross for us.*

"Don't think that I came to abolish the Law or the Prophets. I did not come to abolish but to fulfill. For truly I tell you, until heaven and earth pass away, not the smallest letter or one stroke of a letter will pass away from the law until all things are accomplished."
- Matthew 5:17-18 CSB

- *Jesus predicted His death and the method – evidence that He was God and had total omniscience.*

Matthew 26:1-2

- *The Roman centurions certified His death. There were other witnesses; the execution was "open to the public".*

3: Who is Jesus and What is He Like? Is Jesus God?

"It was now about noon, and darkness came over the whole land until three, because the sun's light failed. The curtain of the sanctuary was split down the middle. And Jesus called out with a loud voice, 'Father, into your hands I entrust my spirit.' Saying this, he breathed his last. When the centurion saw what happened, he began to glorify God, saying, 'This man really was righteous!' All the crowds that had gathered for this spectacle, when they saw what had taken place, went home, striking their chests. But all who knew him, including the women who had followed him from Galilee, stood at a distance, watching these things." - Luke 23:44-49 CSB
1 Peter 3:18

- *Jesus died once and was resurrected once.*

"Because we know that Christ, having been raised from the dead, will not die again. Death no longer rules over him. For the death he died, he died to sin once for all time; but the life he lives, he lives to God." - Romans 6:9-10 CSB

- *All of us participated in His death – we all have sins that need redemption.*

"What then? Are we any better off? Not at all! For we have already charged that both Jews and Gentiles are all under sin," - Romans 3:9 CSB

- *Jesus died and was in the grave 3 days, but His body did not decay like ours when we die.*

"As to his raising him from the dead, never to return to decay, he has spoken in this way, I will give you the holy and sure promises of David. Therefore he also says in another passage, *You will not let your Holy One see decay*. For David, after serving God's purpose in his own generation, fell asleep, was buried with his fathers, and decayed, *but the one God raised up did not decay*." - Acts 13:34-37 CSB

Jesus was resurrected from the dead.

- *Jesus predicted His resurrection before He even died!*

"Jesus said to her, 'I am the resurrection and the life. The one who believes in me, even if he dies, will live. Everyone who lives and believes in me will never die. Do you believe this?'" - John 11:25-26 CSB
Matthew 26:63-64, John 8:21-24

- ***Bodily resurrection. Jesus was resurrected to physical life by the Holy Spirit. This was a miracle because it cannot be explained by nature or science. The power to resurrect Jesus came from the Holy Spirit.***

"The Good News is about his Son. In his earthly life he was born into King David's family line, and he was shown to be the Son of God when he was raised from the dead by the power of the Holy Spirit. He is Jesus Christ our Lord." - Romans 1:3-4 NLT

- ***The resurrection was observed by Mary and the disciples.***
Matthew 28:1-10

- ***Peter said He definitely died, but death could not hold Him. He was an eyewitness to the resurrection.***

"Though he was delivered up according to God's determined plan and foreknowledge, you used lawless people to nail him to a cross and kill him. God raised him up, ending the pains of death, because it was not possible for him to be held by death." - Acts 2:23-24 CSB

"God has raised this Jesus; we are all witnesses of this." - Acts 2:32 CSB
Acts 3:15

- ***Jesus in His resurrected physical body stays on earth for 40 days. 40 days of ministry post-resurrection provide "many convincing proofs".***

"I wrote the first narrative, Theophilus, about all that Jesus began to do and teach until the day he was taken up, after he had given instructions through the Holy Spirit to the apostles he had chosen. After he had suffered, he also presented himself alive to them by many convincing proofs, appearing to them over a period of forty days and speaking about the kingdom of God." - Acts 1:1-3 CSB

- ***Jesus was resurrected in His physical body. He ate food; He had wounds from the crucifixion. He continued to mentor and teach the disciples.***
John 21:12-15 CSB

- ***Paul says that there were over 500 eyewitnesses to the resurrected Jesus.***
1 Corinthians 15:3-6

- ***Paul says "Yes, He was crucified but God raised Him from the dead."***
Acts 13:29-31 CSB

3: Who is Jesus and What is He Like? Is Jesus God?

- ***The resurrection of Jesus is key to our eventual resurrection to new life in Heaven.***

"Now if Christ is proclaimed as raised from the dead, how can some of you say, 'There is no resurrection of the dead'? If there is no resurrection of the dead, then not even Christ has been raised; and if Christ has not been raised, then our proclamation is in vain, and so is your faith. Moreover, we are found to be false witnesses about God, because we have testified wrongly about God that he raised up Christ -- whom he did not raise up, if in fact the dead are not raised. For if the dead are not raised, not even Christ has been raised. And if Christ has not been raised, your faith is worthless; you are still in your sins. Those, then, who have fallen asleep in Christ have also perished. If we have put our hope in Christ for this life only, we should be pitied more than anyone." - 1 Corinthians 15:12-19 CSB

The death and resurrection of Jesus accomplished the aim of Jesus coming to earth to provide the sin solution. He took our sin and made it right (reconciliation).

- ***This was the ultimate rescue operation.***

"He has rescued us from the domain of darkness and transferred us into the kingdom of the Son he loves. In him we have redemption, the forgiveness of sins." - Colossians 1:13-14 CSB

Colossians 1:19-20, Colossians 1:21-23

- ***He is our High Priest. Jesus was sinless and thus the perfect high priest who mediates between people and God. That is what Jesus does for us.***

"He is the kind of high priest we need because he is holy and blameless, unstained by sin. He has been set apart from sinners and has been given the highest place of honor in heaven. Unlike those other high priests, he does not need to offer sacrifices every day. They did this for their own sins first and then for the sins of the people. But Jesus did this once for all when he offered himself as the sacrifice for the people's sins. The law appointed high priests who were limited by human weakness. But after the law was given, God appointed his Son with an oath, and his Son has been made the perfect High Priest forever." - Hebrews 7:26-28 NLT

- ***Jesus our High Priest forever because He was perfect and resurrected.***

Hebrews 7:22-28

- **Jesus the High Priest sacrificed Himself only once!** Then He 'sat down" in Heaven meaning it (the sacrifice) is complete. That is why Jesus said it is finished and why we refer to it as the "finished work of Jesus".

"But our High Priest offered himself to God as a single sacrifice for sins, good for all time. Then he sat down in the place of honor at God's right hand." - Hebrews 10:12 NLT

- **Jesus the High Priest who "has been there and understands us."**
Hebrews 4:14-16

- **Friend of sinners. Since we are all sinners, He indeed is our friend too!**
Luke 7:34

- **Jesus is God of both the dead and the living.**
Romans 14:9

- **Jesus is the Head of the Church.**
Colossians 1:18

Questions:

1. Why is Jesus referred to as "the foundation"?

2. How can Jesus be both the cornerstone of our faith and yet also be a stumbling stone?

3. Explain the futility of believing in Jesus if He was not really resurrected. See 1 Corinthians 15:12-19.

4. Why is Jesus resurrection so important? Read 1 Corinthians 15 and understand Paul's argument.

Questions with suggested answers:

1. Why is Jesus referred to as "the foundation"?

Answer: Foundations are important. In 2021 my place of work, the Mayo Clinic began constructing the Kellen Research Building adjacent to the parking deck where I always park my car. Each day I would look at the large hole in the ground and marveled over the months (yes months) at the painstaking care of the workers to prepare that hole and then pour tons of concrete into what became "the foundation". It seemed sometimes like the project was going slowly. But now its 2023 and the floors are forming, and the progress is going fast. The foundation is no longer in sight – it is covered by the floors, but I know it is there and will support that building and its research for years to come. The key point here is that foundations are very important in buildings and also to your spiritual life. If you do not get the foundation right (Jesus) the rest of your life (or building) will not be stable or productive. Jesus is your spiritual foundation – get Him early into your life and build your life on Him and the rest will follow.

2. How can Jesus be both the cornerstone of our faith and yet also be a stumbling stone?

Answer: It is readily apparent that Jesus is the keystone of the foundation of your spiritual life. He is the basis for the Christian faith and the Bible. So, how could He also be a stumbling stone? It is because since Jesus said that He was the only way to God and eternal life if you do not believe in Him then Jesus becomes a very controversial figure and people will "choke" or "stumble" on this concept.

3. Explain the futility of believing in Jesus if He was not really resurrected. See 1 Corinthians 15:12-19.

Answer: Jesus resurrection shows us that He has the power to be resurrection and will use that power to resurrect us when we die. This is the great hope for the Christ-follower – that no matter what happens to us we will be resurrected to new life in Jesus. That means eternity in Heaven. Eternity means forever.

4. Why is Jesus resurrection so important? Read 1 Corinthians 15 and understand Paul's argument.

Answer: Paul argues first that without the proven resurrection of Jesus we might as well not bother with following Jesus – "we are of all men most miserable". He also argues that if we cannot believe the resurrection of Jesus how can we hope to be resurrected and spend eternity in Heaven. Our resurrection hope is linked to Jesus! But fortunately, we have much eye-witness proof of over 500 people and 40 days of appearances to verify the resurrection. The key here is "The last enemy to be abolished is death." – 1 Corinthians 15:26 CSB. Jesus resurrection overcomes the death that came into the world in Genesis after sin entered. The battle between Satan and God began then, Jesus was predicted to win, and He did so with the resurrection. The resurrection also proves that Jesus death for us on the cross was "acceptable to God as fulfilling the Law". If Jesus was still in the grave, it would signal that He lost to the devil, and we are still in our sin.

Phase 8: The 40 days and the Ascension of Jesus back to Heaven.

The period between the resurrection and the return of Jesus to Heaven is very important. It provides many eyewitnesses to the resurrection and Jesus provided important instructions to the disciples. He is able to tell them about the coming of the Holy Spirit when He returns to Heaven. This emboldens the disciples and solidifies their understanding of Jesus as Messiah. If Jesus had gone from grave to heaven immediately it would be more difficult to believe He was really alive. The passages below are the threads of evidence for these eyewitness accounts.

- *Jesus predicted His return to Heaven.*
"Peace I leave with you. My peace I give to you. I do not give to you as the world gives. Don't let your heart be troubled or fearful. You have heard me tell you, 'I am going away and I am coming to you.' If you loved me, you would rejoice that I am going to the Father, because the Father is greater than I. I have told you now before it happens so that when it does happen you may believe. I will not talk with you much longer, because the ruler of the world is coming. He has no power over me." – John 14:27-30 CSB

- *40 days between resurrection and ascension from Luke in Acts 1.*
"I wrote the first narrative, Theophilus, about all that Jesus began to do and teach until the day he was taken up, after he had given instructions through the Holy Spirit to the apostles he had chosen. After he had suffered, *he also presented himself alive to them by many convincing proofs, appearing to them over a period of forty days and speaking about the kingdom of God."* – Acts 1:1-3 CSB

- *The un-named couple who met Jesus on the road to Emmaus; they received valuable teaching from the risen Jesus.*
Luke 24:13-35

- *Jesus appears to His disciples, now 11 in number, and proves He was physically resurrected by eating and showing them the scars from the crucifixion.*
Luke 24:36-49

3: Who is Jesus and What is He Like? Is Jesus God?

- *Jesus bestows the Holy Spirit on the 11 (actually 10 since Thomas not there).*
"When it was evening of that first day of the week, the disciples were gathered together with the doors locked because they feared the Jews. Jesus came, stood among them, and said to them, 'Peace be with you.' Having said this, he showed them his hands and his side. So the disciples rejoiced when they saw the Lord. Jesus said to them again, 'Peace to you. As the Father has sent me, I also send you.' After saying this, he breathed on them and said, 'Receive the Holy Spirit.' If you forgive the sins of any, they are forgiven them; if you retain the sins of any, they are retained." – John 20:19-23 CSB

- *This happens a second time a week later for Thomas's sake.*
John 20:24-29

- *Jesus gives His final instructions to the disciples, The Great Commission.*
"The eleven disciples traveled to Galilee, to the mountain where Jesus had directed them. When they saw him, they worshiped, but some doubted. Jesus came near and said to them, 'All authority has been given to me in heaven and on earth. Go, therefore, and make disciples of all nations, baptizing them in the name of the Father and of the Son and of the Holy Spirit, teaching them to observe everything I have commanded you. And remember, I am with you always, to the end of the age.'" – Matthew 28:16-20 CSB

"While he was with them, he commanded them not to leave Jerusalem, but to wait for the Father's promise. Which, he said, you have heard me speak about; for John baptized with water, but you will be baptized with the Holy Spirit in a few days. So when they had come together, they asked him, Lord, are you restoring the kingdom to Israel at this time? He said to them, It is not for you to know times or periods that the Father has set by his own authority. But you will receive power when the Holy Spirit has come on you, and you will be my witnesses in Jerusalem, in all Judea and Samaria, and to the end of the earth." – Acts 1:4-8 CSB

- *Ascension – it was another eyewitness event.*
"Then he led them out to the vicinity of Bethany, and lifting up his hands he blessed them. And while he was blessing them, he left them and was carried up into heaven. After worshiping him, they returned to Jerusalem with great joy. And they were continually in the temple praising God." – Luke 24:50-53 CSB
Acts 1:9-11

Question with suggested answer:

How important are the 40 days of ministry that Jesus conducted after His resurrection?

Answer: Well, think about it. Jesus definitely was dead and then He was resurrected by the Holy Spirit. If He would have immediately ascended back, then we would not have the eyewitness accounts. The fact that 40 days elapsed is also key – that is a long time, and He was visible to many. Paul says, "Now I want to make clear for you, brothers and sisters, the gospel I preached to you, which you received, on which you have taken your stand and by which you are being saved, if you hold to the message I preached to you – unless you believed in vain. For I passed on to you as most important what I also received: that Christ died for our sins according to the Scriptures, that he was buried, that he was raised on the third day according to the Scriptures, and that he appeared to Cephas, then to the Twelve. T*hen he appeared to over five hundred brothers and sisters at one time; most of them are still alive, but some have fallen asleep.* Then he appeared to James, then to all the apostles. Last of all, as to one born at the wrong time, he also appeared to me." – 1 Corinthians 15:1-8 CSB

Phase 9: The current work of Jesus – what is Jesus doing now? Where is He today? What's next?

• *He said He was going back to prepare a place for us!*

"Don't let your heart be troubled. Believe in God; believe also in me." In my Father's house are many rooms; if not, I would have told you. I am going away to prepare a place for you. "If I go away and prepare a place for you, I will come again and take you to myself, so that where I am you may be also." – John 14:1-3 CSB
John 14:18-20

• *Advocate – Jesus is your advocate in Heaven. He is always "for you".*

"For Christ did not enter a sanctuary made with hands (only a model of the true one) but into heaven itself, so that he might now appear in the presence of God for us." – Hebrews 9:24 CSB
1 Peter 3:21-22

3: Who is Jesus and What is He Like? Is Jesus God?

• ***Jesus is the exact representation of God; He sits today at God's right hand. Notice He "sits" indicating that His work of saving us is complete.***
"The Son reflects God's own glory, *and everything about him represents God exactly*. He sustains the universe by the mighty power of his command. After he died to cleanse us from the stain of sin, *he sat down in the place of honor at the right hand of the majestic God of heaven.*" Hebrews 1:3, NLT.
Ephesians 1:20-21

• ***Jesus is the Head of the Church (that's all of us believers).***
Ephesians 1:22-23

• ***Peter said that Jesus is back in Heaven until He returns again to restore all things. This will be the greatest miracle.***
Acts 3:21

• ***John's vision of Jesus in Rev 1. This is what Jesus is doing today – alive and powerful. We serve a Risen Jesus who is in Heaven working on our behalf.***
Revelation 1:12-18

"The twenty-four elders fall down before the one seated on the throne and worship the one who lives forever and ever. They cast their crowns before the throne and say, Our Lord and God, you are worthy to receive glory and honor and power, because you have created all things, and by your will they exist and were created." – Revelation 4:10-11 CSB

• ***Jesus is being honored today in Heaven as He sits on the throne. Notice He is called Lamb here. These verses are in Handel's Messiah sung at Christmas.***
"Then I looked and heard the voice of many angels around the throne, and also of the living creatures and of the elders. Their number was countless thousands, plus thousands of thousands. They said with a loud voice, Worthy is the Lamb who was slaughtered to receive power and riches and wisdom and strength and honor and glory and blessing! I heard every creature in heaven, on earth, under the earth, on the sea, and everything in them say, Blessing and honor and glory and power be to the one seated on the throne, and to the Lamb, forever and ever!" – Revelation 5:11-13 CSB

Phase 10: The return of Jesus for His Church and Judge of all People.

This is the most exciting part of the story of Jesus because it has not yet happened. Jesus promised to come back to retrieve us from this earth and its associated sorrows and bring us to Heaven where we will live with Him forever. This is the Great Promise, the hope of all believers. In the Bible this is called the "day of the LORD". You will sometimes here this referred to as "the rapture" but that word is not in the Bible.

- *Jesus is coming back for us. When? Soon but the exact date nobody knows. People will make fun of this fact since it has not yet happened.*

"Above all, be aware of this: Scoffers will come in the last days scoffing and following their own evil desires, saying, 'Where is his coming that he promised? Ever since our ancestors fell asleep, all things continue as they have been since the beginning of creation.'" – 2 Peter 3:3-4 CSB

- *The delay in His return is allowing others to be saved. God is patient.*

"The Lord does not delay his promise, as some understand delay, but is patient with you, not wanting any to perish but all to come to repentance." – 2 Peter 3:9 CSB
2 Peter 3:15 CSB

- *Jesus says – Be Alert for you do not know when this next event will happen. It can happen anytime – like a "thief in the night".*

Mark 13:32-37 CSB

"But the day of the Lord will come like a thief. The heavens will disappear with a roar; the elements will be destroyed by fire, and the earth and everything done in it will be laid bare." – 2 Peter 3:10 NIV
2 Peter 3:10 KJV

- *Don't despair – He could come again at any moment. That is our hope.*

"Look, I am coming soon! Blessed is the one who keeps the words of the prophecy of this book." – Revelation 22:7 CSB

- *What are we to do in the meantime? We wait and live holy lives.*

"Since all these things are to be dissolved in this way, it is clear what sort of people you should be in holy conduct and godliness *as you wait for the day of God* and hasten its coming. Because of that day, the heavens will be dissolved with fire and the elements will melt with heat. But based on his promise, *we wait for new heavens and a new earth*, where

righteousness dwells. Therefore, *dear friends, while you wait for these things*, make every effort to be found without spot or blemish in his sight, at peace." – 2 Peter 3:11-14 CSB
2 Peter 3:17-18

• *John got a glimpse of what heaven will be like.*
- Revelation 21:1-4

Questions:

1. How can Jesus be called both a lion and a lamb?

2. How can Jesus be both a cornerstone and a stumbling stone?

3. Why is it important to understand that God and Jesus are "light" and Satan is "darkness"?

4. In John 15:11-15 who are the shepherd, the wolf, and the sheep?

5. When Jesus was close to His ascension to Heaven, He gave the disciples specific instructions and ended with the "I am with you always". What does that mean for you?

Questions with suggested answers:

1. How can Jesus be called both a lion and a lamb?

Answer: Jesus is the Lamb of God because He was the sacrificial lamb to shed blood as a sacrifice for the sin of all peoples. It is important to also see Him as Lion because if we always picture Jesus as the baby in the manger and gentle, we miss a key characteristic – the Lion aspect. There is only one verses in the Bible that calls Him Lion.

"Then one of the elders said to me, 'Do not weep. Look, *the Lion from the tribe of Judah*, the Root of David, has conquered so that he is able to open the scroll and its seven seals.'"
- Revelation 5:5 CSB

2. How can Jesus be both a cornerstone and a stumbling stone?

Answer: Jesus is called the cornerstone because He is the foundation of our faith. Peter tells the Jewish leaders in the Acts 4 passage that Jesus healed the man in question and that Jesus was the Messiah. He quotes the Old Testament verse in Psalm 118:22 that Jesus was the stone rejected – a link to the fact that the Jews rejected Him as Messiah. A cornerstone of a building historically was the first stone that was carefully set. It was important to make sure the subsequent structure was positioned correctly. That is why Jesus is so important to your life's foundation. Get Him right into your life the rest will follow.

3. Why is it important to understand that God and Jesus are "light" and Satan is "darkness"?

Answer: If Jesus is going to be "the Way" and the "only way to God" then the path to Him must be well-lighted and clear. And it is if you look for it. Satan will always lead you into darkness. As John put it in 1 John when you are in the dark you cannot see and are essentially blind. But the one who hates his brother or sister is in the darkness, walks in the darkness, and doesn't know where he's going, because the darkness has blinded his eyes. - 1 John 2:11 CSB. Jesus had to win over Satan to overcome evil. He did that by winning the temptation battle with Satan and He destroyed the works of Satan. But when people keep on sinning, it shows that they belong to the devil, who has been sinning since the beginning. But the Son of God came to destroy the works of the devil. - 1 John 3:8 NLT

"The time for judging this world has come, when Satan, the ruler of this world, will be cast out." - John 12:31 NLT The completion will come in the future as revealed in Revelation. "Then the devil, who had deceived them, was thrown into the fiery lake of burning sulfur, joining the beast and the false prophet. There they will be tormented day and night forever and ever." - Revelation 20:10 NLT

Satan (aka the devil) works always to kill and destroy whereas Jesus brings life and light. The best verse example on this is John 10:10 "A thief comes only to steal and kill and destroy. I have come so that they may have life and have it in abundance." Another example is the case of the proconsul and the sorcerer Elymas. Notice that the devil, working in this case through Elymas tries always to thwart the work of the Holy Spirit. Paul works a miracle through the power of the Holy Spirit to block Elymas.

"When they had traveled the whole island as far as Paphos, they came across a sorcerer, a Jewish false prophet named Bar-Jesus. He was with the proconsul, Sergius Paulus, an intelligent man. This man summoned Barnabas and Saul and wanted to hear the word of God. But Elymas the sorcerer (that is the meaning of his name) opposed them and tried to turn the proconsul away from the faith. But Saul -- also called Paul -- filled with the Holy Spirit, stared straight at Elymas and said, 'You are full of all kinds of deceit and trickery, you son of the devil and enemy of all that is right. Won't you ever stop perverting the straight paths of the Lord?'" - Acts 13:6-10 CSB

4. In John 15:11-15 who are the shepherd, the wolf, and the sheep?

Answer: This is a good example of a spiritual metaphor. Jesus is the good shepherd, the wolf is the devil and we the people are the sheep.

5. When Jesus was close to His ascension to Heaven, He gave the disciples specific instructions and ended with the "I am with you always". What does that mean for you?

Answer: You can answer this for yourself but for me it is a powerful promise. Jesus never promised us an easy way on this earth. As a Christian we may be ridiculed and persecuted and even martyred. But Jesus promises us that He is there right with us, we are never alone. If you visit the city of Haarlem near Amsterdam, the Netherlands you can visit the house that Corrie and Betsie Ten Boom hid Jews from the Germans in World War II. Eventually they were discovered and sent to a concentration camp where they were tortured, and Betsie dies. Corrie survived and wrote *The Hiding Place* which became a movie. In it she quotes Betsie who says during the depths of the torture, "They placed the stretcher on the floor and I leaned down to make out Betsie's words, '...must tell people what we have learned here. We must tell them that *there is no pit so deep that He is not deeper still*. They will listen to us, Corrie, because we have been here.'" This is the meaning of Matthew 28:20 "I am with you always". John 14:16 says the same for the Holy Spirit.

Names for Jesus - Son of God, Son of Man, and Son of David.

As one reads the verses above about Jesus it will be noticed how He is sometimes called the Son of God or Son of Man or Son of David. What do these titles mean?

Son of God. Depending on the version of the Bible you are using the term 'Son of God' is used many times – 889 for example in the KJV with 48 exact phrases. Obviously there are too many to record here but its easy to find them electronically. Here are a few key examples.

- ***The angels in the annunciation***
"The angel replied to her, 'The Holy Spirit will come upon you, and the power of the Most High will overshadow you. Therefore, the holy one to be born will be called the Son of God.'" - Luke 1:35 CSB

- ***Satan and his demons referred to Jesus as the Son of God.***
Matthew 4:3, Mark 3:11 CSB

- ***Jesus called Himself the Son of God***
John 3:18

- ***The disciples and Martha believed He was the Son of God.***
Matthew 14:33, Mark 1:1

"Rabbi," Nathanael replied, "You are the Son of God; you are the King of Israel!" - John 1:49 CSB
John 11:27

- ***The centurion at the crucifixion***
Matthew 27:54

- ***The apostle Paul***
"...and was appointed to be the powerful Son of God according to the Spirit of holiness by the resurrection of the dead." - Romans 1:4 CSB

Son of Man. This title is recorded some 81 times in all 4 Gospels, 69 times in the Synoptic Gospels (Matthew, Mark, and Luke), and 30 times alone in Matthew. Jesus when He came to earth as a human being was fully human. As mentioned above, He had to grow up, He had emotions, He suffered immeasurable pain for us on the Cross. Thus, Jesus in His humanity as a human sacrifice is the Son of Man. This does not take away from His Deity but rather emphasizes His purpose to be a human sacrifice for our sin.

- ***Jesus understood both titles and is entitled to be called both Son of God and Son of Man.***
"But Jesus kept silent. The high priest said to him, I charge you under oath by the living God: Tell us if you are the Messiah, the Son of God. You have said it, Jesus told him. But I tell you, in the future you will see the Son of Man seated at the right hand of Power and coming on the clouds of heaven." - Matthew 26:63-64 CSB

Matthew 16:13-17

"For the Son of Man has come to seek and to save the lost." - Luke 19:10 CSB

Son of David – His Jewish name. There are 16 times in the CSB (all in the New Testament Gospels) where Jesus is referred to as the Son of David. This title is a fulfillment of the prophecy in 2 Samuel 7 given to David from the prophet Nathan. "Your house and kingdom will endure before me forever, and your throne will be established forever." - 2 Samuel 7:16 CSB. This title is also Messianic in that it confirms that Jesus is the predicted Messiah.

An account of the genealogy of Jesus Christ, the Son of David, the Son of Abraham: - Matthew 1:1 CSB
Matthew 9:27, Matthew 12:23, Matthew 15:22, Matthew 20:30-31, Matthew 21:9, Revelation 22:16

Other titles or names for Jesus. Now that it is clear what Jesus' aims were and His characteristics, we need to review some of the other names for Jesus that you will encounter in Bible reading, in Christian music, and in listening to sermons. These names used in the Bible expand on His attributes What do these mean?

Savior of the World—only the Apostle John records this title.
1 John 4:14

Light – Jesus is always referred to as light.
John 1:4-5

"Jesus spoke to them again: 'I am the light of the world. Anyone who follows me will never walk in the darkness but will have the light of life.'" - John 8:12 CSB
John 12:34-36

• *In Heaven the light of Jesus will be all that is needed for illumination.*
Revelation 21:23-26

Lamb of God whose sacrifice will be for all people.

"The next day John saw Jesus coming toward him and said, 'Here is the Lamb of God, who takes away the sin of the world!'" - John 1:29 CSB
Revelation 7:17

The Way – Jesus is the Way and the Only Way.

"Jesus told him, 'I am the way, the truth, and the life. No one comes to the Father except through me.'"
- John 14:6 CSB
John 8:24

The True Vine. Jesus is our source of spiritual strength.
John 15:1, 5

Bread of Life – a word picture of Jesus as necessary for spiritual vitality.
John 6:32-35

The Gate – Jesus is the One Gate to Heaven, and we are the sheep.
John 10:7-9

The Good Shepherd; The Great Shepherd of the Sheep; The Chief Shepherd
John 10:11-15, Revelation 7:17, Hebrews 13:20-21, 1 Peter 5:4 CSB

Righteous judge
Isaiah 11:5, 2 Timothy 4:8

Lion
Revelation 5:5

Spiritual Rock – Jesus is a solid rock.
1 Corinthians 10:4

Foundation for life and eternity.
1 Corinthians 3:11

Cornerstone and also a Stumbling stone

"Then Peter was filled with the Holy Spirit and said to them, 'Rulers of the people and elders: ...let it be known to all of you and to all the people of Israel, that by the name of Jesus Christ of Nazareth, whom you crucified and whom God raised from the dead -- by him this man is standing here before you healthy. This Jesus is the stone rejected by you builders, which has become the cornerstone.'" - Acts 4:8, 10-11 CSB
Ephesians 2:20, 1 Peter 2:6

"So honor will come to you who believe; but for the unbelieving, The stone that the builders rejected -- this one has become the cornerstone, and A stone to stumble over, and a rock to trip over. They stumble because they disobey the word; they were destined for this." - 1 Peter 2:7-8 CSB

Conqueror of evil and of Satan.
1 John 3:8

Faithful witness; firstborn from the dead; ruler of all.
Revelation 1:5

The Alpha and the Omega – the beginning and the end.
Revelation 22:13

Prince of Peace; Wonderful Counselor
Isaiah 9:6

Other key characteristics of Jesus.

• *Loving - Jesus was loving and had a servant attitude.*
John 13:1-5

• *Unchanging – He will always be the same!*
"Jesus Christ is the same yesterday, today, and forever." - Hebrews 13:8 CSB

• *Jesus is always with us – all the way. We are never alone.*
"Teaching them to observe everything I have commanded you. And remember, I am with you always, to the end of the age." - Matthew 28:20 CSB

• *Authoritative – Jesus exemplifies His authority over religious Law by identifying flaws in the religious teachings of the day by the Pharisees in the Sermon on the Mount chapter 5. He was not afraid to show His authority and superiority. He gives 6 examples and 6 corrections. The first is given below.*

Current Teaching: "*You have heard* - Matthew 5:21 CSB

Correction by Jesus: "*But I tell you,* - Matthew 5:22 CSB

Thomas Witzig

Questions:

1) When viewing some of the great paintings of Jesus why do they often include a corona? The art below of Madonna and Child is from a 15th century painting by an unknown artist. It is now in the National Gallery of Art, Widener Collection (in the public domain; https://www.nga.gov/collection/art-object-page.1189.html). It is also a US Postal Service 2016 Forever Stamp.

2. If you were taking a class on Comparative Religions, what should be said about Christianity? How would you compare it to the Jewish religion or Hinduism or Islam or Buddhism? What are the critical differences?

Questions with suggested answers:

1. When viewing some of the great paintings of Jesus why do they often include a corona?

Answer: This is sometimes referred to as a halo. Because of His deity, the artist believed the Scriptures that said Jesus is God. It can also mean holiness and spiritual light.

2. If you were taking a class on Comparative Religions, what should be said about Christianity? How would you compare it to the Jewish religion or Hinduism or Islam or Buddhism? What are the critical differences?

Answer: Obviously, a Comparative Religion class takes up a whole semester and entire books are written on this subject. To keep our answer short, let's focus on Christianity. Christianity is based on its Founder, Jesus Christ, and His teachings. Jesus was not just a good person, nor just a prophet or god (little g god). Rather, He was and is God (a big G God). He lived a sinless life in the flesh on earth, died for us, was resurrected and is alive today in Heaven with God the Father and God the Holy Spirit. Now how does that compare with the stated religions of the world?

4

Who is the Holy Spirit and What are His Functions?

In the King James Translation of the Bible (the Authorized version of 1611) the Holy Spirit was referred to as the "Holy Ghost". Today, more modern translations use "Holy Spirit" for obvious reasons. The Holy Spirit was present in both the Old and New Testament but there was a difference. In the Old Testament we observe the Holy Spirit coming onto people for specific reasons or tasks; it was not a continual presence. In the New Testament Jesus clearly states that after He returned to Heaven, the Holy Spirit would come to dwell in the Christian from the time of their conversion and be there with the person for the rest of their life. He would not "come and go" as in the Old Testament. Thus, when we become a Christ-follower the Holy Spirit immediately comes into us and is with us at all times. These are powerful verses that tell us all the functions of the Holy Spirit. I trust you will be greatly encouraged by the Holy Spirit.

Who is the Holy Spirit?

• ***The Holy Spirit is the third Person in the Trinity***. The Trinity is composed of God the Father, Jesus (God the Son), and the Holy Spirit. When we become a Christian, we are baptized and during this sacred rite the pastor will baptize the person in the names of the Trinity "I now baptize you in the name of the Father, the Son, and the Holy Spirit." This is based on Matthew 28 where Jesus came near and said to them, 'All authority has been given to me in heaven and on earth. Go, therefore, and make disciples of all nations, baptizing them in the name of the Father and of the Son and of the Holy Spirit, "eaching them to observe everything I have commanded you. And remember, I am with you always, to the end of the age.'" - Matthew 28:18-20 CSB

- ***The Holy Spirit is "Holy" (sacred) and a "Spirit" (not flesh).*** He, like God the Father and Jesus the Son, was present at the creation of the earth.

"The earth was empty, a formless mass cloaked in darkness. And the Spirit of God was hovering over its surface." Genesis 1:2, NLT.
John 3:5-6

- ***Other names used for the Holy Spirit = Counselor, Spirit of truth.***
"When the Counselor comes, the one I will send to you from the Father -- the Spirit of truth who proceeds from the Father -- he will testify about me." - John 15:26 CSB

- ***The Holy Spirit knows the thoughts of God—because He is part of the Trinity.***
"No one can know what anyone else is really thinking except that person alone, and no one can know God's thoughts except God's own Spirit." 1 Corinthians 2:11, NLT.

- ***The Holy Spirit lives in our bodies; more specifically in our hearts. Your body is a temple of the Holy Spirit, and it is holy. This is a very important concept to grasp.***
"He has also put his seal on us and given us the Spirit in our hearts as a down payment."
- 2 Corinthians 1:22 CSB

"Don't you realize that your body is the temple of the Holy Spirit, who lives in you and was given to you by God? You do not belong to yourself, for God bought you with a high price. So you must honor God with your body." - 1 Corinthians 6:19-20 NLT
Romans 8:11, 1 John 3:24, 1 Corinthians 3:16-17 CSB

- ***There is only one Holy Spirit for both Jews and the Gentiles; we share Him.***
"Some of us are Jews, some are Gentiles, some are slaves, and some are free. But we have all been baptized into one body by one Spirit, and we all share the same Spirit." - 1 Corinthians 12:13 NLT

- ***He is like the wind, unseen but felt and mysterious.***
"Jesus answered, 'Truly I tell you, unless someone is born of water and the Spirit, he cannot enter the kingdom of God. Whatever is born of the flesh is flesh, and whatever is born of the Spirit is spirit. Do not be amazed that I told you that you must be born again. The wind blows where it pleases, and you hear its sound, but you don't know where it comes from or where it is going. So it is with everyone born of the Spirit.'" - John 3:5-8 CSB
Acts 2:2-4

4: Who is the Holy Spirit and What are His Functions?

When Do We Get the Holy Spirit?

• *The Holy Spirit is key to becoming a Christ-follower. He convicts us of our sin.*
"Nevertheless, I am telling you the truth. It is for your benefit that I go away, because if I don't go away the Counselor will not come to you. If I go, I will send him to you." *When he comes, he will convict the world about sin, righteousness, and judgment."* - John 16:7-8 CSB

• *Repent and be baptized, and then receive the Holy Spirit in that order.*
"Peter replied, 'Repent and be baptized, each of you, in the name of Jesus Christ for the forgiveness of your sins, and you will receive the gift of the Holy Spirit.'" - Acts 2:38 CSB

• *We receive the Holy Spirit at the time we believe in Jesus.* The Holy Spirit is obtained by faith not by a certain amount of good works or by keeping the Mosaic Law.
"Let me ask you this one question: Did you receive the Holy Spirit by obeying the law of Moses? Of course not! You received the Spirit because you believed the message you heard about Christ." - Galatians 3:2 NLT
Galatians 3:5, Galatians 3:14, Matthew 3:11 CSB

• *Jesus "breathed" the invisible Holy Spirit to the disciples prior to ascending to Heaven.*
"Jesus said to them again, 'Peace to you. As the Father has sent me, I also send you.' After saying this, he breathed on them and said, 'Receive the Holy Spirit.'" - John 20:21-22 CSB

• *The Holy Spirit is given to us because of God's love for us.*
Romans 5:3-5

• *Christ-followers have the Holy Spirit; unbelievers do not.*
"But you, dear friends, remember what was predicted by the apostles of our Lord Jesus Christ. They told you, In the end time there will be scoffers living according to their own ungodly desires. These people create divisions and are worldly, not having the Spirit." - Jude 1:17-19 CSB
1 John 4:1-2, 1 John 2:20, Romans 8:9 CSB

• *Indeed, the presence of the Holy Spirit is proof of salvation and that God is real.*
Acts 10:47-48 CSB

"Peter replied, Repent and be baptized, each of you, in the name of Jesus Christ for the forgiveness of your sins, and you will receive the gift of the Holy Spirit." - Acts 2:38 CSB

"And God has given us his Spirit as proof that we live in him and he in us." - 1 John 4:13 NLT
Romans 8:16-17

- ***You can test the spirit by what it says about Jesus***. Any speech that is degrading about Jesus cannot be coming from the Holy Spirit.
1 Corinthians 12:3

"Dear friends, do not believe every spirit, but test the spirits to see if they are from God, because many false prophets have gone out into the world. This is how you know the Spirit of God: *Every spirit that confesses that Jesus Christ has come in the flesh is from God, but every spirit that does not confess Jesus is not from God.* This is the spirit of the antichrist, which you have heard is coming; even now it is already in the world." - 1 John 4:1-3 CSB

Questions:
1. What is the importance of the Biblical concept of your body being the Temple of the Holy Spirit? Read 1 Corinthians 3:19-20 again.

2. When do you receive the Holy Spirit?

Questions with suggested answers:
1. What is the importance of the Biblical concept of your body being the Temple of the Holy Spirit? Read 1 Corinthians 3:19-20 again.

Answer: First, it tells us that God values our bodies. He created each of us as unique genetic human beings with a genetic code given by God at the time of conception. That code determined our genetic sex, our skin color, whether we would be tall or short compared to others and even some aspects of our metabolism and where fat is distributed on our bodies. We are to care for our bodies and obviously we can determine to some extent how we look, weigh, or act. Secondly, if the body is the temple of the Holy Spirit, we are not to destroy our bodies by taking our own life. Thirdly, these verses speak to the current (2024) subject of gender dysphoria where some people feel the need to change the way their genetic sex characteristics are portrayed to others. Gender dysphoria is a medical condition or disorder and requires medical care and treatment. It is different than any other letter in the LGBTQ acronym. Fourth, harming or killing another person in an act of murder is considered a crime because it destroys the body in which the Holy Spirit dwells.

2. When do you receive the Holy Spirit?

Answer: When you become a Christ follower. The Holy Spirit is Holy and He is a spirit so you will not see Him. As we will see below, the Holy Spirit is key to your knowing the will of God and to help you understand spiritual truth. Remember, there are many "little s" spirits in the world and they are evil. They will tempt you to do evil. There is only one Holy Spirit. You can tell the difference by what they think of Jesus (read 1 John 4 again).

What Does the Holy Spirit Do?

• *Responsible for the miracle of Mary becoming pregnant with Jesus without sexual activity. This is referred to as the virgin birth and represents the Incarnation (God coming to us in the carne or flesh).*
"This is how Jesus the Messiah was born. His mother, Mary, was engaged to be married to Joseph. But before the marriage took place, while she was still a virgin, she became pregnant through the power of the Holy Spirit." - Matthew 1:18 NLT
Matthew 1:19-21, Luke 1:30-35

• *Filled Jesus with joy while He was living in the flesh on the earth. Jesus does not need the Holy Spirit in Heaven. The Holy Spirit brings joy to your life.*
- Isaiah 11:2

"At that same time Jesus was filled with the joy of the Holy Spirit, and he said, 'O Father, Lord of heaven and earth, thank you for hiding these things from those who think themselves wise and clever, and for revealing them to the childlike. Yes, Father, it pleased you to do it this way.'" - Luke 10:21 NLT
Acts 10:38

• *Provided proof that Jesus was the Messiah when He was on the earth. Notice the Spirit is like a dove that mysteriously comes upon Jesus. In religious art, the Spirit is usually depicted as a dove – a way to show on canvas something that is otherwise invisible.*

"And John testified, 'I saw the Spirit descending from heaven like a dove, and he rested on him. I didn't know him, but he who sent me to baptize with water told me the one you see the Spirit descending and resting on -- he is the one who baptizes with the Holy Spirit.'" - John 1:32-33 CSB
Matthew 3:16

• *Responsible for the resurrection of Jesus.*
"The Good News is about his Son. In his earthly life he was born into King David's family line, and he was shown to be the Son of God when he was raised from the dead by the power of the Holy Spirit. He is Jesus Christ our Lord." - Romans 1:3-4 NLT
Romans 8:11

• *Assisted in writing the Bible; He moves us to write.*
"Above all, you know this: No prophecy of Scripture comes from the prophet's own interpretation, because no prophecy ever came by the will of man; instead, men spoke from God as they were carried along by the Holy Spirit." - 2 Peter 1:20-21 CSB

• *We need the Holy Spirit to receive spiritual truth and understand it*. Interestingly, spiritual truth is revealed to those with a childlike nature. In other words, the most intelligent or wealthy people are not necessarily smart in the ways of the Lord. Remember, God first revealed the birth of Jesus to lowly shepherds.
1 Thessalonians 1:5-6

"At that same time Jesus was filled with the joy of the Holy Spirit, and he said, 'O Father, Lord of heaven and earth, thank you for hiding these things from those who think themselves wise and clever, and for revealing them to the childlike. Yes, Father, it pleased you to do it this way.'" - Luke 10:21 NLT

• *Revealed the mystery that Christ is for all people groups.*
Ephesians 3:1-6, Acts 10:45-48

• *The Holy Spirit is a Teacher, a deep search engine.*
1 Corinthians 2:10-16

"But you have received the Holy Spirit, and he lives within you, so you don't need anyone to teach you what is true. *For the Spirit teaches you all things*, and what he teaches is true—it is not a lie. So continue in what he has taught you, and continue to live in Christ." 1 John 2:27, NLT.

4: Who is the Holy Spirit and What are His Functions?

Questions:

1. Why did Jesus say to the Apostles that it was really important that He, Jesus, return to Heaven in John 16:7?

2. Demons are evil spirits. They fell with Satan from Heaven when they rebelled against God (angels have a choice too). Satan and the evil spirits are working against God and against you. So, with that in mind, how do you discern if it is an evil spirit or the true Holy Spirit that is advising you?

3. How do you explain the evil behavior of some people?

Questions with suggested answers:

1. Why did Jesus say to the Apostles that it was really important that He, Jesus, return to Heaven in John 16:7?

Answer: Because although they wanted the resurrected Jesus to stay around on this earth, Jesus said it was more important that they have dwelling in them the Holy Spirit. He is our guide to truth. "When the Spirit of truth comes, he will guide you into all the truth. For he will not speak on his own, but he will speak whatever he hears. He will also declare to you what is to come." - John 16:13 CSB

2. Demons are evil spirits. They fell with Satan from Heaven when they rebelled against God (angels have a choice too). Satan and the evil spirits are working against God and against you. So, with that in mind, how do you discern if it is an evil spirit or the true Holy Spirit that is advising you?

Answer: A. Only the Holy Spirit will honor Jesus and call Him LORD and Savior. "But every spirit that does not confess Jesus is not from God. This is the spirit of the antichrist, which you have heard is coming; even now it is already in the world." - 1 John 4:3 CSB. B. People who are true believers will listen to God; others who are not will not want to hear or obey the truth of the Bible." They are from the world. Therefore what they say is from the world, and the world listens to them. We are from God. Anyone who knows God listens to us; anyone who is not from God does not listen to us. This is how we know the Spirit of truth and the spirit of deception." - 1 John 4:5-6 CSB

3. How do you explain the evil behavior of some people?

Answer: People who do not have the Holy Spirit indwelling them and guiding them revert to natural instincts (read Jude 19 again). Romans 1 tells us the sins we will get into if we follow our natural ways without God.

• *Helps us understand spiritual wisdom. He reveals the deep meaning of things. He is the ultimate search engine.*
"But it was to us that God revealed these things by his Spirit. For his Spirit searches out everything and shows us even God's deep secrets." 1 Corinthians 2:10, NLT.

"The person without the Spirit does not accept the things that come from the Spirit of God but considers them foolishness, and cannot understand them because they are discerned only through the Spirit." - 1 Corinthians 2:14 NIV
1 Corinthians 2:12-13, Ephesians 1:17, Revelation 3:13 NLT

• *Our advocate, but this advocacy is consistent with God's will.*
"And the Father who knows all hearts knows what the Spirit is saying, for the Spirit pleads for us believers in harmony with God's own will." Romans 8:27, NLT.
Romans 8:16, John 14:16-17

• *Gives new life. He is the key to your transformation as a Christ-follower.*
"He saved us, not because of the righteous things we had done, but because of his mercy. He washed away our sins, giving us a new birth and new life through the Holy Spirit. He generously poured out the Spirit upon us through Jesus Christ our Savior. Because of his grace he declared us righteous and gave us confidence that we will inherit eternal life." - Titus 3:5-7 NLT
2 Corinthians 3:17-18

• *Helps guard the truth.*
2 Timothy 1:14

• *Energizes preaching—the Holy Spirit can take the Bible and make it effective.*
"My speech and my preaching were not with persuasive words of wisdom but with a demonstration of the Spirit's power, so that your faith might not be based on human wisdom but on God's power." - 1 Corinthians 2:4-5 CSB
Luke 4:14

4: Who is the Holy Spirit and What are His Functions?

• *Sends out missionaries.*
"Sent out by the Holy Spirit, Saul and Barnabas went down to the seaport of Seleucia and then sailed for the island of Cyprus." Acts 13:4, NLT.
Isaiah 61:1, Acts 8:39, 40

• *Prays for you when you are in deep distress. He knows your needs that are consistent with His will. Pray in the power of the Holy Spirit.*
Romans 8:26-27

"But you, dear friends, must build each other up in your most holy faith, pray in the power of the Holy Spirit.:" - Jude 1:20 NLT
Ephesians 6:18, Ephesians 6:17-19

• *Fruit production—the Holy Spirit produces the fruit of the Spirit.*
"But the *fruit of the Spirit* is love, joy, peace, patience, kindness, goodness, faithfulness, gentleness, and self-control. The law is not against such things. Now those who belong to Christ Jesus have crucified the flesh with its passions and desires. If we live by the Spirit, let us also keep in step with the Spirit. Let us not become conceited, provoking one another, envying one another." - Galatians 5:22-26 CSB

Question with suggested answer:

Discuss the meaning of I Cor 2:14 and apply it how people respond to Bible teachings in society today. "The person without the Spirit does not accept the things that come from the Spirit of God but considers them foolishness, and cannot understand them because they are discerned only through the Spirit." - 1 Corinthians 2:14 NIV

Answer: The Holy Spirit is necessary to really open a person's eyes and heart to the truth of the Bible. That is why so many people ignore the teachings of the Bible and simply "go their own way". They overtly disobey the principles of the Bible – they just do not care what the Bible says nor even if you read it to them, it just doesn't sink in or make sense to them. It's like a "foreign language" to them.

• *The Holy Spirit is your personal coach and trainer – listen to Him!*
"For all those led by God's Spirit are God's sons. You did not receive a spirit of slavery to fall back into fear. Instead, you received the Spirit of adoption, by whom we cry out, 'Abba, Father!' The Spirit himself testifies together with our spirit that we are God's

children, and if children, also heirs -- heirs of God and coheirs with Christ -- if indeed we suffer with him so that we may also be glorified with him." - Romans 8:14-17 CSB

• *Guides your thought life. If you do not have the Holy Spirit, then you are not a believer. Your sin nature will lead you to death.*
Romans 8:5-9

• *The Holy Spirit leads…we follow.*
"Those who belong to Christ Jesus have nailed the passions and desires of their sinful nature to his cross and crucified them there. If we are living now by the Holy Spirit, let us follow the Holy Spirit's leading in every part of our lives." Galatians 5:24, 25, NLT.

• *Works synergistically with God and Jesus to be your guide.*
John 16:13-15

• *Gave direction when people worship and fast!*
"One day as these men were worshiping the Lord and fasting, the Holy Spirit said, 'Dedicate Barnabas and Saul for the special work I have for them.'" Acts 13:2, NLT.

• *The Holy Spirit guides and compels and in some cases, He blocks our intentions. The examples of Paul and Silas, Jesus, Philip, John the Baptist, and Simeon*
"Next Paul and Silas traveled through the areas of Phrygia and Galatia, because the Holy Spirit had told them not to go into the province of Asia at that time." Acts 16:6, NLT.
Acts 20:22, Mark 1:12, Luke 4:1, Acts 8:29, Luke 1:13, 15, Luke 2:25-26

• *The Holy Spirit is a counselor. The Holy Spirit is on call 24/7, 365 days a year. He will never leave you hanging.*
"But the Counselor, the Holy Spirit, whom the Father will send in my name, will teach you all things and remind you of everything I have told you." - John 14:26 CSB

"And I will ask the Father, and he will give you another Counselor, who will never leave you." John 14:16, NLT.

• *Keeps us unified.*
"Therefore I, the prisoner in the Lord, urge you to live worthy of the calling you have received, with all humility and gentleness, with patience, bearing with one another in

love, making every effort to keep the unity of the Spirit through the bond of peace." - Ephesians 4:1-3 CSB

• *Provides us boldness to witness for Jesus.*
Acts 4:31

• *Gives spiritual gifts - each of us receives at least one from the same Holy Spirit to be used for His glory.*
"There are different kinds of spiritual gifts, but the same Spirit is the source of them all." - 1 Corinthians 12:4 NLT

• *Many types of gifts – read this passage to learn them.*
1 Corinthians 12:7-11

• *The Spiritual Gift of Languages. The Holy Spirit enables some to have the gift of speaking in different languages.*
Acts 2:1-4, NLT.

• *The Holy Spirit gives us words to speak, especially when under duress, in prison or in court.*
Luke 21:14, 15, NLT.

"When you are arrested, don't worry about what to say in your defense, because you will be given the right words at the right time. For it won't be you doing the talking—it will be the Spirit of your Father speaking through you." Matthew 10:19, 20, NLT.
Mark 13:11

• *Speaks to us when we worship.*
"One day as these men were worshiping the Lord and fasting, the Holy Spirit said, 'Dedicate Barnabas and Saul for the special work I have for them.'" Acts 13:2, NLT.

• *Selects leaders who are full of the Holy Spirit instead of themselves.*
"Now look around among yourselves, brothers, and select seven men who are well-respected and are full of the Holy Spirit and wisdom. We will put them in charge of this business." Acts 6:3, NLT.
Acts 9:17, Acts 4:31

• *Talk down demons; we need the Holy Spirit when dealing with the devil.*
Acts 13:9-11

"But if I am casting out demons by the Spirit of God, then the Kingdom of God has arrived among you." Matthew 12:28, NLT.

"But you belong to God, my dear children. You have already won a victory over those people, because the Spirit who lives in you is greater than the spirit who lives in the world." - 1 John 4:4 NLT

- ***The gift of the Holy Spirit to each of us is a powerful and very significant gift. It is not trivial; it removes fear.***

"For all those led by God's Spirit are God's sons. You did not receive a spirit of slavery to fall back into fear. Instead, you received the Spirit of adoption, by whom we cry out, 'Abba, Father!'" - Romans 8:14-15 CSB

- *Gives us the ability to love other people.*

Romans 5:3-5

"Dear brothers and sisters, I urge you in the name of our Lord Jesus Christ to join in my struggle by praying to God for me. *Do this because of your love for me, given to you by the Holy Spirit.*" - Romans 15:30 NLT
Colossians 1:7-8

Question with suggested answer:

Do you ever have difficulty loving other people? Or a specific person? Perhaps a family member or co-worker? What does Colossians 1:7-8 say about this?

Answer: This is a little-known concept or passage. It tells us that the Holy Spirit can actually give us the ability to love a person who otherwise might be offensive to us or rub us the wrong way. If you find yourself in a difficult situation with an interpersonal relationship, read this verse and ask the Holy Spirit to help you love them.

- *Gives hope.*

"For we eagerly await through the Spirit, by faith, the hope of righteousness." - Galatians 5:5 CSB

- ***Prevents us from sinning by giving us power to overcome or not to yield to sin. He will free you from the power of sin.***

2 Corinthians 3:17

4: Who is the Holy Spirit and What are His Functions?

"For the power of the life-giving Spirit has freed you through Christ Jesus from the power of sin that leads to death." Romans 8:2, NLT.
Romans 8:11-15

• *Warns us of false teachings that come from the evil one (aka demons).*
"Now the Holy Spirit tells us clearly that in the last times some will turn away from what we believe; they will follow lying spirits and teachings that come from demons." 1 Timothy 4:1, NLT.

• *Helps to control our thought lives.*
"Those who are dominated by the sinful nature think about sinful things, but those who are controlled by the Holy Spirit think about things that please the Spirit. So letting your sinful nature control your mind leads to death. But letting the Spirit control your mind leads to life and peace. For the sinful nature is always hostile to God. It never did obey God's laws, and it never will. That's why those who are still under the control of their sinful nature can never please God. But you are not controlled by your sinful nature. You are controlled by the Spirit if you have the Spirit of God living in you. (And remember that those who do not have the Spirit of Christ living in them do not belong to him at all.)" - Romans 8:5-9 NLT

• *Encourages church growth.*
Acts 9:31

• *Brings mercy.*
Hebrews 10:29

• *We do good things by the Holy Spirit.*
2 Corinthians 6:4, 6

• *We walk by the Holy Spirit's guidance; we are led by Him.*
"I say then, walk by the Spirit and you will certainly not carry out the desire of the flesh. For the flesh desires what is against the Spirit, and the Spirit desires what is against the flesh; these are opposed to each other, so that you don't do what you want. But if you are led by the Spirit, you are not under the law." - Galatians 5:16-18 CSB

• *Knows what God is thinking.*
"No one can know what anyone else is really thinking except that person alone, and no one can know God's thoughts except God's own Spirit." 1 Corinthians 2:11, NLT.

- ***The Holy Spirit as a sword, a symbol of the Bible.***
"Put on salvation as your helmet, and take the sword of the Spirit, which is the word of God." Ephesians 6:17, NLT.

- ***Guardian of your faith.***
"Hold on to the pattern of sound teaching that you have heard from me, in the faith and love that are in Christ Jesus. Guard the good deposit through the Holy Spirit who lives in us." - 2 Timothy 1:13-14 CSB

- ***Preaching is in the power of the Holy Spirit.***
"They were told that these things would not happen during their lifetime, but many years later, during yours. And now this Good News has been announced by those who preached to you in the power of the Holy Spirit sent from heaven. It is all so wonderful that even the angels are eagerly watching these things happen." 1 Peter 1:12, NLT.
Acts 10:44

Examples of the Holy Spirit in action in the Old Testament. Now that we understand the nature and functions of the Holy Spirit, the third member of the trinity, we will look at some of the many examples from Scripture. These are some of the great stories of the Bible. Remember that in the Old Testament, the Holy Spirit was given to people for specific tasks whereas in the New Testament, after Jesus was on the earth, He is given to all of us at the time of conversion.

- ***Bezalel was given the Holy Spirit to design the Tabernacle. He is the first recorded person in the Old Testament to receive the Holy Spirit. Notice what the Holy Spirit did – it provided Bezalel the gift of wisdom and ability (artist and craftsman).***
"Then the LORD said to Moses, Look, I have specifically chosen Bezalel son of Uri, grandson of Hur, of the tribe of Judah. I have filled him with the Spirit of God, giving him great wisdom, ability, and expertise in all kinds of crafts. He is a master craftsman, expert in working with gold, silver, and bronze. He is skilled in engraving and mounting gemstones and in carving wood. He is a master at every craft!" - Exodus 31:1-5 NLT
Exodus 35:30-35

- ***The Holy Spirit was given to the 70 elders to help them judge the people.*** This was the beginning of the Sanhedrin (assembly or council) that eventually would judge Jesus and turn Him over to Pilate (Romans) for crucifixion. The 70 elders received a one-time gift of the Holy Spirit.
Numbers 11:16-17

4: Who is the Holy Spirit and What are His Functions?

"Moses went out and told the people the words of the LORD. He brought seventy men from the elders of the people and had them stand around the tent. Then the LORD descended in the cloud and spoke to him. He took some of the Spirit that was on Moses and placed the Spirit on the seventy elders. As the Spirit rested on them, they prophesied, but they never did it again." - Numbers 11:24-25 CSB

• *Eldad and Medad – they were given the Spirit to predict the future (prophesy).*
Numbers 11:26

• *Isaiah was given the Holy Spirit as a guide to the Israelites.* He brought Good News to the people.
Isaiah 61:1

• *Joseph – Pharaoh realized that the key to Joseph's success was the Holy Spirit.*
Genesis 41:37-39

• *Balaam prophesied under the direction of the Holy Spirit. He did not ask for the Holy Spirit; rather, the Holy Spirit used Balaam.*
Numbers 24:2-4

• *Zechariah – this is a great verse that reminds us that we accomplish things not so much in our own strength but rather by the Holy Spirit.*
Zechariah 4:6

• *Jahaziel's prediction in the Old Testament was from the Holy Spirit.*
2 Chronicles 20:13-15, NLT.

• *Joshua the second commander of the Israelites was given the Holy Spirit to lead the Israelites. This gave him wisdom to lead.*
Numbers 27:18-20, Deuteronomy 34:9

Question with suggested answer:

Read again 2 Chronicles 20:13-15. Where was Jahaziel when the Holy Spirit suddenly came upon him and enabled him to speak truth to the Israelites that prepared them for battle?

Answer: He was "standing before the LORD". If you read the verses just before verse 13 Jehoshaphat was afraid, and he resolved to seek the LORD. Then he proclaimed a fast for all Judah, who gathered to seek the LORD. They even came from all the cities of Judah to seek him. Then Jehoshaphat stood in the assembly of Judah and Jerusalem in the LORD's temple before the new courtyard. - 2 Chronicles 20:3-5 CSB. This passage notes that the people, including Jahaziel and his family, were in the Temple when this happened. This provides a clue for us today– in order to receive that kind of direction from the Holy Spirit we need to be worshipping God and listening to Him and listening for Him to speak to us. That can be meditating on the Word of God at home or in church (temple).

• *Othniel – Caleb's nephew, had the Holy Spirit to help him as a judge of Israel.*
Judges 3:9-10

• *Gideon was given the Spirit that enabled him to entice people to follow him.*
Judges 6:34

• *Jephthah*
Judges 11:29

• *Samson – the Spirit first came quietly and "stirred him"; then it came powerfully upon him, and he became supernaturally strong.*
Judges 13:24-25, Judges 14:5-6

"When he came to Lehi, the Philistines came to meet him shouting. The Spirit of the LORD came powerfully on him, and the ropes that were on his arms and wrists became like burnt flax and fell off. He found a fresh jawbone of a donkey, reached out his hand, took it, and killed a thousand men with it." - Judges 15:14-15 CSB

• *Samson lost physical strength when "the LORD left him". Hair was a metaphor of his strength. Profound continual disobedience led to his downfall.*
"Then she let him fall asleep on her lap and called a man to shave off the seven braids on his head. In this way, she made him helpless, and his strength left him. Then she cried, "Samson, the Philistines are here! When he awoke from his sleep, he said, 'I will escape as I did before and shake myself free.' But he did not know that the LORD had left him."
- Judges 16:19-20 CSB

- **King Saul did well when the Spirit was with him. When you feel the power of the Holy Spirit you need to act. The Holy Spirit's presence is "transformational".**
"The Spirit of the LORD will come powerfully on you, you will prophesy with them, and you will be transformed. When these signs have happened to you, do whatever your circumstances require because God is with you." - 1 Samuel 10:6-7 CSB
1 Samuel 10:10-11

- **The Holy Spirit could also be withdrawn as in the case of Saul (and Samson).**
"Now the Spirit of the LORD had left Saul, and an evil spirit sent from the LORD began to torment him." - 1 Samuel 16:14 CSB

- **Saul's soldiers.**
1 Samuel 19:20-24

- **Elisha asked for a double portion of the Holy Spirit because he realized just how valuable it was for his effectiveness. It was a wise request.**
2 Kings 2:8-14

- **David was anointed as King of Israel and the Holy Spirit empowered him.**
1 Samuel 16:13

- **David was aware of the danger of losing the Holy Spirit.**
"Turn your face away from my sins and blot out all my guilt. God, create a clean heart for me and renew a steadfast spirit within me. Do not banish me from your presence or take your Holy Spirit from me."
- Psalm 51:9-11 CSB

- **David said on his deathbed that it was the Spirit that spoke through him.**
2 Samuel 23:1-4

- **Zerubbabel—it's the Holy Spirit—not a physical army.**
"So he answered me, This is the word of the LORD to Zerubbabel: '*Not by strength or by might, but by my Spirit, says the LORD of Armies.*'" - Zechariah 4:6 CSB

Thomas Witzig

Question with suggested answer:

How did these Old Testament characters notice the Holy Spirit?

Answer: David perceived the Holy Spirit impacting his speech; Samson felt it in his physical strength; Gideon was inspired to lead others and they followed – they must have sensed that he was a great leader. For Saul it was the ability to prophesy (predict the future). In the other cases the leaders somehow felt it. They perceived the strength. It is indeed a mysterious, indescribable feeling that the Holy Spirit provides. Pray that the Holy Spirit will make Himself known to you. Put yourself in a position to listen. That means set time away to read Scripture and pray.

New Testament examples of the Holy Spirit in action.

• ***Elizabeth, the mother of John the Baptist, was filled with the Holy Spirit while pregnant with John and when meeting the pregnant (Jesus) Mary.***
"At the sound of Mary's greeting, Elizabeth's child leaped within her, and *Elizabeth was filled with the Holy Spirit.*" Luke 1:41, NLT.

• ***John the Baptist – had the Holy Spirit before he was even born!***
"But the angel said to him: Do not be afraid, Zechariah, because your prayer has been heard. Your wife Elizabeth will bear you a son, and you will name him John. There will be joy and delight for you, and many will rejoice at his birth. For he will be great in the sight of the Lord and will never drink wine or beer. He will be filled with the Holy Spirit while still in his mother's womb. He will turn many of the children of Israel to the Lord their God." - Luke 1:13-16 CSB

• ***Zachariah, the father of John the Baptist and a priest, prophesied with the power of the Holy Spirit.***
"Then his father, Zechariah, was filled with the Holy Spirit and gave this prophecy:" Luke 1:67, NLT.

• ***Simeon.*** The Holy Spirit came on him because he was righteous, and he was looking forward (not backward) to Jesus. Always look forward to Jesus.
Luke 2:25-27 CSB

4: Who is the Holy Spirit and What are His Functions?

- ***The Holy Spirit dwelt in Jesus. It is symbolized by a dove.***

"Then John said, "I saw the Holy Spirit descending like a dove from heaven and resting upon him. I didn't know he was the one, but when God sent me to baptize with water, he told me, 'When you see the Holy Spirit descending and resting upon someone, he is the one you are looking for. He is the one who baptizes with the Holy Spirit.' I saw this happen to Jesus, so I testify that he is the Son of God." John 1:32-34, NLT.
Acts 10:37-38

- ***The Trinity functions as a singular unit.***

"God raised Jesus from the dead, and we are all witnesses of this. Now he is exalted to the place of highest honor in heaven, at God's right hand. And the Father, as he had promised, gave him the Holy Spirit to pour out upon us, just as you see and hear today."
- Acts 2:32-33 NLT

- ***Barnabas—be like him—full of the Holy Spirit and strong in faith.***
Acts 11:22-24

- ***Stephen—he had wisdom and was able to debate in the public square effectively and with wisdom because of the Holy Spirit. He also saw the resurrected Jesus in Heaven through the power of the Holy Spirit.***

"Now Stephen, full of grace and power, was performing great wonders and signs among the people. Opposition arose, however, from some members of the Freedmen's Synagogue, composed of both Cyrenians and Alexandrians, and some from Cilicia and Asia, and they began to argue with Stephen. But they were unable to stand up against his wisdom and the Spirit by whom he was speaking." - Acts 6:8-10 CSB
Acts 7:54-56

- ***Peter - the Holy Spirit filled him during his preaching—somewhat spontaneously. Peter says he in a sense heard the Holy Spirit speaking to him. We are to be ready anytime for the filling and influence of the Holy Spirit in our lives.***

"Then Peter, filled with the Holy Spirit, said to them, "Leaders and elders of our nation..."
Acts 4:8, NLT.
Acts 10:19-21

- **Paul – *attributed his effective speech to the Holy Spirit.***
"My speech and my preaching were not with persuasive words of wisdom but with a *demonstration of the Spirit's power*, so that your faith might not be based on human wisdom but on God's power." - 1 Corinthians 2:4-5 CSB
Acts 21:4

Questions:

1. Can we have the Holy Spirit?

2. What do you notice about Paul, Stephen, and Peter – great apostles in the book of Acts?

Questions with suggested answers:

1. Can we have the Holy Spirit?

Answer: Of course – you must have the Holy Spirit and you will get the Holy Spirit at the time of belief in Jesus. It is not something that you buy or work for. The only way to obtain the Holy Spirit is to acknowledge faith in Jesus for your sins and become a Christ-follower. Now, how you listen to the Holy Spirit, depend on Him, respond to Him, and acknowledge Him is dependent on your walk with Jesus.

2. What do you notice about Paul, Stephen, and Peter – great apostles in the book of Acts?

Answer: They did great things but never took credit themselves. Everything they did was attributed to the Holy Spirit working through them.

Two sins against the Holy Spirit that you should never commit - blasphemy of the Holy Spirit and lie to the Holy Spirit.

- ***Blasphemy against or insult the Holy Spirit.*** Blasphemy according to Webster's Dictionary is "the act of insulting or showing contempt or lack of reverence for God". *https://www.merriam-webster.com/dictionary/blasphemy* accessed February 19, 2024.

"Therefore, I tell you, people will be forgiven every sin and blasphemy, but the blasphemy against the Spirit will not be forgiven." Whoever speaks a word against the Son of Man, it will be forgiven him; *but whoever speaks against the Holy Spirit, it will not be forgiven him, either in this age or in the one to come.*" - Matthew 12:31-32 CSB

4: Who is the Holy Spirit and What are His Functions?

"Anyone who speaks against the Son of Man can be forgiven, *but anyone who blasphemes the Holy Spirit will not be forgiven.*" - Luke 12:10 NLT
Mark 3:28-30

Blasphemy of the Holy Spirit is an unpardonable sin where the person attributes the miracles of Christ or the Holy Spirit to the devil. The reason this sin is unpardonable is that to believe in Jesus we need the Holy Spirit. If we deny the Holy Spirit and instead believe the devil, it's hard to believe in Jesus. In other words, if you reject the Holy Spirit who is leading you to Jesus then it's impossible to get to Jesus.

• *Lie* – never lie to the Holy Spirit and God—the case of Ananias and Saphira.
Acts 5:3-5, Ephesians 4:30

What are the best summary passages to read and meditate on the Holy Spirit?

• *To get strength from the Holy Spirit meditate on these verses.*
Ephesians 3:14-21

• *To get control of your mind meditate on these verses.*
Romans 8:1-17

Question with suggested answer:

In astrology people search for spirit guides. How are they different from the Holy Spirit?

Answer: The Holy Spirit is the only "Spirit" that you want or need. *You will only be able to get the Holy Spirit by being a Christ-follower.* Do not seek out any other 'spirit guides' as they are potentially an evil spirit. Remember, the Evil One (Satan, the Devil) is always trying to counterfeit the real Holy Spirit and lead us astray. This happened to Saul when he visited the medium (witch) of En-dor in 1 Samuel 28. This is a frightening story, but it is a reminder that people practicing occult practices can indeed bring up supernatural visions. That does not mean you are communicating with the Holy Spirit but rather an evil spirit. Don't go there; stick with the Holy Spirit.

Thomas Witzig

5

What is Truth? A Biblical View

"What is truth?" is the famous statement uttered by Pontius Pilate, the Roman governor of Judea who sentenced Jesus to death ("What is truth?" said Pilate. After he had said this, he went out to the Jews again and told them, "I find no grounds for charging him." - John 18:38 CSB). People today still try to define truth because it is difficult to live in a world that is filled with deception and lies. The Bible clearly declares itself to be true and Jesus says that He is truth; therefore, the Bible and Jesus' teachings are a vital source of truth. Many of these truths are high-level, foundational principles that are easily applied to the situations we face today. Knowing the truth (and why it is truth) is not just important to individuals but also to our nation. "For look, the wicked string bows; they put their arrows on bowstrings to shoot from the shadows at the upright in heart. *'When the foundations are destroyed, what can the righteous do?'*" - Psalm 11:2-3 CSB

How do you tell if something is false? To do so one needs to know the truth. Back when paper money was the standard, thieves would try to pass counterfeit bills. People that worked at the banks to receive the money (they were called bank tellers) were taught how to detect counterfeit money. The instructors spent most of the time teaching them what true money looked like rather than showing them the many examples of false money. By knowing the truth, it was easy to spot a counterfeit. The same goes with Biblical truth. *In this section we will not discuss all the strategies used to deceive, but rather what truth is as defined by the Bible.*

- ***God's nature is truth. He said this to Moses as He was giving him the 10 Commandments. This is exactly the opposite of Satan who is by nature a liar.***

"Moses cut two stone tablets like the first ones. He got up early in the morning, and taking the two stone tablets in his hand, he climbed Mount Sinai, just as the LORD had commanded him. The LORD came down in a cloud, stood with him there, and proclaimed his name, "the LORD." The LORD passed in front of him and proclaimed: The LORD -- the LORD is a compassionate and gracious God, slow to anger and abounding in faithful love and truth," - Exodus 34:4-6 CSB

- ***God's word (the Bible) is truth and can be trusted. God by nature cannot lie.***

"For the word of the LORD holds true, and everything he does is worthy of our trust." Psalms 33:4, NLT.
Psalms 89:14, 2 Samuel 7:28

"In the hope of eternal life that God, who cannot lie, promised before time began." - Titus 1:2 CSB

- ***Satan however is evil, ignores the truth, and lies.***

"Jesus said to them, 'If God were your Father, you would love me, because I came from God and I am here. For I didn't come on my own, but he sent me." Why don't you understand what I say? Because you cannot listen to my word.' You are of your father the devil, and you want to carry out your father's desires. He was a murderer from the beginning and does not stand in the truth, because there is no truth in him. When he tells a lie, he speaks from his own nature, because he is a liar and the father of lies." - John 8:42-44 CSB.

- ***God wants us to know the truth.***

"This is good, and it pleases God our Savior, who wants everyone to be saved and to come to the knowledge of the truth." - 1 Timothy 2:3-4 CSB

- ***God's judgements are based on truth.***

"We know that God's judgment on those who do such things is based on the truth." - Romans 2:2 CSB

- ***We are told to always try to get the truth.***

"Get the truth and never sell it; also get wisdom, discipline, and good judgment." - Proverbs 23:23 NLT

5: What is Truth? A Biblical View

- **We do have a choice in what we believe. David said, "choose truth".**
"I have chosen the way of truth; I have set your ordinances before me." - Psalm 119:30 CSB

- **God values truth and can get angry when people do not tell it.**
"After the LORD had finished speaking to Job, he said to Eliphaz the Temanite: 'I am angry with you and your two friends, for you have not spoken the truth about me, as my servant Job has.'" - Job 42:7 CSB

- **Some truths are innate – they are hard wired in our DNA. We *need to obey these innate truths otherwise we spiral downward.***
"They know the truth about God because he has made it obvious to them. For ever since the world was created, people have seen the earth and sky. Through everything God made, they can clearly see his invisible qualities--his eternal power and divine nature. So they have no excuse for not knowing God." - Romans 1:19-20 NLT
Romans 1:21

Questions:

1. When Vladimir Putin, the President of Russia invaded the neighboring country of Ukraine in February 2022. He denied that Russia was bombing civilian targets. How did the world prove that was true?

2. What is an innate truth? Can you give an example?

3. What is worldliness (being like the world)?

Questions with suggested answers:

1. When Vladimir Putin, the President of Russia invaded the neighboring country of Ukraine in February 2022, he denied that Russia was bombing civilian targets.

Answer: Russia broke the important Biblical command to "love your neighbor". To prove that Russia was bombing civilians, we reviewed real-time camera footage and reporters on the ground in Ukraine to prove that indeed theatres and other civilian targets were being attacked. Biblical truths are concepts and principles that can be applied to situations. For example, "Jesus answered, 'The most important is Listen, O Israel! The Lord our God, the Lord is one. Love the Lord your God with all your heart, with all your soul, with all your mind, and with all your strength. The second is, Love your neighbor as yourself. There is no other command greater than these.'" - Mark 12:29-31 CSB

2. What is an innate truth? Can you give an example?

Answer: Innate truths are those where nearly all humans would agree that something is wrong no matter what religion they are. Even atheists or people who have no regard for Biblical truth, agree that taking a gun and murdering innocent children in a school is wrong. We would not need to show them the 5th Commandment – "Thou shalt not murder", rather they would say "that is just wrong".

3. What is worldliness (being like the world)?

Answer: Many people deny the Biblical standard of truth and instead follow the shifting sands of what is right and wrong. God's standards of truth never change – they are eternal. Kevin DeYoung is a theologian and pastor. He writes, "Worldliness is whatever makes sin look normal and righteousness look strange." We see this in several areas of sexual immorality. Hollywood often portrays casual sex between unmarried people as perfectly normal activity, even on first dates. Unions of people of the same sex used to be wrong but now this has been normalized from a legal standpoint. That is why foundational Biblical truths are important to know and live by because they are unchanging. They help you develop a firm spiritual foundation for living.

Is Jesus truth? Is He trustworthy? If we indeed are going to be a follower of Jesus, we need to be assured that He is the truth.

- *Jesus was filled with truth. John 1:14, Luke 10:21*
- *Jesus is the "the way, the truth and the life". Jesus did not say He was "a way", rather He said, I am "the way".*

"Jesus told him, I am the way, the truth, and the life. No one comes to the Father except through me." - John 14:6 CSB

- *Peter confirms this – Jesus is the only way to be saved. He makes it easy to remember.*

"There is salvation in no one else, for there is no other name under heaven given to people by which we must be saved." - Acts 4:12 CSB

5: What is Truth? A Biblical View

- ***Truth sets us free – from what? From sin and bondage and hell.***
"Then Jesus said to the Jews who had believed him, 'If you continue in my word, you really are my disciples. You will know the truth, and the truth will set you free.'" - John 8:31-32 CSB

- ***Jesus will judge by the truth He gave.***
John 12:48-50 CSB

- ***Jesus always taught truth because He was God and with God.***
John 7:28, 29

- ***Isaiah was speaking about Jesus in this Old Testament verse.***
"Turn to me and be saved, all the ends of the earth. For I am God, and there is no other. By myself I have sworn; truth has gone from my mouth, a word that will not be revoked: Every knee will bow to me, every tongue will swear allegiance. It will be said about me, Righteousness and strength are found only in the LORD. All who are enraged against him will come to him and be put to shame." - Isaiah 45:22-24 CSB

- ***Jesus said, "you must be born again" in order to enter Heaven. This is "truth".***
John 3:5-6

- ***Jesus asks God to purify us by His truths and to worship in truth.***
"Make them pure and holy by teaching them your words of truth." John 17:17, NLT.
John 4:23-24

Questions:

1. God gave us a foundation of Biblical truth in the 10 Commandments. How do they inform laws today?

2. Jesus said He is the "way, the truth, and the life". This bold statement does not leave any option for "additional routes to God". Does that bother you? What does the world think of this?

3. What if something comes up that is not covered in the Bible? How do we apply Biblical principles of truth?

4. Why is it so hard for some people to understand spiritual truth? Read Luke 10:21.

115

"At that same time Jesus was filled with the joy of the Holy Spirit, and he said, "O Father, Lord of heaven and earth, thank you for hiding these things from those who think themselves wise and clever, and for revealing them to the childlike. Yes, Father, it pleased you to do it this way." – Luke 10:21 NLT

5. John 4:23-24 discuss the role of truth in worship. How should this statement guide our songs and preaching in the church?

Questions with suggested answers:

1. God gave us a foundation of Biblical truth in the 10 Commandments. How do they inform laws today?

Answer: The 10 Commandments are succinct but far-reaching because they are principle-based. Commandment 9 for example, "You must not testify falsely against your neighbor." – Exodus 20:16 NLT is vital to courtroom conduct. In a criminal trial a witness is asked to swear that they, the witness, will tell the truth on the witness stand. If they do not, they themselves can be charged with perjury.

2. Jesus said He is the "way, the truth, and the life". This bold statement does not leave any option for "additional routes to God". Does that bother you? What does the world think of this?

Answer: Jesus makes the way to Heaven straightforward for us. You cannot get lost on a one-way road. However, many people would rather make their own way. It is distasteful for many that Jesus said there was only one way. They will often say, "We all want to get to Heaven and there are many roads to God." This question must be addressed as it will come up often. Jesus left us no doubts as to the answer.

3. What if something comes up that is not covered in the Bible? How do we apply Biblical principles of truth?

Answer: The beauty of Biblical truth is that it is principle-based. For example, it says in the second commandment, "You must not make for yourself an idol of any kind or an image of anything in the heavens or on the earth or in the sea." – Exodus 20:4 NLT. It says 'idol of any kind' that means it could be a famous artist/singer/performer or sports star or money etc. This is why the Bible is "timeless" and applies to all generations.

5: What is Truth? A Biblical View

4. Why is it so hard for some people to understand spiritual truth? Read Luke 10:21.

"At that same time Jesus was filled with the joy of the Holy Spirit, and he said, 'O Father, Lord of heaven and earth, thank you for hiding these things from those who think themselves wise and clever, and for revealing them to the childlike. Yes, Father, it pleased you to do it this way.'" – Luke 10:21 NLT

Answer: This is a sobering verse and difficult to understand. But what it is saying is that we need to be humble and trusting like a child is. Not everyone is like this, and most are not even faintly interested in knowing spiritual truth. When talking with someone about spiritual truths, try to gauge their spiritual interest. If it is there, then the Holy Spirit is working. If they reject the truth or are disinterested, then move on; forcing spiritual truth on people is not what we are to do. Read Luke 10:1-16 – it tells us Jesus instruction to the 72 other disciples/missionaries sent out to various towns. It reveals this principle.

5. John 4:23-24 discuss the role of truth in worship. How should this statement guide our songs and preaching in the church?

"But the time is coming–indeed it's here now–when true worshipers will worship the Father in spirit and in truth. The Father is looking for those who will worship him that way. For God is Spirit, so those who worship him must worship in spirit and in truth." – John 4:23-24 NLT

Answer: Our worship should be focused on Jesus and the truth of the Scriptures.

What role does the Holy Spirit play in discerning the Truth?

• *The Holy Spirit is invisible and lives within us. He leads us into truth if we listen.*
"And I will ask the Father, and he will give you another Advocate, who will never leave you. He is the Holy Spirit, who leads into all truth. The world cannot receive him, because it isn't looking for him and doesn't recognize him. But you know him, because he lives with you now and later will be in you." – John 14:16-17 NLT
John 15:26

• *The Holy Spirit educates us about Jesus. He reveals the truth to us.*
"When the Spirit of truth comes, *he will guide you into all truth*. He will not speak on his own but will tell you what he has heard. He will tell you about the future." – John 16:13 NLT

Thomas Witzig

1 Corinthians 2:13, 1 John 2:20, Luke 10:21

• ***Truth always glorifies Jesus — remember that when evaluating statements.***
John 16:14-15 NLT

• ***The Holy Spirit is the interpreter of spiritual truths.***
"But the person without the Spirit does not receive what comes from God's Spirit, because it is foolishness to him; he is not able to understand it since it is evaluated spiritually. The spiritual person, however, can evaluate everything, and yet he himself cannot be evaluated by anyone. For who has known the Lord's mind, that he may instruct him? But we have the mind of Christ." – 1 Corinthians 2:14-16 CSB

• ***Spirit of Truth — willingness to listen to truth is a mark of a believer.***
1 John 4:6 CSB

Questions:

1. Why do some people have such difficulty with accepting the truths of the Bible?

2. Read and slowly meditate on John 14:16-17. What part of these verses is most meaningful to you personally? "And I will ask the Father, and he will give you another Advocate, who will never leave you. *He is the Holy Spirit, who leads into all truth.* The world cannot receive him, because it isn't looking for him and doesn't recognize him. But you know him, because he lives with you now and later will be in you." - John 14:16-17 NLT

Questions with suggested answers:

1. Why do some people have such difficulty with accepting the truths of the Bible?

Answer: They do not have the Holy Spirit. See 1 Corinthians 2:14-16. You can sometimes sense this in another person when they show no interest in spiritual things.

2. Read and slowly meditate on John 14:16-17. What part of these verses is most meaningful to you personally? "And I will ask the Father, and he will give you another Advocate, who will never leave you. *He is the Holy Spirit, who leads into all truth.* The world cannot receive him, because it isn't looking for him and doesn't recognize him. But you know him, because he lives with you now and later will be in you." - John 14:16-17 NLT

5: What is Truth? A Biblical View

Answer: Several key points stand out to me. 1. Advocate – the Holy Spirit is your advocate – He is *for you*. We need people on our side as we go through difficulties in this world. 2. He leads into truth not falsehood. 3) He is a special gift to those of us who follow Christ. Non-Christians do not have the Holy Spirit. He only comes when you believe and decide to follow Jesus. 4) He lives inside – you can never "forget to bring along" the Holy Spirit. He is invisible. No prison or kidnapper or situation can ever get at the Holy Spirit and take Him away from you. 5) He is living. He is always awake and fresh.

How to defend the truth.

• *We are urged to be defenders of Scriptural truth.*
"Dear friends, I had been eagerly planning to write to you about the salvation we all share. But now I find that I must write about something else, urging you to defend the faith that God has entrusted once for all time to his holy people." - Jude 1:3 NLT
2 Corinthians 13:8, 1 Timothy 4:10

• *To defend, you must know the truth. This requires study.*
"So we must listen very carefully to the truth we have heard, or we may drift away from it." Hebrews 2:1, NLT.

• *Teach your children the truths of the Scripture.*
"Imprint these words of mine on your hearts and minds, bind them as a sign on your hands, and let them be a symbol on your foreheads. Teach them to your children, talking about them when you sit in your house and when you walk along the road, when you lie down and when you get up. Write them on the doorposts of your house and on your city gates, so that as long as the heavens are above the earth, your days and those of your children may be many in the land the LORD swore to give your fathers." - Deuteronomy 11:18-21 CSB

"A psalm of Asaph. O my people, listen to my instructions. Open your ears to what I am saying, for I will speak to you in a parable. I will teach you hidden lessons from our past- - stories we have heard and known, stories our ancestors handed down to us. We will not hide these truths from our children; we will tell the next generation about the glorious deeds of the LORD, about his power and his mighty wonders." - Psalm 78:1-4 NLT
3 John 1:4, Proverbs 23:24

- ***Demonstrate that you know the truth by actions and deeds.***

"Dear children, let's not merely say that we love each other; let us show the truth by our actions. Our actions will show that we belong to the truth, so we will be confident when we stand before God." - 1 John 3:18-19 NLT

1 Thessalonians 1:5

- ***Remind people often of the truth - People need repetition.***

2 Peter 1:12

- ***Speak truthfully but do it in love not harshly. Look out for fake news.***

"Then we will no longer be immature like children. We won't be tossed and blown about by every wind of new teaching. We will not be influenced when people try to trick us with lies so clever they sound like the truth. Instead, we will *speak the truth in love*, growing in every way more and more like Christ, who is the head of his body, the church. He makes the whole body fit together perfectly. As each part does its own special work, it helps the other parts grow, so that the whole body is healthy and growing and full of love." - Ephesians 4:14-16 NLT

Questions:

1. Did Jesus ever force people to believe? How does this answer inform how we tell others about Jesus?

2. What characteristics about Biblical truth make it unchanging?

3. There are many voices out there now on social media claiming to be truth. How do we defend Biblical truth?

4. Why is it important to teach our children about the Bible in their youth?

Questions with suggested answers:

1. Did Jesus ever force people to believe? How does this answer inform how we tell others about Jesus?

Answer: Jesus never forced anyone to be a follower of Jesus. Never. Jesus invited.

"Look! I stand at the door and knock. If you hear my voice and open the door, I will come in, and we will share a meal together as friends." - Revelation 3:20 NLT

2. What characteristics about Biblical truth make it unchanging?

Answer: The Bible is principle based and the principles are higher level. This is why the Bible remains so popular and useful even in this modern day of fake news and tweets that are often untrue and can cause much harm.

3. There are many voices out there now on social media claiming to be truth. How do we defend Biblical truth?

Answer: Most people do not know what the Bible says and how applicable to today. By quoting the Scriptures we can not only tell the truth but show people our source of truth.

4. Why is it important to teach our children about the Bible in their youth?

Answer: We are told in the Scriptures to teach children early and often about the great Bible stories and about Jesus. This is because we want them to learn the truth early as they build the spiritual foundation of their lives. We are told to do this in the verses quoted above (Psalm 78) and also from the example of Jesus in Luke 2. We see in that text that by age 12 Jesus was able to discuss spiritual matters with the priests in the Temple. His earthly parents (Joseph and Mary) must have taught their children about the Bible in their home, and they went to the Temple annually even though this was not required by their Jewish religion." Every year his parents traveled to Jerusalem for the Passover Festival. When he was twelve years old, they went up according to the custom of the festival." - Luke 2:41-42 CSB. We are also told that Jesus grew up wise in the Scriptures." Then he went down with them and came to Nazareth and was obedient to them. His mother kept all these things in her heart. *And Jesus increased in wisdom and stature, and in favor with God and with people."* - Luke 2:51-52 CSB.

How to deal with people that do not tell the truth.

Combat false teachers by vigorously teaching the truth.

- *Teach the truth*

"Be diligent to present yourself to God as one approved, a worker who doesn't need to be ashamed, correctly teaching the word of truth." - 2 Timothy 2:15 CSB
2 Corinthians 4:2, Ephesians 4:25

- *Do not suppress the truth; rather, elevate it.*
Romans 1:18-19 CSB

- *Avoid fighting over small matters that don't in the end mean much.*
2 Timothy 2:14, 16

Identify false teachers and remove them from influence or avoid them.

- *If not, the falsehoods will spread "like gangrene".*
"Avoid irreverent and empty speech, since those who engage in it will produce even more godlessness, and their teaching will spread like gangrene. Hymenaeus and Philetus are among them. They have departed from the truth, saying that the resurrection has already taken place, and are ruining the faith of some." - 2 Timothy 2:16-18 CSB

- *Beware of false teachers – they redefine truth and twist it.*
"Woe to those who call evil good and good evil, who substitute darkness for light and light for darkness, who substitute bitter for sweet and sweet for bitter." - Isaiah 5:20 CSB

"There were indeed false prophets among the people, just as there will be false teachers among you. They will bring in destructive heresies, even denying the Master who bought them, and will bring swift destruction on themselves. Many will follow their depraved ways, and the way of truth will be maligned because of them. *They will exploit you in their greed with made-up stories.* Their condemnation, pronounced long ago, is not idle, and their destruction does not sleep." - 2 Peter 2:1-3 CSB

- *False teachers do not even understand what they are doing. They slander the Bible without even really understanding it.*
2 Peter 2:12 CSB

- *False teachers who steer people away from the truth need to be silenced.*
"First, I want to remind you that in the last days there will be scoffers who will laugh at the truth and do every evil thing they desire." 2 Peter 3:3, NLT.
1 Timothy 6:3-5, 1 John 1:8, Titus 1:10-11

"If someone comes to your meeting and does not teach the truth about Christ, don't invite him into your house or encourage him in any way." 2 John 1:10, NLT.
2 Corinthians 4:2

5: What is Truth? A Biblical View

Deal gently with those who oppose the truth.

• *Paul indicates that only God can change the heart.*
2 Timothy 2:25-26

• *People who reject the truth may respond to a brisk rebuke.*
Titus 1:12-14

Questions:

1. The first amendment of the US Constitution gives all people the freedom of speech, "Congress shall make no law respecting an establishment of religion, or prohibiting the free exercise thereof; or abridging the freedom of speech, or of the press; or the right of the people peaceably to assemble, and to petition the government for a redress of grievances." Notice what Paul says in Titus 1:10-11 regarding people who spread false teaching in the Church. How is the Church different than the world?

2. What role does conscience play in obeying the truth?

Questions with suggested answers:

1. The first amendment of the US Constitution gives all people the freedom of speech, "Congress shall make no law respecting an establishment of religion, or prohibiting the free exercise thereof; or abridging the freedom of speech, or of the press; or the right of the people peaceably to assemble, and to petition the government for a redress of grievances." Notice what Paul says in Titus 1:10-11 regarding people who spread false teaching in the Church. How is the Church different than the world?

Answer: We do have freedom of speech in the United States, and you can even spread "fake news" as long as you do not hurt someone and are willing to pay the consequences. But in the Church, we are instructed to not tolerate false teachings. *Why? Because it can ruin the faith of others and lead them to abandon the faith.* That is why we stand on the truth of the Bible, and we need to know the truth so we can properly defend it.

2. What role does conscience play in obeying the truth? Name some high-level principles that are interpreted differently by people.

Answer: Remember that the Bible lays down rules as to right vs wrong that are very specific – such as the Ten Commandments; in other situations, the Bible provides principles without specifics. A good example is food choice. We are to eat healthy foods that God has provided. After sin entered the world, God allowed animals to be harvested for meat. But He did not ever command meat nor did He command a vegetarian diet. Rather, the Bible says this is a matter of conscience.

"They will say it is wrong to be married and wrong to eat certain foods. But God created those foods to be eaten with thanksgiving by people who know and believe the truth. Since everything God created is good, we should not reject any of it. We may receive it gladly, with thankful hearts." 1 Timothy 4:3, 4, NLT.

Another example is dress – we are to be modest but there is no specific 'dress code' in the Bible. "Also, the women are to dress themselves in modest clothing, with decency and good sense, not with elaborate hairstyles, gold, pearls, or expensive apparel," - 1 Timothy 2:9 CSB. So, what is modest? In some cultures, this will be to cover themselves with long dresses; in others it will be acceptable to wear pants or shorts. Finally, in the end we need to be like the Apostle Paul who said, "I always strive to have a clear conscience toward God and men." - Acts 24:16 CSB

How to live in the truth and be well-grounded.

• *Knowing the Bible prevents falling for false teachings. Be careful.*
"Be careful that no one takes you captive through philosophy and empty deceit based on human tradition, based on the elements of the world, rather than Christ. For the entire fullness of God's nature dwells bodily in Christ, and you have been filled by him, who is the head over every ruler and authority." - Colossians 2:8-10 CSB
Colossians 2:7

• *Preaching and teaching that you listen to should be "Christ-centered".*
2 Corinthians 4:5

• *If you really love and care about people, you will speak the truth to them.*
1 Corinthians 13:4-7

• *Put on the belt of truth; it is part of the armor of God and it holds up everything.*
Ephesians 6:13-18

• *Focus on the truth.*
"And now, dear brothers and sisters, one final thing. Fix your thoughts on what is true, and honorable, and right, and pure, and lovely, and admirable. Think about things that

5: What is Truth? A Biblical View

are excellent and worthy of praise. Keep putting into practice all you learned and received from me--everything you heard from me and saw me doing. Then the God of peace will be with you." - Philippians 4:8-9 NLT

- *Fact-check it by the Scriptures - The example of the Bereans.*

"As soon as it was night, the brothers and sisters sent Paul and Silas away to Berea. Upon arrival, they went into the synagogue of the Jews. The people here were of more noble character than those in Thessalonica, since they received the word with eagerness and examined the Scriptures daily to see if these things were so. Consequently, many of them believed, including a number of the prominent Greek women as well as men." - Acts 17:10-12 CSB

- *Walk in the truth don't just talk about it.*
3 John 1:3

- *Focus on real truth from the Bible not what you or others just dream about.*

"The prophet who has only a dream should recount the dream, but the one who has my word should speak my word truthfully, for what is straw compared to grain? " – "this is the LORD's declaration. Is not my word like fire" -- this is the LORD's declaration – "and like a hammer that pulverizes rock?" - Jeremiah 23:28-29 CSB

- *Truth produces godliness.*
Titus 1:1

- *No tricks or gimmicks; just tell the truth without disguising it.*
2 Corinthians 4:1-2

- *If we are living in truth, then our actions will match up.*

"Dear children, let's not merely say that we love each other; let us show the truth by our actions. Our actions will show that we belong to the truth, so we will be confident when we stand before God." - 1 John 3:18-19 NLT
1 John 2:4-6

- *If we know the truth, then we will have confidence of eternity.*

"This truth gives them the confidence of eternal life, which God promised them before the world began--and he cannot lie." Titus 1:2, NLT.

- ***The earthly church, your church, needs to support the truth.***
1 Timothy 3:15

- ***Truth is essential for the country you live in. Isaiah the prophet said that without truth in a society, justice will suffer.***
"Justice is turned back, and righteousness stands far off. For truth has stumbled in the public square, and honesty cannot enter. Truth is missing, and whoever turns from evil is plundered. The LORD saw that there was no justice, and he was offended." - Isaiah 59:14-15 CSB
Psalm 11:2-3

- ***Truth-telling in the courtroom is vital for justice to prevail.***
"But this is what you must do: Tell the truth to each other. Render verdicts in your courts that are just and that lead to peace. Do not make evil plots to harm each other. And stop this habit of swearing to things that are false. I hate all these things, says the LORD." Zechariah 8:16, 17, NLT.

- ***Unbelievers may not understand it because they are blind to the truth.***
"If the Good News we preach is hidden behind a veil, it is hidden only from people who are perishing. Satan, who is the god of this world, has blinded the minds of those who don't believe. They are unable to see the glorious light of the Good News. They don't understand this message about the glory of Christ, who is the exact likeness of God." - 2 Corinthians 4:3-4 NLT

Questions:

1. Why are dreams not a reliable source of enduring truth?

2. Why is telling the truth so important in a courtroom? What can happen to a witness if they are proven to have lied?

Questions with suggested answers:

1. Why are dreams not a reliable source of enduring truth?

Answer: Because they are unreliable. Dreams are important for good quality sleep but if you do even remember the dream they are often weird conglomerations of events that are disconnected and clearly unrelated to truth.

2. Why is telling the truth so important in a courtroom? What can happen to a witness if they are proven to have lied?

Answer: Telling the truth is part of the Ten Commandments – Commandment #9 "Do not give false testimony against your neighbor." - Exodus 20:16 CSB

A country or court system cannot function without truth. That is why if a person is found to have lied, they are charged with perjury.

Thomas Witzig

6

The Ten Commandments
A Concise Overview

The Ten Commandments are the bedrock of Judeo-Christian ethics and provide founding principles for our laws. They were given by God to the Israelites through Moses in the Old Testament books of Exodus chapter 20 and Deuteronomy chapters 4 and 5. They are as Dr. Thomas Constable, Senior Professor of Bible Exposition at Dallas Theological Seminary in Dallas, Texas, says, "commandments not suggestions". He makes the important point that "these commandments were given to the Israelites *as a community*. God intended them to govern the life of the nation, not just the behavior of individual Israelites." (Constables Notes on Exodus https://planobiblechapel.org/constable-notes/ Accessed August 1, 2020). There were 2 Tablets - Tablet 1: Commandments 1-4 the system of theology or "duty to God" and Tablet 2: Commandments 5-10 moral ethics or "duty to neighbor". The order is important – the first Tablet defines godliness; the second defines righteousness – godliness then righteousness. Jesus supported this interpretation in His conversation with the rich young ruler – first godliness (Tablet 1) and then righteousness (Tablet 2). "Just then someone came up and asked him, 'Teacher, what good must I do to have eternal life? Why do you ask me about what is good?' he said to him. There is only one who is good. If you want to enter into life, keep the commandments. 'Which ones?' he asked him. Jesus answered: 'Do not murder; do not commit adultery; do not steal; do not bear false witness; honor your father and your mother; and love your neighbor as yourself.'" - Matthew 19:16-19 CSB. Then when you get to Romans 1 Paul talks about the wrath of God. What is it directed against? Ungodliness first then unrighteousness. "For the wrath of God is revealed from heaven against all ungodliness and unrighteousness of men, who by their unrighteousness suppress the truth." - Romans 1:18 ESV. To understand our laws in the United States and even how those accused of a crime are tried in our court system you need to fully understand the Bible's teachings on the Ten

Commandments. They are relevant today and are on the walls of the Supreme Court building in Washington, DC.

- ***Why are they important? Because they are "God's work".***

"These stone tablets were God's work; the words on them were written by God himself." Exodus 32:16, NLT.

- ***The 10 Commandments were initially dictated by God to Moses on Mount Sinai and followed up with a stone copy for Moses to keep. There were 2 Tablets that is why artwork shows Moses with two tablets of stone.***

"Then as the LORD finished speaking with Moses on Mount Sinai, he gave him the two stone tablets inscribed with the terms of the covenant, written by the finger of God." Exodus 31:18, NLT.

Tablet 1: Duty to God and the definition of godliness. Commandments 1-4.

1. Mental or theoretic idolatry. God is monotheistic; no one else can compare.

"Thou shalt have no other gods before me." - Exodus 20:3 KJV

2. Making or worshipping images. We worship a living God not a statue.

"Thou shalt not make unto thee any graven image, or any likeness of any thing that is in heaven above, or that is in the earth beneath, or that is in the water under the earth:" - Exodus 20:4 KJV

- ***Moses reiterated this commandment to the nation of Israel. It is a very specific and clear warning about idols and applies to us today.***

Deuteronomy 4:15-19

3. God is holy. We are not to swear, blaspheme, or irreverently use of the name of God. We are never to misuse His name or make it of no or common value.

"Thou shalt not take the name of the LORD thy God in vain; for the LORD will not hold him guiltless that taketh his name in vain." - Exodus 20:7 KJV

4. Keeping the Sabbath day (our Saturday) of rest. This is the only commandment of the 10 that is not mentioned for the Church in the New Testament. Instead, the Church honors the first day of the week (Sunday) as the day of rest.

"Remember the sabbath day, to keep it holy." - Exodus 20:8 KJV

"Six days shalt thou labour, and do all thy work: But the seventh day is the sabbath of the LORD thy God: in it thou shalt not do any work, thou, nor thy son, nor thy daughter, thy manservant, nor thy maidservant, nor thy cattle, nor thy stranger that is within thy gates: For in six days the LORD made heaven and earth, the sea, and all that in them is, and rested the seventh day: wherefore the LORD blessed the sabbath day, and hallowed it." - Exodus 20:9-11 KJV

• *In the New Testament the day of rest is Sunday – the first day of the week.*
"When it was evening of that *first day of the week*, the disciples were gathered together with the doors locked because they feared the Jews. Jesus came, stood among them, and said to them, 'Peace be with you.'" - John 20:19 CSB

"*On the first day of the week, we assembled* to break bread. Paul spoke to them, and since he was about to depart the next day, he kept on talking until midnight." - Acts 20:7 CSB
1 Corinthians 16:2

Tablet 2: Duty to Neighbor. Moral ethics or righteousness. Commandments 5-10.

5. Honor your parents.

"Honour thy father and thy mother: that thy days may be long upon the land which the LORD thy God giveth thee." - Exodus 20:12 KJV

6. Thou shalt not murder. The Hebrew word used here is ratsach which means to murder. This provides rationale for the difference in the KJV and the CSB (and all other modern) translations.

"Thou shalt not kill." - Exodus 20:13 KJV

"Do not murder." - Exodus 20:13 CSB

7. Adultery

"Do not commit adultery." - Exodus 20:14 CSB

8. Stealing

"Do not steal." - Exodus 20:15 CSB

9. Lying to hurt someone; false witness (or testimony) as in a court proceeding.

"Do not give false testimony against your neighbor." - Exodus 20:16 CSB

"You must not testify falsely against your neighbor." - Exodus 20:16 NLT

10. Do not covet. The Hebrew word for covet = chamad which means to desire or covet or lust. This is a warning to not overly desire what is not ours.

"Do not covet your neighbor's house. Do not covet your neighbor's wife, his male or female servant, his ox or donkey, or anything that belongs to your neighbor." - Exodus 20:17 CSB

If a society or community follows the Ten Commandments, it will avoid much of the suffering and crime we observe in the world. Most people cannot recite the 10 Commandments today, but they are likely to agree with them, especially **Tablet 2**. A Jewish colleague and I were discussing this topic one day and he said, "I can accept 5-10 but 1-4 are more difficult for me."

Questions:

1. Why the commandment on coveting (The 10th commandment)? What things are coveted today? Is this like jealousy?

2. The first commandment is to not have any gods in your life other than God. What are some issues that could become "gods" in your life that would interfere with your relationship with God?

3. Compare astronomy with astrology. What does God say about it?

4. What happens if you do not follow the 10 Commandments? Read the answer in Deuteronomy 5.

Questions with suggested answers:

1. Why the commandment on coveting (The 10th commandment)? What things are coveted today? Is this like jealousy?

Answer: Commandment 10 is the sin of coveting or lusting and it is very general as the verse gives several examples. To covet is to have too strong a desire. There is nothing wrong with admiration or wanting something; coveting is taking it to the extreme and like many good things in life when they are taken too far it turns negative. The commandments must be taken together and not just in isolation. Coveting extends the commandments on adultery (#7) and stealing (#8) to lusting for sex and money, respectively.

2. The first commandment is to not have any gods in your life other than God. What are some issues that could become "gods" in your life that would interfere with your relationship with God?

Answer: Money, work, success, any habit when taken to extreme such as alcohol, drugs, sex etc. These all can interfere with our relationship with God. And of course, any graven image that is worshipped such as described in the Old Testament. Idols, as seen in many countries around the world, are not frequently seen in the US.

3. Compare astronomy with astrology. What does God say about it?

Answer: Astronomy is the study of the stars and planets and is a scientific discipline. It is also a hobby for many people who buy a telescope and study the heavens and planets. Astrology is different. Webster defines it as, "the divination of the supposed influences of the stars and planets on human affairs and terrestrial events by their positions and aspects." We are not to worship the stars nor try to read any meaning into their movements. Moses clearly stated this to the Israelites - "When you look to the heavens and see the sun, moon, and stars -- all the stars in the sky -- *do not be led astray to bow in worship to them and serve them*. The LORD your God has provided them for all people everywhere under heaven." - Deuteronomy 4:19 CSB. We are to appreciate the beautiful and precise movements of the planets and stars but not try to worship or read personal meaning for our choices or lives.

4. What happens if you do not follow the 10 Commandments? The answer is in Deuteronomy 5.

Answer: "Do not bow in worship to them, and do not serve them, because I, the LORD your God, am a jealous God, punishing the children for the fathers' iniquity to the third and fourth generations of those who hate me, but showing faithful love to a thousand generations of those who love me and keep my commands." - Deuteronomy 5:9-10 CSB. The results of your belief or unbelief is passed on to your children and grandchildren. You can observe this in families. My great-grandparents on both sides of my family immigrated to America in the early 1900's and settled in the Midwest farming communities. They were believers and continued to serve the Lord. Now over 100 years later if you would look at those family trees you would see many believers, pastors, missionaries etc. Maybe your family tree looks different. If so, it's your chance to change the direction of your children and grandchildren by following Jesus. Break the cycle!

Are the Ten Commandments for us today? Are they in the New Testament?

The Law refers to the Old Testament law in its entirety – judicial, ceremonial, and moral. When Jesus came to the earth, He clearly taught in Matthew 5 in the Sermon on the Mount that He was not here to abolish the Law but rather fulfill/complete it. "Don't think that I came to abolish the Law or the Prophets. I did not come to abolish but to fulfill." For truly I tell you, until heaven and earth pass away, not the smallest letter or one stroke of a letter will pass away from the law until all things are accomplished." - Matthew 5:17-18 CSB. Jesus is saying here in effect that the Old Testament law was pointing to Him. Paul says this too - 2 Corinthians 1:18-20 CSB. Jesus was born and served under the Law - Galatians 4:4-5 CSB Jesus lived a perfect life, followed the Law, and died on the cross for our sins as fulfillment of the Law. God had to punish sin to be consistent with His promise. Jesus thus fulfills the judicial law on the cross and it ends. Since the judicial law is fulfilled, there is no need for the ceremonial. This bring us then back to the moral law and we see that it is permanent and perpetual. Jesus confirms the moral law by reciting the 10 commandments. All are repeated in the New Testament (see below) except the commandment to have worship and rest on Saturday as the Sabbath. Instead, we follow the practice of the early Christians to worship on the day of resurrection or Sunday. However, we are not legalistic about the day as many churches (Catholic and Protestant) have Saturday night services so that those working on Sunday can worship. The 10 Commandments are simple yet profound and obeying them saves us and society from much pain and suffering. They are relevant even though written over 4000 years ago. G. K. Chesterton, English writer and lay theologian (29 May 1874 – 14 June 1936) said "When you break the big laws you do not get liberty; you do not even get anarchy. You get the small laws"… "If men will not be governed by the Ten Commandments, they shall be governed by the ten thousand commandments." Let's examine the New Testament texts that reiterate the 10 Commandments.

- *Jesus kept the Commandments but extended it to love. Jesus keeps them by showing love. He stresses agape love rather than law, and the result is joy.*
John 15:9-12

- *Jesus asks us to do the same.*
"If you love me, you will keep my commands." - John 14:15 CSB

- *Paul says if we love people, we will naturally fulfill the commandments. He turns the "do nots" into a "do". This makes it easier – if we love (agape) then we do not steal, lie, murder, or commit adultery.*
"The commandments, Do not commit adultery; do not murder; do not steal; do not covet; and any other commandment, are summed up by this commandment: *Love your neighbor as yourself.*" - Romans 13:9 CSB

The Ten Commandments in the New Testament

1. Thou shalt have no other gods before me. *Jesus repeated this directly to Satan in the wilderness when He was being tempted. He also explains it well – One God and we are to worship Him and not anything else in our lives.*

"Then Jesus told him, 'Go away, Satan! For it is written: Worship the Lord your God, and serve only him.'" - Matthew 4:10 CSB

2. Thou shalt not make unto thee any graven image (no idols).

"Little children, *guard yourselves from idols.*" - 1 John 5:21 CSB
1 Corinthians 10:14, 20

3. Thou shalt not take the name of the Lord thy God in vain. This means we should be reverent and respectful of God. Jesus said in the Disciple's Prayer that we are to keep God's name holy. Swearing or not behaving in a godly manner is disobedient to this Commandment. Its means more than simply using God's name as a swear word.

"Therefore, you should pray like this: Our Father in heaven, *your name be honored* as holy." - Matthew 6:9 CSB
Philippians 2:9-11, Psalm 8:1

4. Remember the Sabbath – this commandment is not directly repeated; rather the New Testament refers to worship on the first day of the week (Sunday) in celebration of the resurrection of Jesus.

"When it was evening of *that first day of the week, the disciples were gathered together* with the doors locked because they feared the Jews. Jesus came, stood among them, and said to them, 'Peace be with you.'" - John 20:19 CSB
Acts 20:7

5. Honor thy father and mother.

"Why do you ask me about what is good? he said to him. There is only one who is good. If you want to enter into life, keep the commandments. Which ones? he asked him. Jesus answered: Do not murder; do not commit adultery; do not steal; do not bear false witness; *honor your father and your mother;* and love your neighbor as yourself." - Matthew 19:17-19 CSB

6. Thou shalt do no murder.

"Which ones? he asked him. Jesus answered: *Do not murder*; do not commit adultery; do not steal; do not bear false witness;" - Matthew 19:18 CSB

7. Adultery

"Which ones? " he asked him. Jesus answered: Do not murder; *do not commit adultery*; do not steal; do not bear false witness;" - Matthew 19:18 CSB

8. Stealing (and cheating).

"Which ones? he asked him. Jesus answered: Do not murder; do not commit adultery; *do not steal*; do not bear false witness;" - Matthew 19:18 CSB
Mark 10:19

9. Do not bear false witness. When we lie, we lie against God – the case of Ananias.

"You know the commandments: Do not murder; do not commit adultery; do not steal; *do not bear false witness;* do not defraud; honor your father and mother." - Mark 10:19 CSB
Luke 18:20, Acts 5:3-4

6: The Ten Commandments – A Concise Overview

10. Do not covet.

"The commandments, Do not commit adultery; do not murder; do not steal; *do not covet*; and any other commandment, are summed up by this commandment: Love your neighbor as yourself." - Romans 13:9 CSB
Romans 7:7

Questions:

1. Examine the Commandments – which ones in our society today in the United States would be consider criminal if broken?

2. Can you give any examples of commandments that if broken are not legally wrong according to current United States' law?

3. Why did God write the 10 Commandments out for Moses on a stone tablet? What happens when a community follows the 10 Commandments? What if they become lax and do not follow them? What are the implications? Give examples.

Questions with suggested answers:

1. Examine the Commandments – which ones in our society today in the United States would be consider criminal if broken?

Answer: Commandments 6 (murder), 8 (stealing) and 9 (lying under oath) are all considered unlawful (illegal) as of 2023 in the United States.

2. Can you give any examples of commandments that if broken are not legally wrong according to current United States' law?

Answer: Adultery is an obvious example. If a person has sexual intercourse outside of the marriage relationship, then this is destructive to the marriage and breaks the 7th commandment. It has many consequences to the marriage, the children and extended families, and the reputation of the people involved. However, adultery in adults is not something that the police show up and charge the offenders with breaking the law. The same goes for non-medical abortion (one performed for no medical condition in the mother or baby). Many would consider it as taking the life of an unborn child whereas others would not. In Minnesota as of January 2023 with the passage of HF1 it is *legal* to have a non-medical abortion up until the baby's first breath, but some would consider it *morally* wrong. This is the reason that abortion for no medical reason will always

137

remain contentious. The majority feel it should be legal; but few would say its moral. Since people in general do not want to be judgmental, they often abdicate the decision to the person involved. It is complicated of course but when talking about it we must be clear – are we talking *legal* and apply to all people or *moral* as based on the Bible. In the past when more people believed in the Bible our laws reflected our morals. However, as we become distanced from God our laws our based on what we want, and we no longer consider God's way. There is then a disconnect between our laws and our morals.

3. Why did God write the 10 Commandments out for Moses on a stone tablet? What happens when a community follows the 10 Commandments? What if they become lax and do not follow them? What are the implications? Give examples.

Answer: God wrote them on stone so that they would be permanent. In those days, stone was used because it was more permanent than paper. If on paper, they would have been subject to decay. God told Moses to place the tablets in the Ark of the Covenant (Deuteronomy 10:4-5). It was the safest place as it was guarded. God intended these commandments to govern society and He wants us to be obedient children. Moses said, "Keep the LORD's commands and statutes I am giving you today, *for your own good*." - Deuteronomy 10:13 CSB. "If only they had such a heart to fear me and *keep all my commands always,* so that they and *their children would prosper forever*." - Deuteronomy 5:29 CSB. God knew we would forget. God wanted them to be repeated and remembered. The same today, memorize them and read them often. They are the bedrock of civil law and as the verse says, "they are for your own good".

7

Prayer – What is it? Why is it important? How to do it?

Prayer is talking to God. To be effective in your Christian life you will need to pray. Praying is key to your spiritual foundation. Jesus said, "One day Jesus told his disciples a story to show that *they should always pray and never give up*." - Luke 18:1 NLT. To emphasize the importance of prayer, the Bible gives us great examples, many directly from Jesus Himself. Most prayers are silent and personal between the individual and God. Public prayers (also called corporate prayers) are audible like those offered in church. Some prayers are short, some are long. This chapter provides key instruction points from the Bible on prayer followed by some great model prayers.

Does God really want to hear from us? Yes!

"My heart has heard you say, '*Come and talk with me.*' And my heart responds, 'LORD, I am coming'" Psalm 27:8, NLT.

Does He listen?

- *Yes, your prayers are reviewed by God and Jesus (the Lamb in this verse) at the throne of God in real time. Prayers are one of the few things that we do on earth that make it to Heaven!*

"He stepped forward and took the scroll from the right hand of the one sitting on the throne. And as he took the scroll, the four living beings and the twenty-four elders fell down before the Lamb. Each one had a harp, and they held gold bowls filled with incense—the prayers of God's people!" Revelation 5:7, 8, NLT.

Thomas Witzig

How should we pray?

The disciples asked Jesus this question and He responded with what is known as the 'Disciple's Prayer' or as it usually referred to, the 'Lord's Prayer'. The prayer is brief – a reminder that we need not pray long prayers. The first translation is from the King James Version and is the one often recited in church. The second is the Christian Standard Bible – a more modern translation.

- ***The Lord's Prayer in the classic King James Version (includes verse 13).***

"After this manner therefore pray ye: Our Father which art in heaven, Hallowed be thy name. Thy kingdom come. Thy will be done in earth, as it is in heaven. Give us this day our daily bread. And forgive us our debts, as we forgive our debtors. And lead us not into temptation, but deliver us from evil: For thine is the kingdom, and the power, and the glory, for ever. Amen." - Matthew 6:9-13 KJV

- ***The Lord's Prayer in the Christian Standard Bible.***

"Therefore, you should pray like this: Our Father in heaven, your name be honored as holy. Your kingdom come. Your will be done on earth as it is in heaven. Give us today our daily bread. And forgive us our debts, as we also have forgiven our debtors. And do not bring us into temptation, but deliver us from the evil one." - Matthew 6:9-13 CSB

- ***The version of the Lord's Prayer from Luke – 'Lord, teach us to pray'.***
Luke 11:1-4 CSB

- ***Jesus said that prayer is private, short, God-honoring, and respectful.***

"Whenever you pray, you must not be like the hypocrites, because they love to pray standing in the synagogues and on the street corners to be seen by people. Truly I tell you, they have their reward. But when you pray, go into your private room, shut your door, and pray to your Father who is in secret. And your Father who sees in secret will reward you. When you pray, don't babble like the Gentiles, since they imagine they'll be heard for their many words. Don't be like them, because your Father knows the things you need before you ask him." - Matthew 6:5-8 CSB

- ***God wants us to pray… but we must initiate it and be willing to wait for an answer.***
Isaiah 30:18

- ***Pray with humility – admit you need God's help. Bow down to be lifted up.***
James 4:10

How often should we pray?

• *Frequently, persistently, for every occasion, and in the power of the Holy Spirit.*
"Pray at all times and on every occasion in the power of the Holy Spirit. Stay alert and be persistent in your prayers for all Christians everywhere." Ephesians 6:18, NLT.

• *Pray with an alert mind and a thankful heart, not when you are dead tired.*
"Devote yourselves to prayer with an alert mind and a thankful heart." Colossians 4:2, NLT.

How long should our prayers be? Not very long.

• *When Peter was drowning his prayer was short and to the point.*
"But when he looked around at the high waves, he was terrified and began to sink. 'Save me, Lord!' he shouted." Matthew 14:30, NLT.

• *David when he was in deep trouble also was brief and to the point.*
"*Save me, God*, for the water has risen to my neck. I have sunk in deep mud, and there is no footing; I have come into deep water, and a flood sweeps over me." - Psalm 69:1-2 CSB

How to start a prayer.

• *Acknowledge God as Jehovah and creator – Hezekiah's example.*
"LORD of Armies, God of Israel, enthroned between the cherubim, you are God -- you alone -- of all the kingdoms of the earth. You made the heavens and the earth." - Isaiah 37:16 CSB

• *Tell God that you love Him—David's example.*
"I love you, LORD, my strength. The LORD is my rock, my fortress, and my deliverer, my God, my rock where I seek refuge, my shield and the horn of my salvation, my stronghold. I called to the LORD, who is worthy of praise, and I was saved from my enemies." - Psalm 18:1-3 CSB

• *Acknowledge that you actually believe God can do what you are asking Him.*
"Now when I had delivered the evidence of the purchase unto Baruch the son of Neriah, I prayed unto the LORD, saying, Ah Lord GOD! behold, thou hast made the heaven and the earth by thy great power and stretched out arm, and there is nothing too hard for thee:" - Jeremiah 32:16-17 KJV

- **Be disciplined and earnest in prayer; not flippant.**
"The end of the world is coming soon. Therefore, be earnest and disciplined in your prayers." 1 Peter 4:7, NLT.

When should we pray?

- **Pray always; for all occasions; pray persistently; for fellow believers.**
"Pray in the Spirit at all times and on every occasion. Stay alert and be persistent in your prayers for all believers everywhere." - Ephesians 6:18 NLT

- **Pray for our children – people brought children to Jesus to pray for them.**
"Then children were brought to Jesus for him to place his hands on them and pray, but the disciples rebuked them. Jesus said, 'Leave the children alone, and don't try to keep them from coming to me, because the kingdom of heaven belongs to such as these.' After placing his hands on them, he went on from there." - Matthew 19:13-15 CSB

- **Ask others to pray for you. Paul did. Pray for your pastors.**
"And *pray for me, too*. Ask God to give me the right words so I can boldly explain God's mysterious plan that the Good News is for Jews and Gentiles alike. I am in chains now, still preaching this message as God's ambassador. So pray that I will keep on speaking boldly for him, as I should." - Ephesians 6:19-20 NLT
1 Thessalonians 5:25

Questions:

1. Is it possible to pray effectively with ear buds in?

2. What are some tips on how you have been able to connect with God?

3. How can the mature (old, retired, elderly etc.) people help with your needs or the needs of the Church?

4. How do I know that my prayers are worthwhile? Are they really accomplishing anything?

Questions with suggested answers:

1. Is it possible to pray effectively with ear buds in?

Answer: Ear buds are nice because they keep the music or podcast private and do not bother others. But they make it hard to pray effectively because of the interference. God wants our full attention so if you are intent on communicating with Him go out into nature or sit in a quiet place and pray. This is the essence of 1 Peter 4:7 quoted above.

2. What are some tips on how you have been able to connect with God?

Answer: Share with others in your group.

3. How can the mature (old, retired, elderly etc.) people help with your needs or the needs of the Church?

Answer: Many people in assisted living or retired have lots of time on their hands. They become "prayer warriors" for the saints. Tell your Grandparents what issues you need prayer for and get them involved. They will feel a new purpose and they will help you in your areas of need.

4. How do I know that my prayers are worthwhile? Are they really accomplishing anything?

Answer: James answers this question – "Therefore, confess your sins to one another and pray for one another, so that you may be healed. *The prayer of a righteous person is very powerful in its effect.* Elijah was a human being as we are, and he prayed earnestly that it would not rain, and for three years and six months it did not rain on the land. Then he prayed again, and the sky gave rain and the land produced its fruit." – James 5:16-18 CSB. In the devotional book of Oswald Chambers edited by James Reimann, "My Utmost for His Highest" he writes on October 17, "When you labor at prayer from God's perspective there are always results. What an astonishment it will be, once the veil is finally lifted, all the souls that have been reaped by you, simply because you have been in the habit of taking your orders from Jesus Christ."

Thomas Witzig

What should I pray for?

Prayers can become rote and mundane but if we look at the list below the Bible gives us lots of recommendations on what to pray for. Use this section as a checklist – are you praying for these items?

• ***Pray for the right words before teaching or preaching the Word.*** This is the basis for why pastors pray (or should!) before they preach.

"And pray for me, too. *Ask God to give me the right words as I boldly explain God's secret plan* that the Good News is for the Gentiles, too." Ephesians 6:19, NLT.

• ***Let the content of your prayer be directed by the Holy Spirit.***
"But you, dear friends, must continue to build your lives on the foundation of your holy faith. And continue to pray as you are directed by the Holy Spirit." Jude 1:20, NLT.

• ***Pray prayers of adoration. God enjoys being praised.***
"LORD, our Lord, how magnificent is your name throughout the earth! You have covered the heavens with your majesty." – Psalm 8:1 CSB

• ***God wants to hear about our cares. What concerns you? Be thankful from the start.***
"Humble yourselves, therefore, under the mighty hand of God, so that he may exalt you at the proper time, casting all your cares on him, because he cares about you." – 1 Peter 5:6-7 CSB
Philippians 4:6-7

• ***Prayers for Healing – the sick should pray and ask for the elders to pray too.***
"Is anyone among you suffering? He should pray. Is anyone cheerful? He should sing praises. Is anyone among you sick? He should call for the elders of the church, and they are to pray over him, anointing him with oil in the name of the Lord." – James 5:13-14 CSB

- ***Prayers of confession – prayers that acknowledge to God that we are sinners and have done wrong. God enjoys hearing us acknowledge that He is great and awesome and that He is a promise keeper. Notice here how Daniel prays.***

"I prayed to the LORD my God, and confessed: 'O Lord, you are a great and awesome God! You always fulfill your promises of unfailing love to those who love you and keep your commands.'" Daniel 9:4, NLT.

"But we have sinned and done wrong. We have rebelled against you and scorned your commands and regulations." Daniel 9:5, NLT.

- ***Prayers for other people in your circle of influence. Pray for each other.***
Colossians 1:3 CSB

"Therefore, confess your sins to one another and pray for one another, so that you may be healed. The prayer of a righteous person is very powerful in its effect." – James 5:16 CSB

- ***Pray to be delivered from the evil one.***
"And forgive us our sins, for we also forgive everyone who is indebted to us. And do not lead us into temptation, but deliver us from the evil one." Luke 11:4, KJV.

- ***Pray for discernment – keen insight.***
Philippians 1:9-11

- ***Pray for strength that comes from the Holy Spirit.***
Ephesians 3:16-21

- ***Pray for help and do it with thanksgiving.***
"Don't worry about anything, but in everything, through prayer and petition with thanksgiving, present your requests to God." – Philippians 4:6 CSB

- ***Pray for travel safety. We need to pray like Ezra prayed before the journey.***
Ezra 8:21-23, Ezra 8:31, 32

- ***Pray that others will come to know Jesus as their solution for sin.***
"Brothers and sisters, my heart's desire and prayer to God concerning them is for their salvation." – Romans 10:1 CSB

- **Pray for those falsely imprisoned – the whole church prayed for Peter.**
"So Peter was kept in prison, but the church was praying fervently to God for him." – Acts 12:5 CSB

- **Pray for Christians to work in evangelism.**
Matthew 9:35-38 CSB

- **Pray for body and soul health. This would include prayers for the sick.**
"Dear friend, I am praying that all is well with you and that your body is as healthy as I know your soul is." 3 John 1:2, NLT.

- **Pray for effectiveness to finish the task God has given you.**
Philippians 1:6

Questions:

1. Why did James say in 4:10 that we need to "admit your dependence on him"?

2. Explain how this verse applies to the answer we get from our requests to God. "Don't worry about anything, but in everything, through prayer and petition with thanksgiving, present your requests to God. And the peace of God, which surpasses all understanding, will guard your hearts and minds in Christ Jesus." - Philippians 4:6-7 CSB.

Questions with suggested answers:

1. Why did James say in 4:10 that we need to "admit your dependence on him"?

Answer: Effective prayer is realizing you need God's help in a situation. It is not that you give up, rather it is the realization that this problem is beyond something that you yourself can handle. We sometimes try to do it all ourselves.

2. Explain how this verse applies to the answer we get from our requests to God. "Don't worry about anything, but in everything, through prayer and petition with thanksgiving, present your requests to God. And the peace of God, which surpasses all understanding, will guard your hearts and minds in Christ Jesus." - Philippians 4:6-7 CSB.

Answer: This is a deep verse with an important nugget of truth that must be understood. As you go through life there are many times when you will not see an answer to your prayers. Sometimes the prayer will be answered "no". We are never guaranteed every prayer will be answered the way we want. But what the verse says is that we can have "peace" about it and that this peace may actually supersede the understanding. In other words, you will not understand but you will be at peace. My wife's mother was killed at the age of 40 in a car accident leaving her father and 8 children. She was a godly woman and a wonderful loving mother. Why would this happen? We often muse that even many years later we do not understand. Yet, God did give the family peace and they have moved on in faith. They got peace but never understanding.

Prayer – Is it Worth It?

• *Prayer is necessary for very difficult situations. In the case of the boy with the evil spirit, the disciples failed to cast out the demon. Note the response of Jesus.*
Mark 9:17-18, 25-29

• *Specific prayers get specific answers. Rachel prayed for a baby—she got one!*
Genesis 30:22, 23

• *God listened and spared Lot even after his major mistake of moving to Sodom. Notice that God listened to the prayers of Abraham (Lot's prayers are not mentioned here).*
Genesis 19:29

• *God responded to David when he prayed.*
Psalm 4:3

• *James says the prayer of a righteous man is worth it.*
"Therefore, confess your sins to one another and pray for one another, so that you may be healed. The prayer of a righteous person is very powerful in its effect." - James 5:16 CSB

How fast does God answer prayer?

• *It depends; it can be instantaneous as in this case of Daniel. This is reassuring that God can hear us and act instantly.*
"As I was praying, Gabriel, whom I had seen in the earlier vision, came swiftly to me at the time of the evening sacrifice. He explained to me, 'Daniel, I have come here to give you insight and understanding. The moment you began praying, a command was given.

I am here to tell you what it was, for God loves you very much. Now listen, so you can understand the meaning of your vision." Daniel 9:21-23, NLT.

"Then he said, 'Don't be afraid, Daniel. Since the first day you began to pray for understanding and to humble yourself before your God, your request has been heard in heaven. I have come in answer to your prayer.'" Daniel 10:12, NLT.

• *God is always listening! Note the case of Paul and Ananias.*
"The Lord said, 'Go over to Straight Street, to the house of Judas. When you arrive, ask for Saul of Tarsus. He is praying to me right now.'" Acts 9:11, NLT.

• *Prayer of Abraham's servant for success gave immediate results.*
Genesis 24:10-15

Questions:

1. Most things in our daily life are routine and do not need pray. We do not typically pray about whether to take a shower or what to eat for breakfast. We do need to pray for guidance with our schedule and safety in the daily travels. Then as described in the Mark 9 passage above, note that Jesus said for very difficult situations we must pray. Pray for what? Pray for help from God and the Holy Spirit. What things fall into that category for you?

2. Can prayer change the mind of God?

Questions with suggested answers:

1. Most things in our daily life are routine and do not need pray. We do not typically pray about whether to take a shower or what to eat for breakfast. We do need to pray for guidance with our schedule and safety in the daily travels. Then as described in the Mark 9 passage above, note that Jesus said for very difficult situations we must pray. Pray for what? Pray for help from God and the Holy Spirit. What things fall into that category for you?

Answer: At this time (August 2023) Russia and Ukraine have been at war for over 1.5 years. This requires daily prayer because so far negotiations of men and women between the two countries have failed. Also, on September 28, 2022, Florida endured Hurricane Ian, possibly the most destructive storm in recorded history of Florida. We all prayed

7: Prayer – What is it? Why is it important? How to do it?

for safety for our loved ones that lived there. It's not hard to decide what needs prayer. Anything in your life that is hard for you to easily solve should be prayed for.

2. Can prayer change the mind of God?

Answer: Sometimes. But it is still up to God in the end. A good example of where God changed His mind in response to prayer is Deuteronomy 9 where Moses tells the Israelites how close God was to destroying them because of their episode of idolatry with the golden calf idol. It is worthwhile reading the entire chapter but here is a sample,

"I fell down like the first time in the presence of the LORD for forty days and forty nights; I did not eat food or drink water because of all the sin you committed, doing what was evil in the LORD's sight and angering him. I was afraid of the fierce anger the LORD had directed against you, because he was about to destroy you. But again the LORD listened to me on that occasion. The LORD was angry enough with Aaron to destroy him. But I prayed for Aaron at that time also." - Deuteronomy 9:18-20 CSB.

As a medical doctor I pray often for my patients. I believe it helps but I have learned that although I may pray really hard that if the person is destined to die and it is "their time" then there is nothing I can do to change that.

What are the barriers to prayer? What are the "prayer busters"?

Pride, anger, controversy, unconfessed sin, marital discord, and praying a prayer that asks God to do something inconsistent with His character. Growing up in Illinois, our landline phone line would go dead sometimes when a storm would cause a tree to snap the telephone line and "cut the cord". It would take a while for the crew to come out and fix it. During that time, all communication would be lost. Today, with our dependence on satellites, we can still experience a drop in communication when we stray outside the area of coverage. Having no internet or cell service turns a wonderful cell phone into something useless. *Connectivity matters much in the area of prayer. Keep the prayer busters out to enhance the effectiveness of your prayers.*

- *Pride: The case of the Pharisees prayer.*
Luke 18:10-12

- *Unconfessed sin can block prayer. It cuts the cord of communication.*
Isaiah 59:1, 2, Psalm 66:18-20

- **Prayers offered in anger may be blocked.**
1 Timothy 2:8

- **Misalignment of our will with God's will. This is why we do not always get what we pray for. The Holy Spirit directs our prayers so that they are in harmony with God's will.**
1 John 5:14

- **Evil spirits may momentarily block the answer: The case of Daniel.**
Daniel 10:12, 13

- **Troubles in your marriage. When the husband and wife are not honoring and respecting each other and not working together the prayers will be "hindered".**
1 Peter 3:7

Questions:

1. How do you feel when you pray, and the answer is "No"?

2. Biblical marriage is based on equality, honor, and respect for each other. The roles can be very different but the two must pull together for a successful and vibrant marriage. Peter warns that if the husband does not respect his wife that prayers may be disrupted. What does this mean?

3. In the Sermon on the Mount (Mt 5:21-24) Jesus teaches about the importance of dealing with "iniquity in the heart" first before worshiping or praying. How can discord with others be a "prayer buster"?

Questions with suggested answers:

1. How do you feel when you pray, and the answer is "No"?

Answers: All prayers are eventually answered. God either says yes, no, wait, or "I will not tell you until eternity". The first thing to do is to make sure that none of the barriers discussed above is not involved. If not, then you will likely need to pray again or pray for acceptance. I find even after 70 years of living that it is quite distressing and depressing to get a rejection to a prayer. One can read about prayer, study it, practice it, but when it's *your* specific prayer that is answered 'no' it always causes anxiety and unrest in your soul. Sometimes a 'No' is as helpful as a 'Yes' and remember there will be many, many times when your prayers are not answered quickly enough or never even answered this side of eternity. For example, read the Book of Job – God never does reveal the answer to the cause of Job's suffering; only we are shown that behind it all was a cosmic battle between Satan and God.

2. Biblical marriage is based on equality, honor, and respect for each other. The roles can be very different but the two must pull together for a successful and vibrant marriage. Peter warns that if the husband does not respect his wife that prayers may be disrupted. What does this mean?

Answer: Each of the common Bible translations use the word "hindered". This means that our prayers may be ineffective if we are not honoring each other. This is an actionable item – in other words, a component of our prayer life that can be fixed. When things get tough the husband and wife must bond closely and prayer earnestly as a team.

3. In the Sermon on the Mount (Mt 5:21-24) Jesus teaches about the importance of dealing with "iniquity in the heart" first before worshiping or praying. How can discord with others be a "prayer buster"?

Answer: In this passage Jesus says that we should not try to do good works (like giving to the church) until we have made sure our heart is clean. He says – "leave the gift and get right with your brother then come back This is called reconciliation. David said, If I had cherished iniquity in my heart, the Lord would not have listened." - Psalm 66:18 ESV. This harboring anger in our heart is a subtle and important "prayer buster". If you feel that your prayers are going unanswered then get your "heart examined" and deal with any unconfessed sin or bad relationships.

How should we respond when we get an answer to prayer?

• *Offer praise and thanksgiving immediately upon receiving an answer—don't wait.*
Daniel 2:23

• *Worship—answered prayer should stimulate worship.*
Genesis 24:26, 27

"Then I bowed my head and worshiped the LORD. I praised the LORD, the God of my master, Abraham, because he had led me along the right path to find a wife from the family of my master's relatives." Genesis 24:48, NLT.

- *Give glory to God—He likes that and notices when we do not do it. The case of the 10 lepers and only one who said, 'thank you'.*
Luke 17:11-19

- *Tell others how God healed you. The example of the man with the skin disease.*
Mark 1:40-45

Question with suggested answer:

Why is it important to thank God and give Him credit for answered prayer?

Answer: The answer is contained in the Luke 17:17-19 passage above. Jesus wanted the men to acknowledge who (God) was responsible for the healing so that He would get credit. Be careful to not credit yourself.

Examples of great prayers of the Bible. How did these people pray?

Jesus – the best example for us.

- *Jesus was an early riser. Notice He prayed in a quiet isolated place.*
"*Very early in the morning*, while it was still dark, he got up, went out, and made his way to a deserted place; and there he was praying." - Mark 1:35 CSB

- *Jesus typically prayed alone and in nature – an olive grove or mountain.*
"They went to the *olive grove* called Gethsemane, and Jesus said, 'Sit here while I go and pray.'" - Mark 14:32 NLT
Luke 9:18, 28

- *Jesus said in the Sermon on the Mount to not use public prayer to bring glory on oneself.*
"Whenever you pray, *you must not be like the hypocrites*, because they love to pray standing in the synagogues and on the street corners to be seen by people. Truly I tell you, they have their reward." - Matthew 6:5 CSB

- *Pray privately. Pray to God the Father not an idol or a mystic.*
"But when you pray, *go into your private room*, shut your door, and pray to your Father who is in secret. *And your Father who sees in secret will reward you.*" - Matthew 6:6 CSB

7: Prayer – What is it? Why is it important? How to do it?

- ***It is not the word count that counts!***
"*When you pray, don't babble* like the Gentiles, since they imagine they'll be heard for their many words." - Matthew 6:7 CSB

- ***God already knows our needs. But He still likes to talk with us.***
"Don't be like them, because your Father knows the things you need before you ask him." - Matthew 6:8 CSB

- ***Jesus prayed as He was receiving the Holy Spirit. Jesus did not need the Holy Spirit in Heaven because He lived there too. But when He took on flesh and became a human, He benefitted from having the Holy Spirit and He welcomed Him.***
"One day when the crowds were being baptized, Jesus himself was baptized. *As he was praying, the heavens opened, and the Holy Spirit,* in bodily form, descended on him like a dove. And a voice from heaven said, 'You are my dearly loved Son, and you bring me great joy.'" - Luke 3:21-22 NLT

- ***Jesus prayed earnestly before the big decision as to whom He should choose as the 12. He pulled an "all-nighter".***
"During those days he went out to the mountain to pray and *spent all night in prayer to God.* When daylight came, he summoned his disciples, and *he chose twelve of them,* whom he also named apostles:" - Luke 6:12-13 CSB

- ***Jesus prayed for others – here it was for the children.***
"One day some parents brought their children to Jesus so he could lay his hands on them and pray for them. But the disciples scolded the parents for bothering him." - Matthew 19:13 NLT

- ***Jesus said to pray persistently when we feel ready to give up.***
"One day Jesus told his disciples a story to show that they should always pray and never give up." - Luke 18:1 NLT

- ***In the midst of crises. He prayed in the greatest crisis of His earthly life.***
"Then Jesus left them a second time and prayed, 'My Father! If this cup cannot be taken away unless I drink it, your will be done.'" - Matthew 26:42 NLT

"Then Jesus left them again and prayed the same prayer as before." - Mark 14:39 NLT

- ***Before teaching. Jesus prayed for His teachings to be accepted and understood. The key to effective prayer is to be childlike and realize our need.***
Matthew 11:25

Questions:

1. What are the key features of the Disciples' Prayer?

2. Where is the best time and place for you to pray?

3. What do you find are the benefits of prayer? What are the difficulties with it?

4. What kinds of things do you pray about? Look again to the prayers of Jesus – are you doing what He did?

5. Often in a crisis we hear people saying, "I am thinking of you" or "you are in my thoughts". How does this differ from "I am praying for you"?

Questions with suggested answers:

1. What are the key features of the Disciples' Prayer?

Answer: Adoration; holiness; a prayer that God's will will be done in the situation you are praying about; forgiveness; the reality of daily temptation; protection from the enemy (the evil one) and the truth that eternity is real and forever.

2. Where is the best time and place for you to pray?

Answer: This is an individual decision – for me it is the quiet of the morning – like Jesus.

3. What do you find are the benefits of prayer? What are the difficulties with it?

Answer: The benefits are numerous but some of the obvious ones are it turns us to God; it makes us realize how dependent we are on Him; it helps us put the situations into eternal perspective. The difficulties with it are not so much finding time to do it but rather waiting on the answers. It is also difficult to know how much good it does. In medicine, we "work as if everything depends on us and pray as if everything depends on God." God expects us to be the best at what we do and we need all the help we can get from Him.

4. What kinds of things do you pray about? Look again to the prayers of Jesus – are you doing what He did?

7: Prayer – What is it? Why is it important? How to do it?

Answer: Personal – discuss with others and get their input. We can always learn from others and share their burdens and they can share ours.

5. Often in a crisis we hear people saying, "I am thinking of you" or "you are in my thoughts". How does this differ from "I am praying for you"?

Answer: Just thinking about a person's dilemma does not really help much other that it may help the person in need to feel like others really do care. When Christians pray, they are asking the Almighty God to do something about the situation. These prayers can be instantaneously answered as they immediately reach the throne of God (Rev 5:8). A recent example was the case of Damar Hamlin, a Buffalo Bills football player who on January 2, 2023, made a tackle in a game and suffered chest trauma. He went into cardiac arrest on the field on national television. His arrest and resuscitation were viewed by millions on live TV. Many of the players knelt down to pray as did the announcers. The medical team was awesome and within seconds he was cared for and resuscitated and whisked off to the hospital. He was discharged a week later and is recovering. Only God knows the number of instantaneous prayers that made it to Heaven with instantaneous review by Jesus. He was healed certainly because of the work of the medical team; only after we get to Heaven will we know the exact role of the prayers. In summary, if we say we are going to pray for people do it don't just think about it.

Jesus Prayer in John 17 for the Believers.

This prayer of Jesus to His Father is recorded by John prior to His betrayal and eventual crucifixion. Jesus prays for glory, for the disciples He is leaving behind and for us. This prayer provides us a glimpse into how much Jesus cares personally for each believer. He does not promise safety and complete success in this world but rather in the next.

• *Jesus prays to His Father. He prays for reciprocal glory.*
John 17:1

• *God is the only true God. Jesus goal for us is that we would know God and Jesus.*
John 17:2-3

• *Jesus' work here is done. He tells us again that He was with God before the incarnation.* Another affirmation of John 1:1.
John 17:4-5

- *Jesus prays for His disciples — His team that He is now leaving behind. He says by this time the disciples did believe.*
John 17:6-8 CSB

- *Jesus prayed specifically for His disciples. Notice that in this prayer, He does not pray for "the entire world" but rather specifically the believers. He is interested in us as individuals again demonstrating the personal nature of Jesus.*
John 17:9

- *Jesus is leaving this world behind. The disciples however remain in the world.*
John 17:10-11

- *He acknowledges that Judas Iscariot (son of destruction) was lost; but this was predicted and fulfilled Scripture.*
John 17:12

- *Jesus never says we will be liked. He says once saved we are "no longer of this world". He prays for the protection of the believers from the evil one.*
John 17:13-19

- *Jesus now turns and prays for the believers. He prays for the unity of believers. This is not to be mistaken for uniformity. He says — You and I are in unity — may they be in unity between themselves and with us. The result is that the unsaved will be attracted.*
John 17:20-21

- *Jesus has glorified us. What does it mean to be glorified? It means to be special in God's sight and the ability to be in unity with others of the same belief.*
John 17:22-23

- *Jesus prays that we, the believer, will see the glory of Jesus. He wants us to be in Heaven with Him where we will see Jesus in all His glory. He reminds us that He was there before this world. When Jesus was here, we got glimpses of His glory.*
John 17:24

- *Jesus says the "world missed out" but we know Him.*
John 17:25

- *Jesus wants His agape love to be in us. We are to be loving to others.*
John 17:26

7: Prayer – What is it? Why is it important? How to do it?

Questions:

1. Have you ever prayed John 17:1 for yourself? Or for a specific issue at work? "Jesus spoke these things, looked up to heaven, and said: 'Father, the hour has come. *Glorify your Son so that the Son may glorify you.*" - John 17:1 CSB

2. Are Christians still persecuted today? Can you give some examples of "Now I am coming to you, and I speak these things in the world so that they may have my joy completed in them? I have given them your word. *"The world hated them because they are not of the world, just as I am not of the world."* I am not praying that you take them out of the world but that *"you protect them from the evil one."* They are not of the world, just as I am not of the world. "Sanctify them by the truth; your word is truth. As you sent me into the world, I also have sent them into the world. I sanctify myself for them, so that they also may be sanctified by the truth." - John 17:13-19 CSB

Questions with suggested answers:

1. Have you ever prayed John 17:1 for yourself? Or for a specific issue at work? "Jesus spoke these things, looked up to heaven, and said: "Father, the hour has come. *Glorify your Son so that the Son may glorify you,*" - John 17:1 CSB

Answer: This verse is helpful to us because it puts our request in line with our ultimate goal which is to glorify God in our lives. Eric Liddle was a runner who ran for Scotland in the 1924 Paris Olympics. His story is told in the famous movie "Chariots of Fire". In the movie he tells his sister, "I believe God made me for a purpose, but He also made me fast. And when I run, I feel His pleasure." Liddle went on to win the Olympics and died a martyr in China as a missionary. Are you feeling "God's pleasure" in your life's work? You should be and you should pray that God's blessing you will in turn bring glory to Him.

2. Are Christians still persecuted today? Can you give some examples of "Now I am coming to you, and I speak these things in the world so that they may have my joy completed in them. I have given them your word. *The world hated them because they are not of the world, just as I am not of the world.* I am not praying that you take them out of the world but that *you protect them from the evil one.* They are not of the world, just as I am not of the world. Sanctify them by the truth; your word is truth. As you sent me into the world, I also have sent them into the world. I sanctify myself for them, so that they also may be sanctified by the truth." - John 17:13-19 CSB

Answer: This prayer was particularly applicable as we witnessed the hatred in the world and the killing of innocent children and people when President Putin ordered the invasion of Ukraine in February 2022. We realized that this was the doing of an evil man of the likes of Hitler and Stalin that was visible world-wide on video. There was no hiding this war; it was and remains open and brutal. We prayed (and continue to pray) for the safety of Ukraine but are reminded in these verses that we as Christians will be hated by the world and that our goal is heaven. There are many other examples of believers who suffer for the cause of Christ. We are to pray for them as Jesus did.

The Prayer of Moses in Psalm 90.

This is such a great prayer – read it often and meditate on it. Read all 17 verses at once (it will take less than 2 minutes). Psalm 90:1-17 CSB

- *God is our refuge – He has always been here for every generation. Moses acknowledges that all of us will die. Realizing our mortality is important.*
Psalm 90:1-3

- *Time does not matter much to God. We should focus on eternity rather than today.*
Psalm 90:4-6

- *God is concerned about our secret sins.*
Psalm 90:7-9

- *Longevity – the result of senescence is that we have a relatively fixed life span. Just think – in 2022 most of us only live about 80 years (81 for women; 77 for men in 2021). Some (but very few) people are especially blessed and live to be 100!*
Psalm 90:10

- *We need to respect God.*
Psalm 90:11

- *Moses said we need to think on this so that we are wise in our use of time.*
Psalm 90:12

- *Moses prays for compassion.*
- Psalm 90:13

7: Prayer – What is it? Why is it important? How to do it?

• *A prayer for the start of the day. Shout for joy – it's a new day!*
Psalm 90:14-15

• *A prayer for the workplace.*
Psalm 90:16-17

Questions:

1. This prayer of Moses starts with some depressing words about our end. What is Moses trying to get us to realize and think about?

2. The last 4 verses are triumphant and very important. In verses 14-15, what is Moses telling us about how we are to approach each day?

3. How does verse 17 inform the occupation (work) that you do? What is Moses asking God to do with respect to this work?

Questions with suggested answers:

1. This prayer of Moses starts with some depressing words about our end. What is Moses trying to get us to realize and think about?

Answer: The fragility and briefness of life. At best we get 80 years (in 2023 it is 79 years in the United States) and of course we are not guaranteed any more than today. Realizing that will put your thinking about the importance of things in perspective. Having believed in Jesus as the sacrifice for your sin and living for Him is very important to your foundation. You do not ever want to wait until your deathbed to come to Christ. If you know you are going to Heaven when you die, you have stamped your spiritual passport with the blood of Christ, then you can really live without fear of death. I have witnessed many people who are dying. They are not awake enough to have any spiritual discussion.

2. The last 4 verses are triumphant and very important. In verses 14-15, what is Moses telling us about how we are to approach each day?

Answer: Approach each day with joy and thankfulness. Take one day at a time and your troubles will be minimized.

3. How does verse 17 inform the occupation (work) that you do? What is Moses asking God to do with respect to this work?

Answer: He is asking God to make our work meaningful and important to God. Having pride and meaning in our work is important to our satisfaction.

The Disciples Corporate Prayer for Boldness in Acts 4.

Peter and John had been thrown in prison for healing a lame man in Acts 3. They were released and when they returned to the church, they (the disciples and the believers) prayed this corporate prayer. This prayer has an unusual request – *it is a prayer for boldness*. The disciples in the early Church were living in dangerous times of religious persecution. They were doing miracles in the name of Jesus yet being persecuted, not by the government, but by the Jewish religious leaders! The disciples realized that to be effective they had to continue preaching but they understood the need for boldness. The Holy Spirit delivered the answer. We need to pray together as a church and pray for boldness today. Read all of Acts 3 because it is so interesting; the actual prayer starts in verse 23. This prayer provides key guidelines for open prayers in the Church or a group. Before the request, God is praised, and Scripture is quoted. This is then followed by a specific prayer, and finally the prayer gives credit to Jesus not us.

- ***The prayer begins with all praise going to God and not to man.*** This is like the prayer of Jeremiah "Ah Lord GOD! behold, thou hast made the heaven and the earth by thy great power and stretched out arm, and there is nothing too hard for thee:" - Jeremiah 32:17 KJV
Acts 4:23-24

- ***Quoting of Scripture –a good tactic to use in praying. Rulers think they can mock God and get away with it. Here Luke quotes Psalm 2:1-2.***
Acts 4:25-26

- ***Prayer gives us boldness to preach.***
Acts 4:27-29

- ***The miracles, attributed to God, were given to empower and embolden.***
Acts 4:30

- ***When we pray like this the Holy Spirit comes and with it the answer to their request – boldness. This is an example of an immediate answer to prayer.***
Acts 4:31

7: Prayer – What is it? Why is it important? How to do it?

Questions:

1. The disciples were doing miracles by healing the sick, why was this such a problem to the Jewish leaders?

2. How do you explain the boldness the Church exhibited in this period of intense persecution? Is the Church behaving this way today?

3. Who do the disciples say killed Jesus? Read Acts 4:27 again for the answer.

Questions with suggested answers:

1. The disciples were doing miracles by healing the sick, why was this such a problem to the Jewish leaders?

Answer: It was a sign of the power of God and the Holy Spirit, and it gave credence to the Jesus movement and that He was indeed resurrected and alive. It meant that just by killing Jesus, Christianity was not "going away."

2. How do you explain the boldness the Church exhibited in this period of intense persecution? Is the Church behaving this way today?

Answer: They prayed specifically for boldness and the Holy Spirit gave it to them immediately. This boldness of the Church is variably evident around the world. We need to pray for it where we are.

3. Who do the disciples say killed Jesus? Read Acts 4:27 again for the answer.

Answer: They rightfully say "all of us" – Jews and non-Jews (Gentiles) alike.

The Prayer of Jonah 2 when he was drowning – it's never too late to pray.

Jonah was sent to be a missionary to the city of Nineveh (modern day Mosul, Iraq). He refused to go and disobeyed by boarding a ship out of Joppa, a city today in Israel on the Mediterranean coast. God punished him by throwing him overboard in a storm on the Mediterranean Sea and he was swallowed by a large sea monster of some type. In chapter 2 his prayer is recorded. There is much to be learned from this prayer.

- *We can pray anytime anywhere.*

Jonah 2:1

- ***God hears the prayer of distress.***
Jonah 2:2

- ***Jonah was in this situation due to disobedience, yet God's hand was behind it.***
Jonah 2:3

- As he is drowning, Jonah decides to pray one more time. Never give up on God.
Jonah 2:4-5, 7

- ***God answered this last second prayer of Jonah. He can answer ours too.***
Jonah 2:6-7

- ***Prayer can change you attitude and direction. Jonah recommits to following God.***
Jonah 2:8-9

- ***God has command over nature. Jonah was out of trouble.***
Jonah 2:10

Questions:

1. Have you ever been in a tight spot where you needed to fling up a prayer? What happened?

2. Some passages in Scripture are ideal to pray over and apply to your life. Read Psalm 23 and focus on the key words and apply them. It may help to print out this prayer and circle the key words. Do it in a group or with your family.

Questions with suggested answers:

1. Have you ever been in a tight spot where you needed to fling up a prayer? What happened?

Answer: During our lives there will be many times when we are in a really difficult situation. Like Jonah, we need to pray and do it quickly. God answers those prayers. What we promise during them we need to fulfill. I'd like to hear your story and I'm sure your friends will benefit from you sharing it. I recall a story a Bible Study teacher told our class many years ago in reference to this type of prayer. Herb was an Air Force pilot in WWII and his plane was shot and was engulfed in flames. Like Jonah, he quickly uttered a prayer for God to "save him". He bargained with God, "God, if You will get me out of this situation, I will follow You for the rest of my life." God answered his prayer and Herb indeed followed His Lord until his death at age 99. He influenced many young people including me. As long as we are alive, it is "never too late to pray".

2. Some passages in Scripture are ideal to pray over and apply to your life. Read Psalm 23 and focus on the key words and apply them. It may help to print out this prayer and circle the key words. Do it in a group or with your family.

Answer: I like the KJV because that is the way I memorized it. A Psalm of David. "The LORD is my **shepherd**; I shall **not want**. He **maketh me to lie down** in green pastures: he **leadeth me** beside the still waters. He **restoreth my soul**: he **leadeth me** in the paths of righteousness **for his name's sake**. Yea, though I walk through the **valley of the shadow of death, I will fear no evil**: for **thou art with me**; thy rod and thy staff they **comfort** me. Thou preparest a table before me in the presence of mine enemies: thou anointest my head with oil; my cup runneth over. **Surely goodness and mercy** shall follow me all the days of my life: and I will **dwell in the house of the LORD forever**." - Psalm 23:1-6 KJV

Key points – they are "stopping points" in this prayer – Jehovah is my shepherd – personal and my leader. He is "for me" personally. Maketh me to lie down –this tells me that sometimes God has to put me in a situation to rest up, relax, recharge. Leadeth – God leads, I follow. That's what I am a "follower" of Jesus. For His name's sake – God wants me to be true so that His name is glorified. Valley of the shadow of death – these are the tough times, the cancer, the chemotherapy, the transplant, the business failure – but the prayer says we are not to fear because God is with me/us. Goodness and mercy will come. And lastly, don't miss the end of this –its glory with Jesus in Heaven – its eternity. It's a reminder to always keep an eternal focus.

Thomas Witzig

8

Genesis 1-11 Interpreting Current Issues with a Biblical Worldview

The book of Genesis, the first Book in the Bible, is about beginnings and provides a foundation for a Biblical worldview. The setting is modern day Iraq (Babylon in the Bible times) an area of the world referred to as the Cradle of Civilization. In order to understand many current issues in the 21st century it is important to read and understand the first 11 chapters of Genesis. The topics therein form the foundation of entire disciplines of study such as archeology, linguistics, dietary science, animal science, sociology, aging, and DEI (diversity, equity, inclusion). Yes, DEI are Biblical principles. As Bill Newton, pastor and author said in his book *Endure* page 37, "God is so wise! He is the author of diversity, even though we think we just discovered it in America in the 21st century. He created us all as different creatures. Those differences are what makes the church rich with talent, wisdom, gifts, and challenges." Genesis also describes how sin got into the world and totally disrupted the entire creation. Reading and understanding Genesis 1-11 will help you establish your worldview. Just what is a worldview? It is the set of beliefs or framework that determines how we view the world around us. It is the lens through which we interpret events and how we live our lives. With a Biblical worldview, we view the world based on the truths of the Bible. There are many other worldviews and many helpful resources and charts comparing them on the internet. In this section, you will learn what the Bible says about the following topics (**Figure 6**) and be able to articulate your worldview based on a solid foundation of Biblical truth:

- Origins of the earth and its inhabitants. The theory of creation and the who, what, and why of the creation.

- The creation of the first man Adam and the first woman Eve. The complementarity of the sexes and the equality of men and women.

- The creation of humans with both a body and a spirit.

- The Trinity – God in Three Persons (God the Father, God the Son Jesus, and God the Holy Spirit) are all present at the Creation.

- Monotheism – we read of no other God than the God of Genesis. Christianity is a monotheistic religion.

- What was earth designed for? What is its purpose?

- The genetic code and the concept of genetic kinds.

- The origin of sexual identity (genetic sex) and the definition of Biblical marriage.

- Why humans are special and different than animals.

- Human responsibility for caring for the world and its inhabitants.

- Where did Satan come from? Did he have a choice in his destiny?

- The choice we are all given to sin or not to sin.

- The consequences of sin – the results of God's wrath are death, degradation of creation, diet changes, and shame. Shame comes with sin and was not part of the original creation.

- God's plan to save us from His wrath - the need for a blood sacrifice to atone for sin. Sin required a sacrifice – and that was blood of an animal.

- The need for a Savior for all time to abolish the need for continued animal sacrifice. This Savior was Jesus (the Messiah) and the need for Him to come to save us from eternal death starts in Genesis.

- The universal Flood and its impact on geology.

- Single race theory - we are all descendants of Adam and Eve and then the eight people that survived the Flood. This is why there is no basis for racism.

- The origins of capital punishment as practiced by governments.

8: Genesis 1:11 Interpreting Current Issues with a Biblical Worldview

- The three major judgements – the Fall and its consequences; the universal Flood; the Tower of Babel and the subsequent separation of people into groups by language.

- Calling out of a people (Israel) to raise up Jesus to save us from our sins.

- The concept of work and need for rest from work.

- Accelerated aging - why we only live about 80 years now compared to the original 900+

Key Issues in Genesis
by Chapter

Chapter	Topics (above line)	Topics (below line)
1	7 Days of Creation	Origins; Humans created in the image of God
2	Adam; Eve; Soul; Gender	Genetic; Gender
3	Garden of Eden; Two Trees; Choices; Biblical Marriage; Vegetarian Diet; No Shame	Choices; Diet
3	Satan tempts Adam and Eve to disobey; they sin resulting in: Punishments, Shame, Animal sacrifice, Closing of Eden	Choose to Sin; Pain and Pestilence
4	Abel murdered; Cain punished; The arts; Seth born; Polygamy enters; Public worship	Murder; The arts; Distorted Marriage; Worship
5	Genealogy	Family Matters
6/7/8	Evil reigns; God judges with the Flood and reduced lifespan of humans	Judgement/Flood; Righteousness matters; Senescence
9	Noahic Covenant	Rainbow; Diet Change; Animal Fear
10/11	Tower of Babel; Table of Nations	Linguistics; Cultural Styles

Figure 6: The topics and issues in the first 11 chapters of Genesis.

Guiding principles for reading Genesis 1-11.

God does not tell us everything about these subjects, but He did tell us enough to develop a framework of thinking and what is necessary for life. Remember, we use many things in our lives that we do not fully understand. In this section, similar to others in this book, we will take a "*Mostly Scripture*" approach which means we will look primarily at what the Bible says about the topic. The Creation theory is described in detail in the Bible in only 2 chapters – Genesis 1 and 2. There are additional confirming verses from some of the Prophets in the Old Testament and Jesus and other authors in the New Testament. The only theory discussed is creation by the Holy Trinity. Reverend Stan Keys speaking at a conference in 2006 (and I paraphrase) "God devoted 2 chapters (Genesis 1 and 2) to creation, while 40 chapters are devoted to the design and building of the tabernacle. God took 6 days to create the universe; 40 days to deliver the instructions on how to build the tabernacle. He is more concerned with our worship than exact mechanisms of origins."

- **When did the Creation happen?** Scholars date the creation of Adam to about 4000 BC and the Universal Flood to 2500 BC. The Bible is not a complete history of the world and there were other civilizations occurring during the Bible times. *The main theme of the Bible is Jesus from Genesis to Revelation.* There are many other books on ancient civilizations one can read and study. Indeed, it is important to understand when other key historical events occurred compared with Biblical events.

In Chapter 1, God says the Trinity (discussed in Chapters 2-4) did the creation and that the process was orderly. Each day God reviewed the results and certified that it was good. What is important here? (A) God was responsible for the creation not some other random cosmic force; (B) Creation was rational, orderly, and progressive; (C) The concept of DNA and kinds. God's design is for organisms to reproduce progeny with the same DNA content. *A kind begets the same kind.* This is due to faithful DNA replication. There is no doubt that there is change and evolution *within kinds* that allow diversity and fitness. Whenever discussing the topic of evolution, ask, "Are you referring to the development of a "kind" or "change within a kind"? "Is the question about how the world was originally created or what is visible and testable today?" Origin science (historical science; inferred science) is the realm of philosophy and uses testable scientific techniques to infer about what could have happened in the beginning. The origin of the earth cannot be reproduced in the lab. Research that we do daily in the lab is referred to as testable or operational science. Genesis 1 is about the development/creation of the *kinds*. How exactly God did this is a mystery and requires faith to believe (Hebrews 11:3). On the other hand, changes within kinds are frequently observed in nature, can be studied, and proven scientifically. The best recent example is the mutation of the virus that causes COVID-19 infection from wild-type (original version) to delta variant to omicron. The virus evolved but it remained a virus. It did not turn into a bacteria or fungus. It stayed within its kind. This sort of evolution is different than the evolution of the species that Jean Baptiste Lamarck and Charles Darwin wrote about in the 1800's to explain the origins of the universe and the variation we see today. The Bible leaves a full explanation of this out as it does other things such as "Were these days 24 hours

8: Genesis 1:11 Interpreting Current Issues with a Biblical Worldview

long"? and "How long between verse 1 and 2"? The way Genesis 1 is written it seems the days were 24 hours long, but there is much contention about this. I do not recommend fussing about it.

- ***Why was the earth created? To be inhabited. God wanted fellowship with us.***

"For this is what the LORD says -- the Creator of the heavens, the God who formed the earth and made it, the one who established it (he did not create it to be a wasteland, but *formed it to be inhabited*) -- he says, 'I am the LORD, and there is no other.'" - Isaiah 45:18 CSB

Figure 7: Summary of what was created on each of the 6 days of Creation in Genesis 1-2.

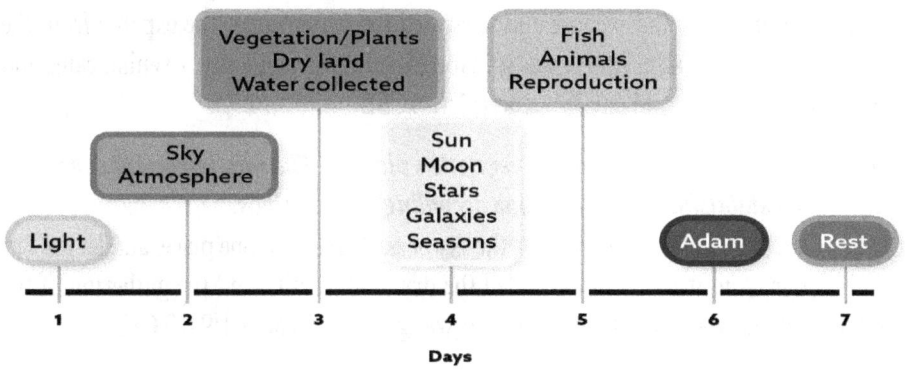

How was the world created? —Genesis 1.

- ***Who created the earth? God (Hebrew = elohiym) did!***

"In the beginning *God* created the heavens and the earth." - Genesis 1:1 CSB The word '*Beginning*' in Hebrew is *re'shiyth* which means 'first'. It all started with God. The Trinity was eternal (without beginning or end) whereas the earth had a beginning.

- ***What was the earth like before Creation? It was empty and the only population was the Trinity – God the Father, God the Son (Jesus), and God the Holy Spirit.***

"Now the earth was formless and empty, darkness covered the surface of the watery depths, and the Spirit of God was hovering over the surface of the waters." - Genesis 1:2 CSB

- ***Creation Day 1 was "lights on"; God is always Light, and Light was first. In the Bible God and Jesus are always represented as light and evil and Satan as darkness.***

"Then God said, 'Let there be light,' and there was light. God saw that the light was good, and God separated the light from the darkness. God called the light 'day,' and the darkness he called 'night.' There was an evening, and there was a morning: one day." - Genesis 1:3-5 CSB

- ***Creation Day 2: The Atmosphere—clouds are the water above, and lakes, rivers, oceans, and subterranean streams are the water below. There was no rain yet.***

"Then God said, Let there be an expanse between the waters, separating water from water. So God made the expanse and separated the water under the expanse from the water above the expanse. And it was so. God called the expanse sky. Evening came and then morning: the second day." - Genesis 1:6-8 CSB

- ***Creation Day 3: Land is formed; vegetation planted. The very important concept of genetics is established— reproduction according to their kinds.***

"Then God said, Let the water under the sky be gathered into one place, and let the dry land appear. And it was so. God called the dry land 'earth,' and the gathering of the water he called 'seas.' And God saw that it was good." - Genesis 1:9-10 CSB

"Then God said, Let the earth produce vegetation: seed-bearing plants and fruit trees on the earth bearing fruit with seed in it according to their kinds. And it was so. The earth produced vegetation: seed-bearing plants *according to their kinds* and trees bearing fruit with seed in it *according to their kinds*. And God saw that it was good. Evening came and then morning: the third day." - Genesis 1:11-13 CSB

- ***Creation Day 4: Creation of the sun and the moon and seasons. Their purpose was to create a schedule of daylight and nightlife, a rhythm so precise and predictable.***

"Then God said, Let there be lights in the expanse of the sky to separate the day from the night. They will serve as signs for seasons and for days and years. They will be lights in the expanse of the sky to provide light on the earth. And it was so. God made the two great lights -- the greater light to rule over the day and the lesser light to rule over the night -- as well as the stars. God placed them in the expanse of the sky to provide light on the earth, to rule the day and the night, and to separate light from darkness. And God saw that it was good. Evening came and then morning: the fourth day." - Genesis 1:14-19 CSB

• *Creation Day 5*: *Birds, sea creatures and land animals; the principle of reproduction of kinds is introduced to multiply and "fill the earth".*
"Then God said, Let the water swarm with living creatures, and let birds fly above the earth across the expanse of the sky. So God created the large sea-creatures and every living creature that moves and swarms in the water, according to their kinds. He also created every winged creature according to its kind. And God saw that it was good. God blessed them: Be fruitful, multiply, and fill the waters of the seas, and let the birds multiply on the earth. Evening came and then morning: the fifth day." - Genesis 1:20-23 CSB

"Then God said, Let the earth produce living creatures *according to their kinds*: livestock, creatures that crawl, and the wildlife of the earth according to their kinds. And it was so. So God made the wildlife of the earth according to their kinds, the livestock according to their kinds, and all the creatures that crawl on the ground according to their kinds. And God saw that it was good." - Genesis 1:24-25 CSB

God designed the earth to be filled with life and diversity. Today, we marvel at nature and its wide variety of species and kinds. It is likely (although not specifically mentioned) that the creation of life was "with age". In other words, the original kinds were created of reproductive age rather than having to grow up. It is critical to note the scientific principle of "kinds" again noted in verses 20-23. The creation was according to "kinds" and each kind reproduces according to its kind. When sheep reproduce, more sheep are born; humans produce humans, etc. This is genetically confirmed as we examine the DNA content of the cells from each kind. We have 46 chromosomes/cell including the two sex chromosomes, 'X' and 'Y'. 46XX is human genetic female; 46XY is a human genetic male. A gorilla is close but still distinct with 48 chromosomes/cell. Gorillas always beget gorillas. A mouse has 40 chromosomes; koalas and kangaroos have 16 chromosomes (the same as an onion!); frogs, 20; tomatoes, 24; giraffes, 30. Each of these kinds are genetically unique and reproduce faithfully. If they do not, we have a mutant, which almost always does not survive as well. For example, a child with Down's

Syndrome has one extra chromosome 21 leading to a remarkably consistent appearance and a shortened survival.

Questions:

1. When did God create the world?

2. Where was Jesus before the Creation described in Genesis 1?

3. How can I respond to my professor who states that the world was created through scientific evolution?

4. Differentiate between evolution of kinds vs evolution within a kind.

5. Can a believer be a great scientist?

6. Differentiate between testable science vs inferred science.

7. How do you explain or debate statements that "this organ or gene was conserved through evolution"?

8. In Genesis 1:16 the Bible says, "God made the two great lights -- the greater light to rule over the day and the lesser light to rule over the night -- as well as the stars." - Genesis 1:16 CSB This is referring to the sun, moon, and stars. Some say that the Bible is scientifically wrong here because we now know that the moon reflects light from the sun rather than generates any light itself. How do you explain that?

Questions with suggested answers:

1. When did God create the world?

Answer: The Bible does not say; but science tries to determine the age of the universe through astronomy and archeology and various dating methods. As Pastor Rick Henderson (Autumn Ridge Church Rochester, MN) says, "Origins is more about 'what and why' than 'how and when'. God chose to tell us in general concepts about creation but in the end, He spends little time telling us dates and methods. This remains a mystery."

2. Where was Jesus before the Creation described in Genesis 1?

Answer: The three members of the Trinity were not created – they were pre-existent - eternal. In Jesus prayer to God in John 17 He makes it clear. "Now, Father, glorify me in your presence *with that glory I had with you before the world existed.*" - John 17:5 CSB

3. How can I respond to my professor who states that the world was created through scientific evolution?

Answer: The Bible says that God created the world *ex nihilo* – Latin for out of nothing. These exact words are not in the Bible (but rather inferred from Hebrews 11:3 below), but nowhere does it say that God first made all the elements then constructed things. Studying how the world was made is difficult because it occurred in the past and cannot easily be tested in the lab. It is not testable science. This experiment is impossible to conduct. We cannot ask God to re-create as described in Genesis 1. We can do experiments in the lab with amino acids and try to generate DNA and organisms. We can study the universe and work backwards and try to infer how the universe came about. Indeed, scientists have launched the James Webb telescope and are peering into the far reaches of the universe to get clues on its origins. But in the end, these are but models. God chose to let this be a mystery. Both camps believe either creation by God or evolution of the species *by faith*.

"By faith we understand that the universe was created by the word of God, so that what is seen was made from things that are not visible." - Hebrews 11:3 CSB

What *can* we study? *Studying evolution within a kind or comparing anatomy and gene function is very testable and goes on all the time.* This is hard-core research and presents no problem for the scientist who is a Christian. This is not origins research; rather, this is testable science.

4. Differentiate between evolution of kinds vs evolution within a kind.

Answer: Evolution or change within a kind is very common and necessary. Sometimes it is good, but often bad. Cancer cells evolve to become resistant to certain chemotherapy, but they still remain the same kind of cancer. Lymphoma cells can transform from low grade to high grade, but they do not change from lymphoma to breast cancer. Bacteria have over the years become resistant to penicillin (the first antibiotic developed) but they remain bacteria. Our own immune system adapts (evolves) to handle and cope with these changes by making new antibodies. Lastly, influenza and COVID-19 viruses change often which requires new vaccines planned each season. They still are viruses. We do not observe changes of one kind becoming another in nature.

5. Can a believer be a great scientist?

Answer: Of course, because scientists today do testable science – science that can be repeated again and again. We know that water boils at 100 degrees C (212F) at sea level. If anyone doubts that we can go to the kitchen and prove it. Even Darwin recommended continuous study on both the Biblical and scientific fronts. "To conclude, therefore, let no man out of a weak conceit of sobriety or an ill-applied moderation, think or maintain, that a man can search too far or be too well-studied in the book of God's word, or in the book of God's works; divinity or philosophy; but rather let men endeavor an endless progress or proficiency in both." Finding Darwin's God by Kenneth R. Miller. I heard Dr Francis Collins, past Director of the United States National Institutes of Health repeat and add to this quote on a podcast on CMDA Matters on May 27, 2021. "Being absolutely faithful to Scripture and also trusting that science can teach us the truth about nature and knowing that those are all things that God has given us - both the Book of God's words the Bible and the Book of God's works which is Nature, and they really cannot be in conflict or else we misunderstood something."

6. Differentiate between testable science vs inferred science (**Table 1**).

Answer: Inferred science is often used to support various theories of how the world came into being. For example, the James Webb Telescope in 2022 begun sending remarkable photos of the deep edges of our universe never seen before. They are giving us information on galaxies and other planets, whether there is water there and any signs of inhabitants (so far none). If you read the discussion of these findings scientists will extrapolate from these data on how the earth came into being. They cannot "remake" the earth, but they can use scientific data to extrapolate backwards and infer how it might of happened. The more data we gather the better our extrapolations will be. Those who believe that God did the Creation also use these data. They search the heavens and the rocks and use the most modern methods to infer how long-ago creation happened etc. Both use faith since we cannot and do not ask God to "start over and do it again". Testable or operational science is easier to explain. No matter what your religion (or

8: Genesis 1:11 Interpreting Current Issues with a Biblical Worldview

even if you are an atheist) you can do testable science because replication of the results and showing others and writing up your results are all part of operational science. Most science is operational, and God wants us to be exceptional scientists.

Table 1: Origins science vs Testable science.

Origins Science (Historical or Inferred)	Testable Science (Operational)
Since the earth cannot be remade or directly and reproducibly tested in the lab, origins science draws on testable science to infer backwards to address questions of origins.	Can be tested and proven; can be reproduced by others
Less commonly discussed or debated	What we do 99.9% of the time
Based on Biblical accounts in Genesis and what testable science reveals.	Not religious based; all faiths (and atheists) can work together
Faith based (Hebrews 11:3)	Testable but still elements of faith

7. How do you explain or debate statements that "this organ or gene was conserved through evolution"?

Answer: This phrase is used often in classes on comparative anatomy or in scientific publications that discuss the function of a gene. In order to understand function of a gene, the gene or its homologue is studied in a lower life form (fruit flies; zebrafish or rodents). These can provide important information to understand disease and design new treatments. If it is a critically important gene to the function of the organism the scientist may comment that since it was found in both lower and higher forms of life that it must be really important and thus was "conserved" (as opposed to "lost") during the evolutionary process. A scientist who believes that God was the creator will study the gene in a similar way but conclude that it was important enough for the Creator to use it in all the various life forms. For example, the wheel is vital to the function of a wheelbarrow and an oxcart as well as any modern racecar. We do not look at the oxcart and the car and say they evolved from one to another; rather, we say the wheel is critical and we modify it as needed to serve the vehicles. As you go through museums of natural history around the world and view the displays of comparative anatomy, focus on learning the importance of the function of the anatomical part rather than debating its origins. Whether it happened through creation or Darwinian evolution cannot itself be reproduced.

8. In Genesis 1:16 the Bible says, "God made the two great lights -- the greater light to rule over the day and the lesser light to rule over the night -- as well as the stars." - Genesis 1:16 CSB This is referring to the sun, moon, and stars. Some say that the Bible is scientifically wrong here because we now know that the moon reflects light from the sun rather than generates any light itself. How do you explain that?

Answer: The Bible sometimes speaks to us just as we see things. The moon appears to the eye to be a "light" and indeed, light is coming to us as a reflection from the sun. The Bible does not say that the moon is generating light itself – it simply says that when we go outside at night and look up into the heavens, we see light from the moon and stars. We now know the mechanism. Another example when David says, "From the rising of the sun to its setting, let the name of the LORD be praised." - Psalm 113:3 CSB. We know scientifically that the sun does not "rise" or "set" but to our eye it does and we go out often to watch the "sunset" or take a "sunset cruise". Even our apps on our phones and the official weather services refer to the time of "sunrise" and "sunset". It is easier to say what we see than to say, "earth rotation out of sunlight" and "earth rotation into sunlight".

Introduction to Days 6 and 7: God designed the earth with hierarchy. The Hebrew word for "man" is *'adam'* and means man or mankind (i.e., any human). Adam and Eve were different because they were made in the image of God; the other animals were not. Humans have great responsibility to manage the earth and the lower animals. Therefore, people who believe the Bible, are (and should be) staunch supporters of conservation of the earth and the animals that live therein. However, the earth and animals were not designed to be worshipped but rather managed and cared for. The original food recipes were all fruits and vegetables; no meat because that would have required killing an animal. This design occurred before the "Fall" i.e., before sin entered the world and before death. Note also that God designed humans to be either genetically male (46XY) or genetically female (46XX). These verses have implications for worship, for human responsibility, and for informing how we approach those with gender dysphoria.

God also introduced the concept of rest by creating Day 7. Work and rest were part of the order of the world that God created. This is an early reminder to avoid overworking.

• *Creation Day 6: Creation of Adam in the image of God (or like God). Two sexes were created— genotype male (46XY) and genotype female (46XX) and both were blessed and given the responsibility of ruling and managing the lower creation. They were also ordered to procreate.*

"Then God said, '*Let us make man in our image*, according to our likeness. They will rule the fish of the sea, the birds of the sky, the livestock, the whole earth, and the creatures that crawl on the earth.' So God created man in his own image; he created him in the image of God; he created them male and female. God blessed them, and God said to them, 'Be fruitful, multiply, fill the earth, and subdue it. Rule the fish of the sea, the birds of the sky, and every creature that crawls on the earth.'" - Genesis 1:26-28 CSB

Question with suggested answer:

What does the Bible say about transgender people?

Answer: The Bible says, "So God created man in his own image; he created him in the image of God; he created them male and female." - Genesis 1:27 CSB. This means all people are created in the "image of God" and that is special and different than animals and insects and fish etc. Science teaches us that in normal reproduction (genetic errors are beyond the scope of this discussion) our genetic sex, the sex we are born with, is either XX female or XY male depending on whether a sperm with an X sex chromosome united with the X in the female egg or if a sperm with a Y sex chromosome united with the X in the female egg. Thus, whether viewed from the Bible or strictly from science genetic sex is binary – male XY or female XX. If you are asked your genetic sex, there are only two choices – male or female. There can be no "nonbinary" genetic sex box. That is where the Bible leaves the discussion. But we know today that some people view themselves as a different gender than their genetic sex. They may be XY male but feel more like a XX female. This disorder is referred to in the medical world as gender dysphoria. Dysphoria is distress or anxiety; gender dysphoria is discomfort about your gender. The Mayo Clinic states (accessed February 20, 2024), "Gender dysphoria is the feeling of

discomfort or distress that might occur in people whose gender identity differs from their sex assigned at birth or sex-related physical characteristics."
https://www.mayoclinic.org/diseases-conditions/gender-dysphoria/symptoms-causes/syc-20475255.

This diagnosis (gender dysphoria) is included in the Diagnostic and Statistical Manual of Mental Disorders (DSM-5) published by the American Psychiatric Association. *Thus, gender dysphoria is a medical condition that should be evaluated and treated by medical professionals in a team approach.* The treatment is typically counseling; rarely, sex hormones or surgery. Hormones and surgery can change the body phenotype (what the person looks like) but cannot change the genetic sex. The confusion in current society over transgender issues is related to how these cases are handled in children (minors) and the eligibility of transgender athletes to compete in competitive sports given the hormonal and muscle mass differences in transgender women (XY males who change what they look like to become female). Additional confusion arises because transgender individuals are often lumped into the LGBTQ acronym that stands for – lesbian, gay, bisexual, transgender, and queer (questioning). The LGB people groups are lifestyle choices not medical diagnoses; transgenderism is a manifestation of gender dysphoria, a medical diagnosis that is treated by medical professionals.

June is Pride Month, and this dates back to a proclamation of President Bill Clinton in 1999 to declare June as "Gay and Lesbian Pride Month". In 2009, President Barack Obama updated the title to Lesbian, Gay, Bisexual, and Transgender Pride Month." This blending of the groups is unfortunate and confuses many because we don't typically openly celebrate or showcase people with medical disorders such as those with gender dysphoria. We do have special months or days to raise awareness for a disease or raise funds for research and there are many special groups for Alzheimer's Disease, various cancers etc. Indeed, there needs to be more research into helping patients with gender dysphoria. I believe it is important to separate the "T" from the "LGB" in our discussions. In summary, the issue is evolving and complicated and the Bible only goes so far as clearly discussing genetic sex, but we find no examples of people changing their sex appearance in the Bible. The Bible does have much discussion of the sex acts that are considered sinful (see the chapter on Biblical sex in Volume 2).

• ***Creation Day 6: Fruits and vegetables were the initial planned food source. Our original created bodies were designed to live without needing meat.***

"God also said, 'Look, I have given you every seed-bearing plant on the surface of the entire earth and every tree whose fruit contains seed. This will be food for you, for all the wildlife of the earth, for every bird of the sky, and for every creature that crawls on the earth -- everything having the breath of life in it -- I have given every green plant for food.' And it was so. God saw all that he had made, and it was very good indeed. Evening came and then morning: the sixth day." - Genesis 1:29-31 CSB

Questions:

1. Why was the original diet meatless?

2. Who is responsible today for caring for the earth and its animals and plants? Who should be leaders in the field?

3. What is the difference between caring for the earth as instructed in Genesis 1:28 and worshipping nature?

4. How does the hierarchy of creation inform law today? What if a bear is attacking a child while she hikes a trail in a national park. Is it ok to pepper spray the bear or even shoot the bear if the child's life is in danger? What if a person is taunting a buffalo in Yellowstone National Park and it turns on them and gores them with its horns?

5. How does the hierarchy of creation inform law today? Why is it illegal to harvest elephant tusks in Africa to sell for decorations?

6. Is it wrong to have a zoo?

7. Is it wrong to milk a cow? Take eggs from a chicken for human consumption? Take honey off of a beehive?

8. Can animals be used to test a vaccine?

Questions with suggested answers:

1. Why was the original diet meatless?

Answer: There had been no sin, thus no need for blood sacrifice. There were no carnivores in the original creation.

2. Who is responsible today for caring for the earth and its animals and plants? Who should be leaders in the field? How do you see this happening in the world around you.

Answer: Christians should know and understand their original task as described in Genesis 1:28. We care for the earth because our survival depends on it. The conservation methods (caring for the world) are different depending on where you live. In Southern Minnesota where I live, we have lots of wind, so we generate electricity with wind power. If you live in warmer areas, solar power is easy to develop. Seed companies are constantly trying to develop crops that can resist disease so as to increase production. In 2023 we suffered increased pollution from the Canadian wildfires that burned uncontrolled, and the smoke drifted over the United States. Thus, conservation can be tricky; the avoidance of controlled forest burns was thought to be good in that they saved trees, but this eventually led to hotter more destructive fires when they did happen.

3. What is the difference between caring for the earth as instructed in Genesis 1:28 and worshipping nature?

Answer: The Christian must take his/her responsibilities for climate management seriously and scientifically without worshiping nature and thus letting it become an idol.

The worship of nature is a form of idolatry and thus a form of ungodliness. They exchanged the truth of God for a lie, and worshiped and served what has been created instead of the Creator, who is praised forever. Amen. - Romans 1:25 CSB

4. How does the hierarchy of creation inform law today? What if a bear is attacking a child while she hikes a trail in a national park. Is it ok to pepper spray the bear or even shoot the bear if the child's life is in danger? What if a person is taunting a buffalo in Yellowstone National Park and it turns on them and gores them with its horns?

Answer: We value human life over lower animals. However, how we act depends on the situation. The child being attacked by the bear in an unprovoked incident is different than the Yellowstone buffalo incident. In the latter, the buffalo are part of the park and were minding their own business (grazing) when people approached them and purposely got in their way. This led to a natural response – the buffalo chased them away. In that incident the park rangers did not kill the buffalo after rescuing the people. That is why we post warnings to not goad the animals.

5. How does the hierarchy of creation inform law today? Why is it illegal to harvest elephant tusks in Africa to sell for decorations?

Answer: This is animal cruelty – clearly wrong.

6. Is it wrong to have a zoo?

Answer: It depends how the zoo is built. Is it fair to the animals? In many zoos the animals have been wounded or have no chance of survival in the wild. Zoos teach all of us about animals and can be a strong promoter of animal welfare.

7. Is it wrong to milk a cow? Take eggs from a chicken for human consumption? Take honey off of a beehive?

Answer: We take the excess for our consumption. We make sure that the farm animals all are fed and cared for properly. God blesses those animals with excess production which we can use for food. If we leave the excess, it goes to waste; it is given to us for food. Every animal needs to eat something that the ground or another animal produces. Creation is interdependent. This is not considered abuse in and of itself.

8. Can animals be used to test a vaccine?

Answer: The purpose of testing a vaccine or any medical device or new drug on animals is to prove their safety prior to use on humans. The rules are set by the Animal Welfare Act and all institutions that do animal research must follow the rules to minimize pain and suffering in animals. The research team must provide rationale as to why animals of any type are needed for the research and if so, what it is the plan to minimize pain and suffering. Typically, as much testing as possible is done on cell lines in the lab followed by lower animals (worms and rodents). Only when a drug or device is felt to be a candidate for human use does the final testing occur in mammals. This testing is done humanely and carefully so as to minimize pain and suffering.

Genesis 2 - The dual nature of men and women – body and soul.

• *Creation Day 7: A Day of rest; God built in rest for all creation from the very beginning. Thus, we see "work" and "rest" were part of the original design.*
"So the heavens and the earth and everything in them were completed. On the seventh day God had completed his work that he had done, *and he rested on the seventh day from all his work that he had done*. God blessed the seventh day and declared it holy, for on it he rested from all his work of creation." - Genesis 2:1-3 CSB

• *No rain in the original design. The ground was watered by an underground watering system. Farming was the original work.*
"These are the records of the heavens and the earth, concerning their creation. At the time that the LORD God made the earth and the heavens, no shrub of the field had yet grown on the land, and no plant of the field had yet sprouted, *for the LORD God had not made it rain on the land*, and there was no man to work the ground." - Genesis 2:4-5 CSB

"But mist would come up from the earth and water all the ground." - Genesis 2:6 CSB

• *Adam is created with a physical body (from the ground) and a spiritual body that was "breathed into him" by God. This is referred to as the dual nature of man.*
"Then the LORD God formed the man out of the dust from the ground and breathed the breath of life into his nostrils, and the man became a living being." - Genesis 2:7 CSB

This message concerning the fate of Israel came from the LORD: "This message is from the LORD, who stretched out the heavens, laid the foundations of the earth, *and formed the spirit within humans*." Zechariah 12:1, NLT.

"Who put wisdom in the heart or gave the mind understanding?" Job 38:36, CSB.

"He has made everything appropriate in its time. He has also put eternity in their hearts, but no one can discover the work God has done from beginning to end." - Ecclesiastes 3:11 CSB

"For just as the body without the spirit is dead, so also faith without works is dead." - James 2:26 CSB

• The first garden was in Eden; that was Adam and Eve's first home.

"The LORD God planted a garden in Eden, in the east, and there he placed the man he had formed."
- Genesis 2:8 CSB

- **The first choice—respect for God's instruction regarding the tree of knowledge.**
"The LORD God caused to grow out of the ground every tree pleasing in appearance and good for food, including the tree of life in the middle of the garden, as well as the tree of the knowledge of good and evil." - Genesis 2:9 CSB

Questions:

1. Is it wrong to take a day off each week? Why did God design a day of rest?

2. What does it mean that creation was likely "with age"?

3. Describe in a short paragraph what the original, ideal world was created to be.

4. What does it mean that we humans are composed of "body and spirit"?

Questions with suggested answers:

1. Is it wrong to take a day off each week? Why did God design a day of rest?

Answer: The principle of rest is embedded in the Creation, and we should be eternally grateful to God that this is enshrined in Genesis. We have learned the hard way about the dangers of not resting and thankfully employers now appreciate the benefits. There are times when rest is difficult as in military service or disasters where people have to overwork. Eventually we need to get that rest to recharge. If we are not healthy in mind and body, how can we help others?

2. What does it mean that creation was likely "with age"?

Answer: This is actually not specifically explained in the Bible. What it means that Adam and Eve were not created as newborns and "dropped" into the Garden of Eden. They like the animals and plants were likely created already mature and ready to reproduce.

3. Describe in a short paragraph what the original, ideal world was created to be.

Answer: Humans were made in the image of God and were different than the animals and plants. Humans were to be the caretakers of the Garden. Adam and Eve were a perfect marriage, and it was between a genetic male (XY) and a genetic female (XX).

The pair were naked and were not ashamed of it. Their diet was vegetarian without any meat, so no animals were sacrificed. The plants they ate were able to reproduce. There were no weeds. They were given a choice, and it was a simple one – they were restricted to no eating from the tree of knowledge and evil. Satan was there also and because of his choice to rebel against God, he had been ejected from heaven and was roaming the earth. He and the demons (other fallen angels) he brought with him were there to tempt Adam and Eve leading them to sin. Sin then disrupted this perfect world.

4. What does it mean that we humans are composed of "body and spirit"?

Answer: Humankind have a dual nature—body and soul. The physical came from the earth and will return to the earth. The spirit of humans comes from God and returns to God at the time of death. This is a unique feature of us and is not mentioned to have been part of the design of fruits and vegetables or other animals. Our bodies age but our spirit (soul) is forever. This is why when we get sick and see our bodies deteriorating, we can still with joy look forward to eternity because we know there our soul will live on. It also means that no one can take our soul even though they may kill our body.

"Therefore we do not give up. Even though our outer person is being destroyed, our inner person is being renewed day by day. For our momentary light affliction is producing for us an absolutely incomparable eternal weight of glory. So we do not focus on what is seen, but on what is unseen. For what is seen is temporary, but what is unseen is eternal." - 2 Corinthians 4:16-18 CSB

Deuteronomy 6:5

"Don't fear those who kill the body but are not able to kill the soul; rather, fear him who is able to destroy both soul and body in hell." - Matthew 10:28 CSB

Does God give us choices? Genesis 2 continued.

Introduction

In this chapter we learn about things we don't control and things we do control. We had no choice in the parents we were given, where we were born, into what religion (if any), and whether our parents loved us. We also had no choice as to the era in history we were born into and lived. Such was the situation for Adam and Eve. They were created by God and placed into the Garden of Eden. Then they were given a choice – just like you and I are given.

- **God placed Adam and Eve in Eden in a garden. Humans had no choice in this.**
"The LORD God planted a garden in Eden, in the east, and there he placed the man he had formed." - Genesis 2:8 CSB

- **Man was placed into the Garden and was to be a farmer or gardener. Humans were to "watch over" the earth (see also Gen 1:28 above).**
"The LORD God took the man and placed him in the garden of Eden *to work it and watch over it.*" Genesis 2:15, CSB.

- **Eden was in the east near 4 rivers and precious stones and metals - gold, bdellium, and onyx.**
"A river went out from Eden to water the garden. From there it divided and became the source of four rivers. The name of the first is Pishon, which flows through the entire land of Havilah, where there is gold. Gold from that land is pure; bdellium and onyx are also there. The name of the second river is Gihon, which flows through the entire land of Cush. The name of the third river is Tigris, which runs east of Assyria. And the fourth river is the Euphrates." - Genesis 2:10-14 CSB

- **Trees were good for food; there was 2 special trees—the Tree of Life and the Tree of the Knowledge of Good and Evil.**
"The LORD God caused to grow out of the ground every tree pleasing in appearance and good for food, including the tree of life in the middle of the garden, as well as the tree of the knowledge of good and evil." - Genesis 2:9 CSB

- **God gave humans freedom of choice, but the choices had consequences.**
"And the LORD God commanded the man, '*You are free* to eat from any tree of the garden, *but you must not eat from the tree of the knowledge of good and evil*, for on the day you eat from it, you will certainly die.'" - Genesis 2:16-17 CSB

Questions:

1. Who was Satan, and did he have choices too?

2. When did evil enter the universe? Read Genesis 2:17. "But you must not eat from the tree of the knowledge of good and evil, for on the day you eat from it, you will certainly die." - Genesis 2:17 CSB

3. Where is the Garden of Eden today?

4. What do we learn about work in Genesis 2?

5. What are the consequences of God's command to Adam and Eve in Genesis 2:15?

"The LORD God took the man and placed him in the garden of Eden to work it and watch over it." - Genesis 2:15 CSB

6. What were the uncontrollable situations in your life?

7. What era are you living in and how does that change things?

Questions with suggested answers:

1. Who was Satan, and did he have choices too?

Answer: God created the heavens and the earth with choice. Remember that sin begins in Heaven before the Creation with Satan and his demons. Satan was a fallen angel. We know this from just a few verses in the Bible. The key eyewitness to this comes from Jesus. "The seventy-two returned with joy, saying, 'Lord, even the demons submit to us in your name.' He said to them, 'I watched Satan fall from heaven like lightning. Look, I have given you the authority to trample on snakes and scorpions and over all the power of the enemy; nothing at all will harm you. However, don't rejoice that the spirits submit to you, but rejoice that your names are written in heaven.'" - Luke 10:17-20 CSB. Jesus tells us that before Creation Satan was given a choice and decided to revolt and was booted out of Heaven. The stage was set for a cosmic battle of God vs Satan, and this battle would play out on the Earth shortly after Creation. God also gives Adam and Eve a choice. This choice involved clear instructions and a test of obedience. They were created innocent; if they broke that commandment, they would become guilty and understand good and evil.

2. When did evil enter the universe? Read Genesis 2:17. "But you must not eat from the tree of the knowledge of good and evil, for on the day you eat from it, you will certainly die." - Genesis 2:17 CSB

Answer: Evil happened before the Creation because Satan was already present in the Garden ready to tempt. God warns Adam and Eve of this.

3. Where is the Garden of Eden today?

Answer: Nobody knows. The description of 1 river that split into 4 is geologically unusual since most rivers are formed by joining. "...nobody has been able to look at modern maps of the regions mentioned in Genesis and figure out exactly where the Garden of Eden was, at least by the present topography of the lands of the Middle East. Only one river of the four, the Euphrates, is known by the same name in modern times."
—*Gaines R. Johnson, The Bible, Genesis and Geology.*

4. What do we learn about work in Genesis 2?

Answer: Humans were to work—it was part of the Creation. The first occupation was as a gardener or farmer. It remains a very admirable occupation.

5. What are the consequences of God's command to Adam and Eve in Genesis 2:15?

"The LORD God took the man and placed him in the garden of Eden to work it and watch over it." - Genesis 2:15 CSB

Answer: We are to be the best conservationists. That means we do things to manage our natural resources, to not waste food, to avoid pollution. However, notice that God does not tell us to worship creation or nature. We worship God, we respect nature, we help it and control it.

6. What were the uncontrollable situations in your life?

Answer: The answers are personal.

7. What era are you living in and how does that change things?

Answer: Anyone born today is growing up in a world with advanced technology, COVID-19, Ebola, the Russia vs Ukraine war of 2022-2024, Hamas vs Israel war of October 7, 2023, starvation as in Africa and Haiti. None of us control these situations.

The creation of Eve—why, when, and how? Genesis 2 continued.

In these next verses, we learn the hierarchy of creation and why humans are at the top. These foundational verses inform how we should treat animals, how to deal with animal control and farm animals. It also makes us responsible for using organisms for experimentation. God explains within the first two chapters of the Bible, the uniqueness of humans from other creation, the basis of marriage and the design of the family. We are told that by design, humans are created male or female and different from other animals. Biblical marriage was to be monogamous (one man and one woman), heterosexual (between male and female), mutually beneficial (they were to help each other), and distinct from the parents (a new family unit).

- *Humans were unique from the other Creation; they had a different nature and mind. Adam realized after naming the animals that there was no one like him to be friends with. Something was missing.*

"The LORD God formed out of the ground every wild animal and every bird of the sky, and brought each to the man to see what he would call it. And whatever the man called a living creature, that was its name. The man gave names to all the livestock, to the birds of the sky, and to every wild animal; *but for the man no helper was found corresponding to him.*" - Genesis 2:19-20 CSB

- *Eve was thus created for Adam because he was lonely; she was to be a help to him and be "like him" i.e., she had a human nature, not an animal nature. The Hebrew word for help is `ezer' which means 'one who helps'.*

"Then the LORD God said, "It is not good for the man to be alone. I will make a helper corresponding to him." - Genesis 2:18 CSB

- *Eve was the first female and was created from Adam's tissue, not from dust. It was a miracle. 'Ish' is Hebrew for man;'ishshah' is Hebrew for woman (or female or wife). The Anglo-Saxon word "woman" means "man with a womb" or "womb man". This term denotes the key fact that she was taken out of man and was not a new creation from dust. She also had female sex organs (ovaries, fallopian tubes, and a uterus) so that she could bear children something a male cannot do.*

"So the LORD God caused a deep sleep to come over the man, and he slept. God took one of his ribs and closed the flesh at that place. Then the LORD God made the rib he had taken from the man into a woman and brought her to the man. And the man said: This one, at last, is bone of my bone and flesh of my flesh; this one will be called 'woman,' for she was taken from man." - Genesis 2:21-23 CSB

- *Adam realized since she was "from his flesh" that she was part of him. This helped Adam to bond to Eve. Bonding is an important part of a marriage relationship.*

Adam Clarke (1762 – 1832) was a British Methodist theologian who wrote "…God could have formed the woman out of the dust of the earth, as he had formed the man; but had he done so, she must have appeared in his eyes as a distinct being, to whom he had no natural relation. But as God formed her out of a part of the man himself, he saw she was of the same nature, the same identical flesh and blood, and of the same constitution in all respects, and consequently having equal powers, faculties, and rights. This at once ensured his affection and excited his esteem."

"And the man said: This one, at last, is bone of my bone and flesh of my flesh; this one will be called 'woman', for she was taken from man." Genesis 2:23, CSB.

• Biblical marriage, as clearly defined in Genesis 2:24 is between a man and a woman and involves sexual intercourse and forms a new distinct family unit. Note the lack of shame. "...for shame can only arise from a consciousness of sinful or irregular conduct." Adam Clarke

"This is why a man leaves his father and mother and bonds with his wife, and they become one flesh. Both the man and his wife were naked, yet felt no shame." - Genesis 2:24-25 CSB

• Jesus confirmed the Biblical marriage plan in Mark 10.
"But Jesus told them, He wrote this command for you because of the hardness of your hearts. But from the beginning of creation God made them male and female. For this reason a man will leave his father and mother and the two will become one flesh. So they are no longer two, but one flesh. Therefore, what God has joined together, let no one separate." - Mark 10:5-9 CSB

Genesis 2 summary. All these events occurred before Adam and Eve fell into sin.

- Creation of man and woman with both a physical body and a soul.
- A description of Creation theory of the origin of the Earth.
- Work: God designed that human should work. Adam's original job was in agriculture.
- Choice: Humans were given a choice to be obedient or sin. Evil is present before the Fall due to Satan's disobedience.
- Naming of the animals.
- Defining Biblical marriage.

Questions:

1. Genesis 1 and 2 describe how God created the world as we know it. How do people who do not believe in God postulate that the earth was formed?

2. Why is it important to define "evolution" in any discussion of origins?

3. What happens when you leave the God out of creation and your life?

4. Given the verses in Genesis 2 and Mark 10, how does the Biblical definition of marriage differ from the legal definition in the United States?

5. How did God create Eve from a rib of Adam?

6. What does "one flesh" refer to in Genesis 2:24 "This is why a man leaves his father and mother and bonds with his wife, and they become one flesh." - Genesis 2:24 CSB

7. What does "corresponding to" refer to in "Then the LORD God said, 'It is not good for the man to be alone. I will make a helper corresponding to him.'" - Genesis 2:18 CSB

8. Can a person control their genetic sex (the sex they are born with)?

9. What other texts in the Bible support that God was the Creator?

Questions with suggested answers:

1. Genesis 1 and 2 describe how God created the world as we know it. How do people who do not believe in God postulate that the earth was formed?

Answer: The Biblical Theory of Origins (Creation) is covered in only 2 chapters in Genesis. It postulates that the earth and universe were created about 4000 BC (6000 years ago). There are other theories of Origins – namely that the world we observe today is the result of evolution of the species through natural selection. This is the theory of Darwinian Evolution, and it requires millions of years. The third school of thought is Theistic Evolution where Natural Selection occurred but was driven by God. There is hearty debate over these theories. The problem is that all participants must use all the techniques available today to model their theories. The universe cannot be recreated in the lab, and no one can sit around and show evolution over millions of years. So, what do we do? We create models, we peer back (such as with the James Webb telescope) and try to build evidence for our theories. God says in Hebrews 11:3 "By faith we understand that the universe was created by the word of God, so

that what is seen was made from things that are not visible." - Hebrews 11:3 CSB. We understand by faith not by total proof. Whether you are reading articles from creationists or from Darwinian evolution theorists, the discussion soon turns to "testable science". Both use what we can see and test today to look back and try to understand origins of the universe. For example, go to https://earthhow.com/history-of-the-universe/ (accessed November 5, 2022 and the version I read was last updated May 12, 2022). This beautifully illustrated article discusses the Big Bang as the initiator of evolution. They tell us, "So if energy and mass are tied to each other, where did it all come from? The answer is: we made it all up from an event called the Big Bang!" The rest of the article is scientific. There is no mention as to the source of the ingredients present on which the Big Bang acted upon. Another example comes from the excellent online NASA resource on the James Webb Telescope. "After the Big Bang, the universe was like a hot soup of particles (i.e., protons, neutrons, and electrons). When the universe started cooling, the protons and neutrons began combining into ionized atoms of hydrogen (and eventually some helium). These ionized atoms of hydrogen and helium attracted electrons, turning them into neutral atoms - which allowed light to travel freely for the first time, since this light was no longer scattering off free electrons. The universe was no longer opaque! However, it would still be some time (perhaps up to a few hundred million years post-Big Bang!) before the first sources of light would start to form, ending the cosmic dark ages. Exactly what the universe's first light (i.e. stars that fused the existing hydrogen atoms into more helium) looked like, and exactly when these first stars formed is not known. These are some of the questions Webb was designed to help us to answer."
https://jwst.nasa.gov/content/science/firstLight.html) accessed November 9, 2022. Here again we see where scientists jump from the Big Bang which they cannot explain to testable science which they can explore. Creation scientists do the same – they read Genesis 1-2 which is impossible to test in the lab and then jump to testable science to demonstrate the marvelous intelligent design we see in our bodies and the universe around us. The initial origin is the part that will always be a mystery, always faith based.

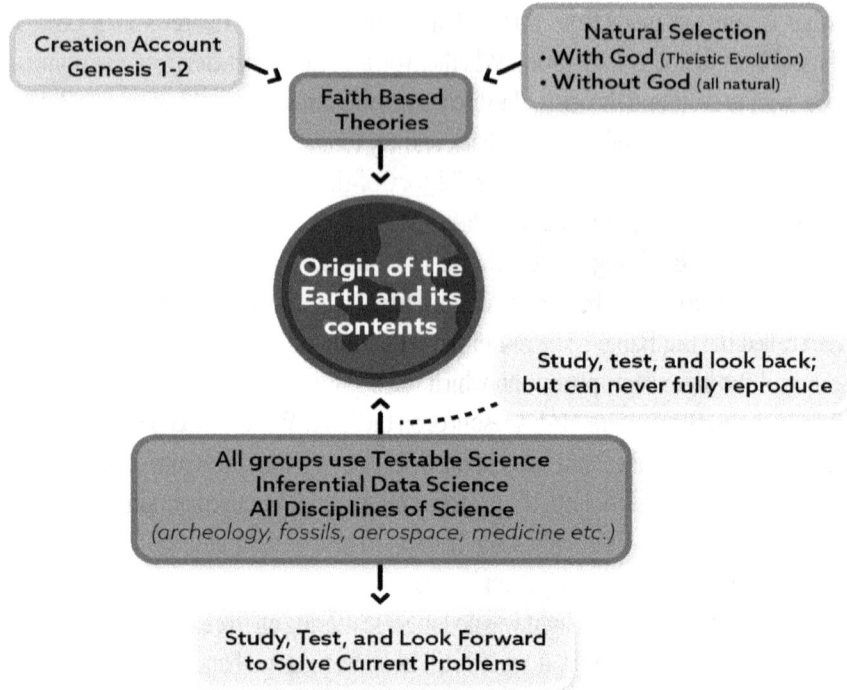

Figure 8: Schema of the various faith-based theories of the origins of the universe.

What is the crux of this discussion? It is God. The pure evolutionist leaves out God and leaving out God leaves out Jesus and our salvation. The Creationist leaves in God and Jesus and reads the rest of the Bible and applies it to our lives. Kenneth R. Miller wrote in *"Finding Darwin's God"* Harper Perennial Books 2007, page 14, "Darwin's wide influence comes from…one simple fact. Evolution displaced the Creator from His central position as the primary explanation for every aspect of the living world. In so doing, Darwin lent intellectual aid and comfort to anti-religionists everywhere…." "For thousands of years, human beings thought of themselves as the children of God. After Darwin, they were children of 'genetic chance and environmental necessity.'"

Discussing the topic of origins makes for interesting discussion, but the Bible seems to push us to move on to all the other important themes of Genesis. In my experience as a physician for over 40 years, I find that this topic is rarely discussed because we spend our time doing testable science and applying it to the care of patients. Testable science is repeatable and provable but still requires faith in the scientific processes. God expects us to do great science to help people and the world. What one does find in the medical scientific literature and research is the discussion of gene function in other cellular and animal systems. We call this comparative anatomy. In order to study a gene in human disease, we can find a homolog in a lower animal such as a fruit fly or worm or zebrafish and test function and then use that vital information in human medicine. Scientists will often write or say in a lecture that this gene has been "conserved through evolution". This means that the gene was so important that it survived evolution of that animal. The creation scientist would say that the gene was so important it was used in the creation of multiple kinds of animals. Same science, different interpretations on the theory of origins.

Table 2: Summary of the scientific approaches to origins science. Both groups of theorists use modern scientific tests and analyses to look backward to support their theory. However, since the origin of the universe cannot be done over it is impossible to prove. Thus, both theories in the end are faith-based.

Creation Theory	Naturalist Theory
God, Jesus, and the Holy Spirit were the Designers and did the creation.	Natural processes accomplished what we see today.
Creation was perfect and complex at the beginning; then sin and corruption. Perfection first, then death enters.	Simplicity in form first; then depends on death and destruction to allow the strong to survive and develop. Death first, then improvement.
The earth is young	The earth is millions of years old
Evolution occurs within a kind but not one kind changing to another.	Kinds evolved to become other kinds
Finds supportive evidence in the fossil record	Finds supportive evidence in the fossil record
Comparative anatomy is interpreted as a common creator	Comparative anatomy is interpreted as evolution from a lower to a higher kind
Defines humans as made in the image of God; different than lower life forms	Humans are just part of the evolutionary continuum
Describes the dual nature of humans – body and soul and how that happened	Difficult to explain the acquisition of the soul.
Faith-based	Faith-based

Table 3: Implications of which theory one believes.

Creation Theory	Naturalist Theory
Bible says God did the creation and I understand this by faith (Hebrews 11:3) even though I do not understand how it was really done.	I do not believe in God, so I need an alternative explanation and natural selection makes the most sense to me.
I believe in the rest of the Bible also	I may or may not believe in God
I believe in testable science and will do my best to learn and practice it. I can and will work with those who believe alternative theories.	I believe in testable science and will do my best to learn and practice it. I can and will work with those who believe alternative theories.
I will seek to explain Creation by doing testable science and apply it to the theory of Creation.	I will seek to explain natural selection by doing testable science and apply it to the theory of natural selection.
I will train to be the best scientist possible. I will learn to think critically.	I will train to be the best scientist possible. I will learn to think critically.
I will focus on testable science to benefit humankind	I will focus on testable science to benefit humankind

2. Why is it important to define "evolution" in any discussion of origins?

Answer: It is very important because the whole discussion or answer that you give will depend on the nature of the question. Which evolution are you asking about? Are you talking about "origins" or are you talking about "post-creation" as to whether we see changes in society or changing of thinking or change of kinds? If we are talking about how the world we see today came into being then, "no, I do not believe in the theory of natural selection where one kind changes into another kind." The theory of creation is based on a perfect creation without death that is then corrupted by sin which led to death in all creation. The theory of natural selection is based on lots of death with the emergence of a selected group of plants and animals.

Troy Lacey writes, "Science in the narrow sense involves some observable or repeatable event against which we can measure our theories. But when there is no direct access to the original event, the best scientists can do is to offer speculative reconstructions of the past. These imaginative reconstructions cannot be either verified or falsified in a strict scientific way. They may be plausible or implausible, but they are not scientifically proveable . . . because they cannot be checked over against the original event." Answers in Depth February 1, 2018 (https://answersingenesis.org/what-is-science/first-usage-origins-vs-operational-science/).

Now if you are asking me if I believe in post-origins change and natural selection of course I do. These are facts proven by testable science. We have watched bacteria gain resistance to antibiotics as they experience natural selection. The COVID-19 virus is doing the same. Tumors become resistant to chemotherapy. That is why people of all persuasions can work together in a lab to do testable science without arguing. You will find little discussion in science labs over origins; you will find lots of discussion about hypotheses and test results and experimental design as we search to make this a better world to live in. Remember, Jesus was interested in the unfit people of the world. His miracles took people who were blind, lame, or even dead and healed them. He was for the "survival of the unfit" as we are in medicine. We fight disease daily so that the weak and sick can get well and thrive.

3. What happens when you leave the God out of creation and your life?

Answer: You get ungodliness and "natural selection" which is survival of the fittest with lots of death and destruction. Paul describes "going natural" in Romans 1 and it is not a pretty picture. "For though they knew God, they did not glorify him as God or show gratitude. Instead, their thinking became worthless, and their senseless hearts were darkened." - Romans 1:21 CSB. The result is that people who deny God think they are really smart when they are not, and they start to worship idols. "Claiming to be wise, they became fools and exchanged the glory of the immortal God for images resembling mortal man, birds, four-footed animals, and reptiles." - Romans 1:22-23 CSB. If a person continues down this path of thinking and acting naturally the result is what you see in the world today. Read the remaining verses of Romans 1; these acts are the result of a depraved mind.

4. Given the verses in Genesis 2 and Mark 10, how does the Biblical definition of marriage differ from the legal definition in the United States?

Answer: Just because something is legal does not mean it is moral. United States law was originally based on the Biblical definition of marriage as stated in Genesis 2 and Mark 10. The United States changed the definition; the Bible did not. As John Piper, theologian, and pastor writes "There is no such thing as same-sex *marriage*. There can be *same-sex unions,* but you have to change the Biblical definition of marriage to call it same-sex marriage." So, when we talk with people, clarify the definitions – are you talking about Biblical marriage? A US law defined marriage? A civil union? The changing of the definition of marriage from a legal perspective happened over a rather short 45-year period as outlined below. It provides a good example of how rapidly Biblical truth can be eroded.

• 1969 Stonewall Riots – the unofficial beginning of the struggle for gay rights and marriage equality.

• 1971 the Minnesota Supreme Court - same-sex marriage bans are constitutional.

• 1996 President Clinton signs the Defense of Marriage Act (DOMA), *prohibiting* the recognition of same-sex marriages at the federal level, into law.

• 2000 Vermont instituted same-sex civil unions.

• 2003 Massachusetts became the first state to legalize same-sex marriage.

• 2008 President Obama opposes DOMA; supports civil unions; opposes changing the law regarding marriage given its religious roots.

• 2013 Supreme Court rules DOMA unconstitutional.

• 2015 Supreme Court heard arguments on April 28, 2015, in the case of Obergefell v. Hodges. On June 26, the court ruled 5-4 in favor of the plaintiffs, stating that both bans on same-sex marriages and bans on recognizing same-sex marriages were unconstitutional. Justice Anthony Kennedy said, "The *right to marry* is a fundamental right inherent in the liberty of the person, and under the Due Process and Equal Protection Clauses of the Fourteenth Amendment couples of the same sex may not be deprived of that right and that liberty." The issue became about rights, freedom of choice, and personal happiness.

Today, we have two views of marriage – the Biblical one and the legal one. Christians are not against people's happiness nor liberty, but definitions are important. This drift from Biblical standards to cultural standards comes because there is a general reduction in what people even know about what the Bible actually says and how much they value Biblical truth and authority. So, what are the consequences? Well, nobody died because of this decision, and we should treat people who make this decision with respect and focus on their personal salvation. They typically will not ask our opinion of what they are doing. Our focus should be on bringing them to Jesus and we trust He will work appropriately in their life if they decide to follow Him.

5. How did God create Eve from a rib of Adam?

Answer: The Bible does not say. Ribs have marrow and bone marrow has stem cells but the creation of a woman from a male marrow would indeed be miraculous because males are 46XY and females are 46XX. It is also difficult for a person who believes in natural selection to explain the development of both a woman and a man at the same time that would allow for reproduction. To have that happen by chance is beyond comprehension and must be taken by faith. We can ask Jesus when we get to Heaven.

6. What does "one flesh" refer to in Genesis 2:24 "This is why a man leaves his father and mother and bonds with his wife, and they become one flesh." - Genesis 2:24 CSB

Answer: The Hebrew word translated 'one flesh' is *dābaq* and it is usually translated "cleave" or "stick together" or be joined to one another. It is a beautiful concept that when we marry someone we are to stick together and function as one unit helping each other to succeed and meet the needs of each other. It is also symbolic of the sexual relationship between a man and a woman in a Biblical marriage.

7. What does "corresponding to" refer to in this scripture? "Then the LORD God said, 'It is not good for the man to be alone. I will make a helper corresponding to him.'" - Genesis 2:18 CSB

Answer: Physically speaking, men and women have sex organs that correspond to each other but are different. Males have testicles to manufacture sperm and male hormones and women have ovaries to make eggs and female hormones. The male sex organ corresponds to the woman's sex organs. Besides these differences in physical features there are other differences that provide what we often refer to in medicine as synergy.

This means the two together are better than the sum of the parts. Each person brings unique strengths and weaknesses into a marriage, and this makes the team much more effective. We also see this in any team sport. A football lineman has much more brute physical strength than the field goal kicker but together they score lots of points.

8. Can a person control their genetic sex (the sex they are born with)?

Answer: Your genetic sex (46XY for genetic male and 46XX genetic female) is assigned at the time of fertilization. All female eggs carry one copy of the X chromosome; a sperm carries either an X or a Y chromosome. Thousands of sperm are injected into the female and only one fertilizes with the egg. If it is a Y sperm, then a genetic male embryo results, if an X sperm, then a female embryo. Sometimes medical institutions will record this in your medical record as your "sex assigned at birth". Your "sex" refers to your genetic sex. Genetic sex is binary – either XY and male or XX and female. There is no option to be non-binary from a genetic standpoint. Now, of course people can change how they appear to themselves in the mirror and to other people. This physical appearance is called our phenotype. We can change our appearance to others by dressing like the other sex, changing our hair style, take hormones, or have plastic surgery. Thus, people who do not like their genetic sex can change their phenotype, but they cannot alter their genetic sex.

9. What other texts in the Bible support that God was the Creator?

Answer: The Bible says in the New Testament of Hebrews that Jesus did the creation. "Long ago God spoke many times and in many ways to our ancestors through the prophets. And now in these final days, he has spoken to us through his Son. God promised everything to the Son as an inheritance, and through the Son he created the universe. The Son radiates God's own glory and expresses the very character of God, and he sustains everything by the mighty power of his command. When he had cleansed us from our sins, he sat down in the place of honor at the right hand of the majestic God in heaven." - Hebrews 1:1-3 NLT

"Above all, be aware of this: Scoffers will come in the last days scoffing and following their own evil desires, saying, Where is his 'coming' that he promised? Ever since our ancestors fell asleep, all things continue as they have been since the beginning of creation. They deliberately overlook this: *By the word of God the heavens came into being long ago and the earth was brought about from water and through water.*" - 2 Peter 3:3-5 CSB

"Christ is the visible image of the invisible God. He existed before anything was created and is supreme over all creation, for through him God created everything in the heavenly realms and on earth. He made the things we can see and the things we can't see--such as thrones, kingdoms, rulers, and authorities in the unseen world. Everything was created through him and for him. He existed before anything else, and he holds all creation together." - Colossians 1:15-17 NLT

"In the beginning the Word already existed. The Word was with God, and the Word was God. He existed in the beginning with God. God created everything through him, and nothing was created except through him." - John 1:1-3 NLT
Deuteronomy 10:14, Deuteronomy 32:6, Ecclesiastes 12:1, Isaiah 37:16, Isaiah 40:28, Isaiah 45:18, Psalm 33:6-9, Psalm 104, Revelation 4:11

When and how did sin and Satan enter the world? Genesis 3.

After giving the rules for living in the Garden, God lets humans choose whether to obey or not. Satan tricked Eve and then Adam knowingly sins. The situation is the same today—Satan injects doubt into our minds about God's plans and rules. When we do sin, the results are shame, guilt, embarrassment, and an urge to run away and hide (just like Adam and Eve did). The original sin brought death to all humans and animals. Indeed, sin remains deadly today—watch out for it and deal with it. The great news is that despite our sin, God still loves us and wants us back! He will come after us— look for Him! Respond to Him and never put off the decision to follow Him.

- *Satan, the serpent in this passage, had already rebelled against God at the time he tempted Adam and Eve in the Garden of Eden – the first home of Adam and Eve. Note the technique Satan used—a question that raises doubt— "Did God really?" He also lied to her, a common strategy of Satan.*

"Now the serpent was the most cunning of all the wild animals that the LORD God had made. He said to the woman, 'Did God really say, you can't eat from any tree in the garden?'" Genesis 3:1, CSB.

- ***Eve knew the rules of the Garden. The choice was hers and the result was death.***
"The woman said to the serpent, We may eat the fruit from the trees in the garden. But about the fruit of the tree in the middle of the garden, God said, 'You must not eat it or touch it, or you will die.' " Genesis 3:2-3, CSB.

- ***Satan works by lying. He will lie to us all the time. Here he suggests that God is holding something back from humans.***
"No! You will not die, the serpent said to the woman. In fact, God knows that when you eat it your eyes will be opened and you will be like God, knowing good and evil." Genesis 3:4-5, CSB.

- ***There is usually time to ponder the temptation… Eve did… then gave in and believed the lie of Satan. The fruit "looked good, so why not?" Eve was deceived whereas Adam knew and still did it.***
"The woman saw that the tree was good for food and delightful to look at, and that it was desirable for obtaining wisdom. So she took some of its fruit and ate it; she also gave some to her husband, who was with her, and he ate it." Genesis 3:6, CSB.

- ***Results of this first sin were shame and guilt.***
"Then the eyes of both of them were opened, and they knew they were naked; so they sewed fig leaves together and made coverings for themselves." Genesis 3:7, CSB.

- ***Sin resulted in embarrassment and attempts to avoid God.***
"Then the man and his wife heard the sound of the LORD God walking in the garden at the time of the evening breeze, and *they hid from the LORD God* among the trees of the garden." Genesis 3:8, CSB.

- ***God pursues us when we sin; He does not give up on us; God also uses questions even though He already knows the answer.***
"So the LORD God called out to the man and said to him, 'Where are you?' And he said, 'I heard you in the garden, and I was afraid because I was naked, so I hid.' Then he asked, 'Who told you that you were naked? Did you eat from the tree that I commanded you not to eat from?'" Genesis 3:9-11, CSB.

Questions:

1. Why did God give Adam and Eve a choice? Do you feel you have choices?

2. What is the primary temptation technique used by Satan in this chapter. What is Satan like?

3. What were the very first symptoms that the disease of sin had entered Adam and Eve?

4. What is the difference between the sin of Eve and the sin of Adam?

Questions with suggested answers:

1. Why did God give Adam and Eve a choice? Do you feel you have choices?

Answer: God did not want to create robots who "had to love and obey Him". How would you feel if your friends or spouse were forced to love you? God wanted to have a relationship with Adam and Eve, so He gave them a fairly simple set of instructions. They failed thus bringing sin into the world. God knew Adam and Eve would fail and thus had a plan in place to save them and that plan is Jesus.

2. What is the primary temptation technique used by Satan in this chapter. What is Satan like?

Answer: He appeals to the sense of self in both Adam and Eve. Satan used the technique of asking a question that sows doubt in the mind. He made them think that God was cheating them out of something. In turn, both of them doubt God and put themselves in charge instead of God. Satan always will try to turn us away from Biblical truth and instead encourage us to follow our natural tendency. What is Satan like?

• *He is a created being, an angel that was previously in Heaven. He revolted against God and he, along with the angels who went with him, were ejected from Heaven.*

• *He is smart and tricky (cunning as the Bible says).* He uses questions to get you to question God and the Bible. He tried to insert doubt into your mind. Most temptations are pleasure-related and indeed are usually physically pleasurable. He tries to get you to feel entitled to that pleasure.

• *Satan is a liar and a murderer.* He will often tell you that God has misled you. The idea that God is a killjoy. Jesus said this about Satan - "You are of your father the devil, and you want to carry out your father's desires. *He was a murderer from the beginning and does not stand in the truth, because there is no truth in him.* When he tells a lie, he speaks from his own nature, *because he is a liar and the father of lies.*" - John 8:44 CSB

• **His mission is to destroy you.** Jesus accurately describes Satan's mission in John 10:10 "The thief comes only to steal and kill and destroy; I came so that they would have life, and have it abundantly." - John 10:10 NASB20.

3. What were the very first symptoms that the disease of sin had entered Adam and Eve?

Answer: Shame. A realization that they were naked. A desire to run and hide.

4. What is the difference between the sin of Eve and the sin of Adam?

Answer: Eve is scammed (deceived). We see her pondering the temptation and then she gives in. "The woman saw that the tree was good for food and delightful to look at, and that it was desirable for obtaining wisdom. So she took some of its fruit and ate it; she also gave some to her husband, who was with her, and he ate it. Then the eyes of both of them were opened, and they knew they were naked; so they sewed fig leaves together and made coverings for themselves." - Genesis 3:6-7 CSB Adam's sin is somewhat worse because he sinned willingly. "And he said to the man, Because you listened to your wife and ate from the tree about which I commanded you, 'Do not eat from it': The ground is cursed because of you. You will eat from it by means of painful labor all the days of your life." - Genesis 3:17 CSB. There are other verses in the Bible that clearly tell us that both Adam and Eve sinned.

"For I desire faithful love and not sacrifice, the knowledge of God rather than burnt offerings. *But they, like Adam, have violated the covenant*; there they have betrayed me." - Hosea 6:6-7 CSB

"Therefore, just as *sin entered the world through one man*, and death through sin, in this way death spread to all people, because all sinned. In fact, sin was in the world before the law, but sin is not charged to a person's account when there is no law. Nevertheless, *death reigned from Adam* to Moses, even over those who did not sin in the likeness of *Adam's transgression*. He is a type of the Coming One." - Romans 5:12-14 CSB

Thomas Witzig

Who suffers from original sin? Genesis 3.

Sin always has far-reaching consequences—to people, to the land, and to animals (all creation). The first sin of our forefather and foremother was devastating. Sin affects everything from the basic marriage relationship to childbirth and farming to land and animals. So, what do we do? With this understanding and the help of the LORD, we resist Satan. We look out for him—the doubts he plants, and his attempts to get us to sin. We guard against marital strife, *and we now have an understanding as to why we see nature struggling against pollution, pests, and weather.* We also see in this story the prediction that God will send Jesus to crush Satan. That fact gives us hope!

- ***The reaction to sin is to blame someone; Adam blames God for Eve; Eve blames Satan for deceiving her.***

"The man replied, 'The woman you gave to be with me—she gave me some fruit from the tree, and I ate.' So the LORD God asked the woman, 'What is this you have done?' And the woman said, 'The serpent deceived me, and I ate'" Genesis 3:12-13, CSB.

- ***What were the consequences of sin to Satan? He was cursed and forced to live as a snake. In this verse, "hostility" represents Jesus and Jesus will eventually crush Satan. This is the first mention of Jesus in the Bible.***

"So the LORD God said to the serpent: Because you have done this, you are cursed more than any livestock and more than any wild animal. You will move on your belly and eat dust all the days of your life. I will put hostility between you and the woman, and between your offspring and her offspring. He will strike your head, and you will strike his heel." Genesis 3:14-15, CSB.

- ***Consequences of sin for women - pain in childbearing and difficulty in marriage. Men will have the tendency to dominate women and this problem will disrupt marital harmony.***

"He said to the woman: I will intensify your labor pains; you will bear children with painful effort. Your desire will be for your husband, yet he will rule over you." Genesis 3:16, CSB.

- ***Consequences of sin to nature. Farming will be difficult—weeds, bugs, crop failure, too much or too little rain. Again, God tells us that Adam sinned willingly.***

"And he said to the man, 'Because you listened to your wife and ate from the tree about which I commanded you, Do not eat from it: The ground is cursed because of you. You will eat from it by means of painful labor all the days of your life. It will produce thorns and thistles for you, and you will eat the plants of the field. You will eat bread by the sweat of your brow until you return to the ground, since you were taken from it. For you are dust, and you will return to dust'" Genesis 3:17-19, CSB.

• *Adam names his new wife Eve, the mother of all.*
"The man named his wife Eve because *she was the mother of all the living.*" Genesis 3:20, CSB.

• *Consequences to the animal world—the first animals died to give their skin as a covering for Adam and Eve.*
"The LORD God made clothing from skins for the man and his wife, and he clothed them." Genesis 3:21, CSB.

Questions:

1. Are men and women equal in God's eyes?

2. If that is true (men and women are equal) then why do we see domination of women by men?

3. Who is the "hostility" that God said He would put between humans and Satan?

4. Was Jesus created?

5. What does Genesis 3:14-15 tell us about when God decided to save the world?

6. Did both Adam and Eve sin in the Garden? If so, how were they different?

7. What were the consequences of sin on the physical world? How did creation also suffer from the sin of humans?

8. Why do the righteous suffer too?

Questions with suggested answers:

1. Are men and women equal in God's eyes?

Answer: Yes. God created males and females in the image of God with equality yet with different functions and strengths. Many of these differences are physiologic and biologic such as hormonal balance, sex organ structural differences, and ability to bear children. These differences make for great marriages as well as procreation. God's design is equality with different responsibilities. The Acts 29 church website has a nice succinct summary of this Biblical concept (Distinctive 4) – "Both men and women are together created in the divine image and are therefore equal before God as persons, possessing the same moral dignity and value, and have equal access to God through faith in Christ. Men and women are together the recipients of spiritual gifts designed to empower them for ministry in the local church and beyond. Therefore, men and women are to be encouraged, equipped, and empowered to utilize their gifting in ministry, in service to the body of Christ, and through teaching in ways that are consistent with the Word of God. While husbands and wives are responsible to God for spiritual nurture and vitality in the home, God has given to the man primary responsibility to lead his wife and family in accordance with the servant leadership and sacrificial love characterized by Jesus Christ. This principle of male headship should not be confused with, nor give any hint of, domineering control. Rather, it is to be the loving, tender, and nurturing care of a godly man who is himself under the kind and gentle authority of Jesus Christ." https://www.acts29.com/about-us/distinctives/ accessed November 24, 2022.

When you play on a team or work as a team member you will soon learn the importance of the concept of "equality with different responsibilities". On a football team there is only one quarterback; a soccer team has one goalie and indeed they are important but so are all the other players that must work hard to make the team a winner. It's the same in a marriage – equal partners but different roles.

2. If that is true (men and women are equal) then why do we see domination of women by men?

Answer: As part of the curse resulting from original sin, God says that men will have the tendency to put down women and abuse them. We see this in Afghanistan when the Taliban took over in August 2021, they began limiting the occupations girls could have, they dictated their dress, and limited their education. In the Fall of 2022 Iranian women revolted against the "morality police" and refused to cover their face with the hijab. This led to ongoing protests against this restriction of basic freedoms.

3. Who is the "hostility" that God said He would put between humans and Satan?

Answer: Jesus.

4. Was Jesus created?

Answer: No, Jesus was a part of the Trinity from the beginning of Genesis and was with God from all time.

"In the beginning was the Word, and the Word was with God, and the Word was God. He was with God in the beginning. All things were created through him, and apart from him not one thing was created that has been created." – John 1:1-3 CSB

5. What does Genesis 3:14-15 tell us about when God decided to save the world?

Answer: God in His foreknowledge knew sin would occur and Jesus was the plan to save the world from the beginning.

"For God loved the world in this way: He gave his one and only Son, so that everyone who believes in him will not perish but have eternal life." - John 3:16 CSB

6. Did both Adam and Eve sin in the Garden? If so, how were they different?

Answer: The Bible says that both sinned, but in different ways. The woman (Eve) was deceived by Satan and sinned; Adam sinned willingly by also participating. He sinned "with his eyes wide open". Both paid the penalty.

7. What were the consequences of sin on the physical world? How did creation also suffer from the sin of humans?

Answer: As a result of sin animal sacrifice begins and thus bloodshed and death for animals. Meat comes into the diet and thus animals (fish, chickens, beef, etc.) all become a food source for us that results in death for them. Climate change begins especially after the Flood. Human aging kicks in and human life markedly shortens from the original design. The Apostle Paul writes this nice summary to the church at Rome: Romans 8:18-23 NLT. But the future is bright! Jesus will in the end restore Creation to its pre-sin situation as predicted in Isaiah 11:6-9 CSB. Notice that Jesus, the Messiah, will restore animals to pre-carnivore era and we will be full of the knowledge of God. Won't that be interesting!

8. Why do the righteous suffer too?

Answer: This is an age-old question that we all ask when we see the innocent suffer. There are many causes for suffering, and some are due to sinful behavior and thus have an obvious cause. We may suffer simply for being a Christian and if so we are not to be concerned. "But if anyone suffers as a Christian, let him not be ashamed but let him glorify God in having that name." - 1 Peter 4:16 CSB When innocent people suffer, we call it "idiopathic suffering" or "suffering without an obvious cause".

The key reason for this is found in the Genesis 3 passage you just read – because of sin the earth (people and creation) was subjected to a curse and because of that disease enters the world. Peter says "don't be surprised" by this – expect it. "Dear friends, don't be surprised when the fiery ordeal comes among you to test you as if something unusual were happening to you. Instead, rejoice as you share in the sufferings of Christ, so that you may also rejoice with great joy when his glory is revealed." - 1 Peter 4:12-13 CSB

There are many other passages on suffering that may be helpful. See Days 497, and days 414-421 of *Mostly Scripture QD*.

The power of sin and the importance of sacrifice: Genesis 4.

Genesis 4 succinctly explains the importance of blood sacrifice rather than all kinds of non-bloody items. This theme runs throughout the Old Testament and ends with Jesus shedding blood as He was crucified on the cross as the ultimate blood sacrifice. In Genesis 4:7 God describes how sin and Satan are "crouching at the door" trying to devour us. This vibrant word picture should make us very wary of sin. As God says, "You must rule over it." This implies the need for discipline as part of our strategy. We need to look at our lives and daily activities and identify opportunities to sin. How are we "ruling over it". God stands ready to assist us.

- *Adam and Eve are banished from Eden—another result of their sin. Nobody has ever seen the Tree of Life, nor do we know where it was or is today.*

"The LORD God said, 'Since the man has become like one of us, knowing good and evil, he must not reach out, take from the tree of life, eat, and live forever.' So the LORD God sent him away from the garden of Eden to work the ground from which he was taken. He drove the man out and stationed the cherubim and the flaming, whirling sword east of the garden of Eden to guard the way to the tree of life.'" Genesis 3:22-24, CSB.

- *The first recorded child of Adam and Eve was a boy named Cain. The Hebrew word translated "intimate with" is yada` which means "to know or learn to know". Here it refers to knowing sexually. The second child was Abel. Both worked on the farm—Abel as a shepherd; Cain as a gardener/farmer.*

"The man was intimate with his wife Eve, and she conceived and gave birth to Cain. She said, I have had a male child with the LORD's help. She also gave birth to his brother Abel. Now Abel became a shepherd of flocks, but Cain worked the ground." Genesis 4:1-2, CSB.

- *The first sacrifice God provided was animal skins; here we see produce and animals used as sacrifices for sin.*

"In the course of time, Cain presented some of the land's produce as an offering to the LORD. And Abel also presented an offering—some of the firstborn of his flock and their fat portions. The LORD had regard for Abel and his offering," Genesis 4:3-4, CSB.

- *God tells Cain and Abel that He prefers a blood sacrifice. We are not told why but it is the beginning of blood sacrifice that ends with Jesus. Blood sacrifice results from the death of an animal and thus is much more meaningful and significant than some garden produce. Today, there is no need for blood sacrifice thanks to blood that was shed by Jesus on the cross centuries later. God uses probing questions to Cain to try and get him to do the right sacrifice.*

"But he did not have regard for Cain and his offering. Cain was furious, and he looked despondent. Then the LORD said to Cain, 'Why are you furious? And why do you look despondent? If you do what is right, won't you be accepted? But if you do not do what is right, sin is crouching at the door. Its desire is for you, but you must rule over it.'" - Genesis 4:5-7 CSB

Thomas Witzig

- ***The word "desire" in 4:7 is a powerful word description of sin. The Hebrew word here is 'těshuwqah' and means "longing of a beast to devour or sexual longing of a man for a woman or a woman for a man". God warns Cain of the power of sin. He tells Cain that he "must rule over it".***

"If you do what is right, won't you be accepted? But if you do not do what is right, sin is crouching at the door. *Its desire is for you, but you must rule over it.*" Genesis 4:7, CSB.

In the Bible's condensed version of the history of humankind, it only takes 4 chapters until the first murder occurs. The line of Cain will be drowned out in the universal Flood; Abel never had descendants because he was killed before marriage. Rather, Seth is the son of Adam and Eve that will carry forward to Noah and the post-Flood lineages through Shem, Ham, and Japheth. The line from Shem then culminates in Jesus.

- ***Cain commits the first recorded premeditated murder in the history of mankind. Today, this would be considered murder in the first degree.***

"Cain said to his brother Abel, 'Let's go out to the field.' And while they were in the field, Cain attacked his brother Abel and killed him." - Genesis 4:8 CSB

- ***God noticed the sin and He approached Cain gently with questions. Notice again the reference to bloodshed.***

"Then the LORD said to Cain, Where is your brother Abel? I don't know, he replied. Am I my brother's guardian? Then he said, What have you done? *Your brother's blood cries out to me from the ground!*" - Genesis 4:9-10 CSB

- ***God punishes Cain; Cain appeals his sentence – the first recorded judicial appeal.***

"So now you are cursed, alienated from the ground that opened its mouth to receive your brother's blood you have shed. If you work the ground, it will never again give you its yield. You will be a restless wanderer on the earth. But Cain answered the LORD, My punishment is too great to bear! Since you are banishing me today from the face of the earth, and I must hide from your presence and become a restless wanderer on the earth, whoever finds me will kill me." Genesis 4:11-14, CSB.

- ***Cain becomes a marked man.***

"Then the LORD replied to him, In that case, whoever kills Cain will suffer vengeance seven times over. *And he placed a mark on Cain* so that whoever found him would not kill him." - Genesis 4:15 CSB

8: Genesis 1:11 Interpreting Current Issues with a Biblical Worldview

• ***Cain leaves the LORD's presence—a dangerous move. Nod in Hebrew means flight or wandering, and it is not known today where Nod was or is nor do we know the location of the Garden of Eden.***

"Then Cain went out from the LORD's presence and lived in the land of Nod, east of Eden." - Genesis 4:16 CSB

• ***All of these descendants will die in the Flood. This Lamech will later be shown to be the first to practice polygamy. He is different than the Lamech descended from Seth. Enoch is not the same Enoch of Genesis 5 that went to Heaven without dying.***

"Cain was intimate with his wife, and she conceived and gave birth to Enoch. Then Cain became the builder of a city, and he named the city Enoch after his son. Irad was born to Enoch, Irad fathered Mehujael, Mehujael fathered Methushael, and Methushael fathered Lamech." - Genesis 4:17-18 CSB

Questions:

1. There are two sayings "raising Cain" and "you are a marked person" that come from this chapter. What do they mean as used today?

2. Cain is an example of someone who could not control his anger. It was "too hot" and it resulted in murder. Is anger allowed in the Bible? Did Jesus get angry? How should handle anger and what should we be angry about?

3. The Bible says that since sin entered the world with Adam and Eve, we are all "born sinners". Where is that encoded in our DNA?

4. Sin has many consequences as listed below. What are we to do about it besides accepting Jesus sacrifice for our individual sin?

Questions with suggested answers:

1. There are two sayings "raising Cain" and "you are a marked person" that come from this chapter. What do they mean as used today?

Answer: "Raising Cain" is an old expression which means to cause trouble or act in an aggressive manner. It comes from the story you read about Cain and Abel. Being a "marked man or person" also originates from this and means you are being targeted.

2. Cain is an example of someone who could not control his anger. It was "too hot" and it resulted in murder. Is anger allowed in the Bible? Did Jesus get angry? How should handle anger and what should we be angry about?

Answer: The keys to dealing with anger are to identify what you are really angry about; make sure you are slow to get angry and do not sin in your anger. Anger, like many emotions, has a spectrum and both "no anger" and "too quick anger" are bad; slow anger over righteousness (or lack thereof) is the key. God's wrath or anger is against sin and ungodly behavior (see Days 114-120 in *Mostly Scripture QD* for a full discussion).

3. The Bible says that since sin entered the world with Adam and Eve, we are all "born sinners". Where is that encoded in our DNA?

Answer: It is not a genetic trait in the sense of a mutation. The tendency to sin is somehow "hardwired" into our nature such that all of us need the forgiveness that Jesus brings." For all have sinned and fall short of the glory of God." - Romans 3:23 CSB "If we say, 'We have no sin,' we are deceiving ourselves, and the truth is not in us." - 1 John 1:8 CSB. If you have difficulty understanding just observe children above the age of 2!

4. Sin has many consequences as listed below. What are we to do about it besides accepting Jesus sacrifice for our individual sin?

Answer: We are to fight against the sin. We develop vaccines for COVID-19, we develop new drugs for cancer, we genetically engineer crops to produce more food for the starving etc.

Table 4: Consequences of sin entering the world.

The Fall of Adam and Eve
The woman would experience pain in childbirth; distorted desire towards her husband
The man would have a tendency to dominate; food production disrupted by weeds
Marriage prone to abuse; polygamy; sexual sins
Shame
All creation groans and suffers disease; pestilences; famine; and death
Animal sacrifice: meat enters diet of humans and some animals
Fighting between humans; the desire for revenge; the need for the Mosaic Law to control chaos
Animals fight each other; survival of the fittest
The Universal Flood
Aging (senescence) and a shortening of life span to around 80 years
The Tower of Babel rebellion
Multiple languages making communication difficult; development of people groups based on language.

When did artistic gifts appear? —Genesis 4.

We often think that people who lived thousands of years ago were all primitive. Not so. The artistic gifts appear early in civilization and are described in Genesis 4. In this chapter we also encounter the first abuse of Biblical marriage – polygamy. Although rarely observed (and in most states illegal) polygamy is still common in many areas of the world today. It was not God's original design for marriage and when it occurred in the Bible it was usually abusive to women and did not have a happy ending.

- ***The development of technology and arts is described early in the history of the world. Jubal develops musical instruments and Tubal-cain was a metal worker.***

"Lamech took two wives for himself, one named Adah and the other named Zillah. Adah bore Jabal; he was the father of the nomadic herdsmen. His brother was named *Jubal; he was the father of all who play the lyre and the flute.* Zillah bore *Tubal-cain, who made all kinds of bronze and iron tools.* Tubal-cain's sister was Naamah." - Genesis 4:19-22 CSB

- ***Lamech from Cain is the first polygamist. He also committed manslaughter which is murder that is not premeditated (like Cain) but due to his response to an attack. There are two Lamechs in Genesis—the one from Cain was evil and started polygamy. The other Lamech was from Noah and good comes from the line of Seth.***

"Lamech took two wives for himself, one named Adah and the other named Zillah." - Genesis 4:19 CSB

"Lamech said to his wives: Adah and Zillah, hear my voice; wives of Lamech, pay attention to my words. For I killed a man for wounding me, a young man for striking me. If Cain is to be avenged seven times over, then for Lamech it will be seventy-seven times!" - Genesis 4:23-24 CSB

- ***The birth of Seth. Since Abel is dead and Cain's family ends in the Flood, the line of Seth is the only one to survive. The 10th generation from Seth is Noah, the only family to live beyond the Flood. Seth is born when Adam was 130 years old. We are all descendants of Seth!***

"Adam was intimate with his wife again, and she gave birth to a son and named him Seth, for she said, 'God has given me another child in place of Abel, since Cain killed him.'" - Genesis 4:25 CSB

- ***People turn to God during the time of Seth.***

"A son was born to Seth also, and he named him Enosh. *At that time people began to call on the name of the LORD.*" - Genesis 4:26 CSB

8: Genesis 1:11 Interpreting Current Issues with a Biblical Worldview

Figure 9: Simplified inheritance from Adam and Eve to Noah.

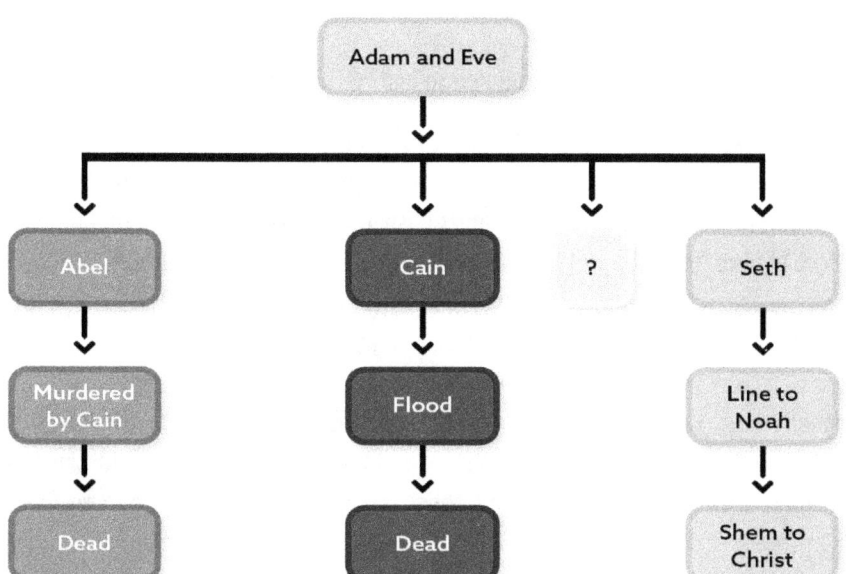

Questions:

1. Why is polygamy illegal in the United States?

2. What does it mean that people began to call on the name of the LORD at the time of Seth (about 6000 years ago).

3. Why is Seth the only line that moves on?

Questions with suggested answers:

1. Why is polygamy illegal in the United States?

Answer: Because it is abusive to women It was never the plan for Biblical marriage.

2. What does it mean that people began to call on the name of the LORD at the time of Seth (about 6000 years ago).

Answer: It seems to indicate that after people saw the results of sin in Cain and Lamech that some turned back to God and began to worship Him.

3. Why is Seth the only line that moves on?

Answer: Seth's line goes to Noah and only Noah's family survives the universal flood (see **Figure 9**).

How long was the human body designed to last? Genesis 5.

Genesis 5 links the history of the Adam and Eve and their descendants to the story of Noah. There are with hundreds of years in-between; some have counted about 1656 years from Adam to the Flood (Rev. James Ussher's *Annals of the World*, first published in 1658.) Moses, the author of Genesis, only gives the reader the high points because the purpose of the genealogy is to get to Jesus. Genealogies are in the Bible for a purpose. Although boring to read, they establish that all humans are united through a common origin. The key points are that many people lived into the 900-year range, yet all eventually died. This provides a clue that the original body was built to last at least 900 years, but death became inevitable once sin entered. What happened to cause this shortening of lifespan? Medical research today is still studying and trying to reverse this aging process.

- *Adam and Eve were created in the 'likeness of God' - the rest of the animal and plant kingdom was not. This is a unique feature of humans. The Bible says we were made with a genetic sex that is male or female. The first thing that God did was bless them.*

"This is the document containing the family records of Adam. On the day that God created man, he made him in the likeness of God; he created them male and female. When they were created, he blessed them and called them mankind." Genesis 5:1-2, CSB.

- *Adam became a father at 130 years of age and died at age 930. Reproduction was consistent with his DNA— "Seth was in the likeness of Adam" or "he looks like his father!" No mention of any wives other than Eve. He lived to be 930.*

"Adam was 130 years old when he fathered a son in his likeness, according to his image, and named him Seth. Adam lived 800 years after he fathered Seth, and he fathered other sons and daughters. So Adam's life lasted 930 years; then he died." - Genesis 5:3-5 CSB

- **Seth lives 912 years; begets Enoch and this line eventually comes to Noah, the only family to survive the Flood.**
"Seth was 105 years old when he fathered Enosh. Seth lived 807 years after he fathered Enosh, and he fathered other sons and daughters. So Seth's life lasted 912 years; then he died." - Genesis 5:6-8 CSB

- **Enoch is righteous and bypasses death. Only two people have avoided physical death- the other was Elijah. Why did God do this? We are not told.**
"Enoch was 65 years old when he fathered Methuselah. And after he fathered Methuselah, Enoch walked with God 300 years and fathered other sons and daughters. So Enoch's life lasted 365 years. Enoch walked with God; then he was not there because God took him." Genesis 5:21-24, CSB.

- **Everyone eventually dies—even Methuselah—the oldest recorded life.**
"Methuselah was 187 years old when he fathered Lamech. Methuselah lived 782 years after he fathered Lamech, and he fathered other sons and daughters. So Methuselah's life lasted 969 years; then he died." Genesis 5:25-27, CSB.

- **Noah was the 10th generation from Adam. Seth's genealogy ends with Noah, the one person whom God found worthy to survive the flood. This was a different Lamech than the one descended from Cain. Notice how the curse from sin had tainted creation and made farm work difficult.**
"Lamech was 182 years old when he fathered a son. And he named him Noah, saying, 'This one will bring us relief from the agonizing labor of our hands, caused by the ground the LORD has cursed.' Lamech lived 595 years after he fathered Noah, and he fathered other sons and daughters. So Lamech's life lasted 777 years; then he died. Noah was 500 years old, and he fathered Shem, Ham, and Japheth." - Genesis 5:28-32 CSB

Questions:

1. Why did people live so much longer in Genesis times?

2. What does it mean that we are created in the likeness (image) of God?

Questions with suggested answers:

1. Why did people live so much longer?

Answer: We do not know for certain, but it is later said that during these some 1600 years the earth was watered by ground irrigation (not rain). The Flood will change that and remove the vapor barrier allowing solar radiation to penetrate the Earth. After the Flood and by the time we get to the Psalms it is mentioned that 80 years is about the average. "Our lives last seventy years or, if we are strong, eighty years. Even the best of them are struggle and sorrow; indeed, they pass quickly and we fly away." - Psalm 90:10 CSB. It is rather disappointing that we have not been able to change this age limit despite modern medicines.

2. What does it mean that we are created in the likeness (image) of God?

Answer: Humans were created with the ability to think and communicate with God. We have the ability to reason; we have a conscience and a soul. Thus, we are in God's image. Insects, fish, chickens etc. do not have the same level of communication skills that we do and are thus not considered to have been created in the image of God.

Who were the "Sons of God" and how did they contribute to the need for the Flood? Genesis 6.

"When mankind began to multiply on the earth and daughters were born to them, the sons of God saw that the daughters of mankind were beautiful, and they took any they chose as wives for themselves. And the LORD said, 'My Spirit will not remain with mankind forever, because they are corrupt. Their days will be 120 years.' The Nephilim were on the earth both in those days and afterward, when the *sons of God* came to the daughters of mankind, who bore children to them. They were the powerful men of old, the famous men." - Genesis 6:1-4 CSB

The 'Sons of God' in Genesis 6:1,2 are not identified and this is a difficult passage to explain. Dr. Thomas Constable, Professor Emeritus at Dallas Theological Seminary (*Constable's Notes on Genesis* 2019 page 119) says, "Scholars have debated this passage heatedly, but there is not yet decisive evidence that enables us to make a dogmatic decision as to the correct interpretation." The reader can read more on the theories of this topic in the Constable article (https://planobiblechapel.org/constable-notes/). The passage seems to document the degradation of men; thus, providing rationale for the Flood and a reboot of the human population through the line of Shem.

8: Genesis 1:11 Interpreting Current Issues with a Biblical Worldview

- ***Human lifespan will drop from 900 to 120 years due to man's sin and corruption.***
"And the LORD said, 'My Spirit will not remain with mankind forever, because they are corrupt. *Their days will be 120 years.*'" - Genesis 6:3 CSB

- ***God, like us has emotions too. Human wickedness causes God to regret making man.***
"When the LORD saw that human wickedness was widespread on the earth and that every inclination of the human mind was nothing but evil all the time, *the LORD regretted that he had made man on the earth, and he was deeply grieved.* Then the LORD said, 'I will wipe mankind, whom I created, off the face of the earth, together with the animals, creatures that crawl, and birds of the sky -- for I regret that I made them.'" - Genesis 6:5-7 CSB

- ***Noah was righteous and walked with God; thus, he found favor with God.***
"Noah, however, found favor with the LORD. These are the family records of Noah. Noah was a righteous man, blameless among his contemporaries; *Noah walked with God.* And Noah fathered three sons: Shem, Ham, and Japheth." - Genesis 6:8-10 CSB

Questions:

1. Why does Genesis 5 and 6 skip so many events and fast forward to Noah?

2. What does it mean that Noah "walked with God"?

3. Why do humans only live an average of about 80 years when they lived 900+ before the Flood?

Questions with suggested answers:

1. Why does Genesis 5 and 6 skip so many events and fast forward to Noah?

Answer: Moses takes us quickly (although hundreds of years have passed) to Noah. Why? Because the Bible is about Jesus, the Messiah. It's always pointing to Jesus. The important point is to get to Noah, then to Shem from whom the line of Jesus Christ descends. Why is this important for us today? It explains the need for the population reboot (the Flood) and how God worked to bring us Jesus, our sacrifice for sin that makes eternity possible. It also demonstrates to us why Noah was chosen among all the others in the genealogies. He was different, he was righteous; the others fell short.

2. What does it mean that Noah "walked with God"?

Answer: "These are the family records of Noah. Noah was a righteous man, blameless among his contemporaries; Noah walked with God." - Genesis 6:9 CSB Walking with God means we follow Him. We let God lead. Noah was really good at this which is why it says "Noah, however, found favor with the LORD." - Genesis 6:8 CSB.

There are other excellent verses on this topic of walking with God: Joshua 22:5 CSB and Micah 6:8 CSB.

3. Why do humans only live an average of about 80 years when they lived 900+ before the Flood?

Answer: This is a difficult scientific question. The oldest recent human was Misao Okawa a Japanese woman who lived to be 117 years old and died in late March 2015. In 2022 the average lifespan of a woman in the US was 81 years and 77 for men. It has dropped to 79 due to COVID-19 pandemic. The medical field of aging conducts research on why our bodies decay more now than before. Is it diet? Radiation from the sun? Pollution? This is a judgement of God, but the mechanism(s) are unclear.

Why did God send the universal Flood? —Genesis 6.

People today who sin without provision for that sin will endure judgment someday. In Noah's day, God judged sin too, but not always immediately. In this case, He did it after hundreds of years of disobedience by the people who inhabited the early earth. He spared a remnant of righteous people and made a covenant with them. The Universal Flood (the Flood) was a world-wide disaster which had major implications that persist even today (**Figure 10**). The Flood represents the second major judgement God performed after the sin of Adam and Eve.

8: Genesis 1:11 Interpreting Current Issues with a Biblical Worldview

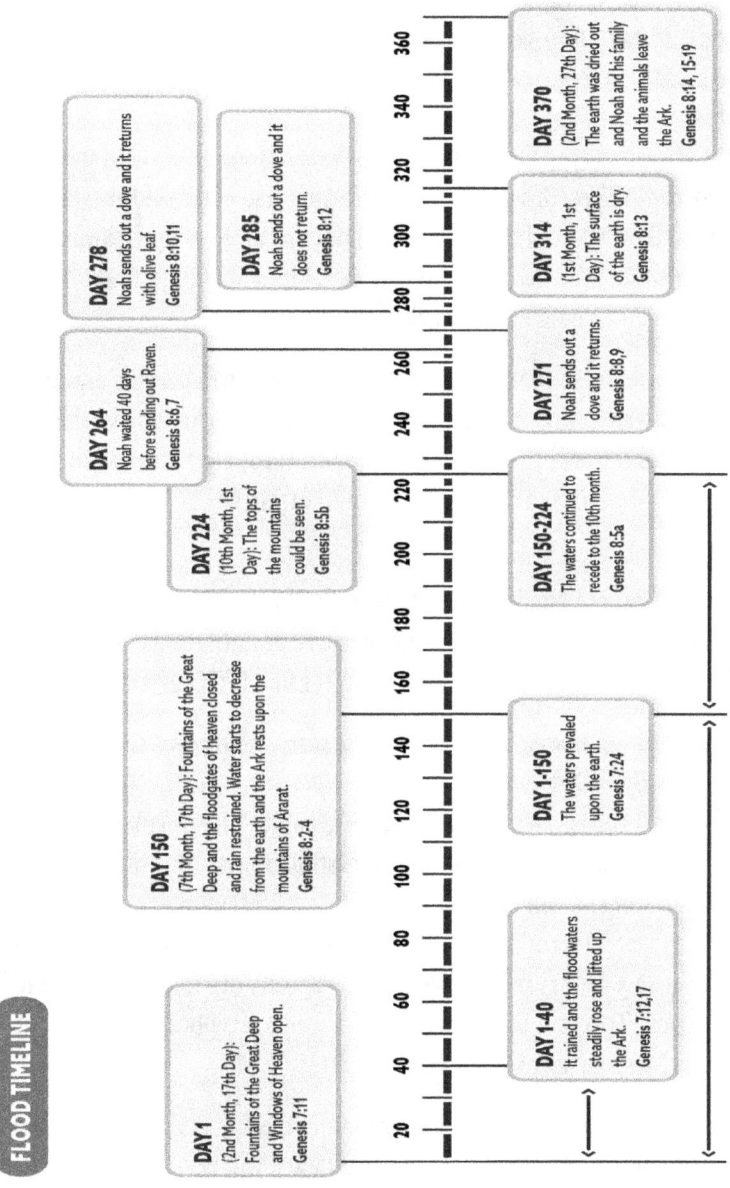

Figure 10: Universal Flood Timeline in days.*

.*Compiled by David Wright. © Answers in Genesis, used by permission

- ***God announces to the righteous Noah that He plans on destroying the earth due to uncontrolled evil. It was 1656 years from creation to the Flood and much evil had developed. God decided to re-boot the earth's population via one righteous family – the family of Noah.***

"Now the earth was corrupt in God's sight, and the earth was filled with wickedness. God saw how corrupt the earth was, for every creature had corrupted its way on the earth. Then God said to Noah, 'I have decided to put an end to every creature, for the earth is filled with wickedness because of them; therefore I am going to destroy them along with the earth.'" - Genesis 6:11-13 CSB

"As the days of Noah were, so the coming of the Son of Man will be. For in those days before the flood they were eating and drinking, marrying and giving in marriage, until the day Noah boarded the ark. They didn't know until the flood came and swept them all away. This is the way the coming of the Son of Man will be." - Matthew 24:37-39 CSB

"Just as it was in the days of Noah, so it will be in the days of the Son of Man: People went on eating, drinking, marrying and giving in marriage until the day Noah boarded the ark, and the flood came and destroyed them all." - Luke 17:26-27 CSB

- ***God provides the Ark—a source of refuge from the surrounding death and destruction for Noah and his family.***

The instructions were precise. The Ark was to be 300 cubits long. A cubit was a unit of measurement from the elbow to the tip of the longest finger and thus varied from 17.5 to 20.6 inches. Depending on which definition the Ark at 300 cubits was about 450-510 feet long. That length could accommodate 3 NASA Space Shuttles and the triple-decker height was higher than a 4-story house. The storage capacity of such a ship was equal to 450 semi-truck loads. To get a better idea you can tour a replica of the Ark at the Answers in Genesis Museum near Cincinnati.

"Make yourself an ark of gopher wood. Make rooms in the ark, and cover it with pitch inside and outside. This is how you are to make it: The ark will be 450 feet long, 75 feet wide, and 45 feet high. You are to make a roof, finishing the sides of the ark to within eighteen inches of the roof. You are to put a door in the side of the ark. Make it with lower, middle, and upper decks." - Genesis 6:14-16 CSB

- ***Noah was to bring reproductive pairs of animals by kinds. The plethora of individual species we observe today would subsequently develop after the Flood from these kinds.***
"You are also to bring into the ark two of all the living creatures, male and female, to keep them alive with you. Two of everything -- from the birds *according to their kinds*, from the livestock *according to their kinds*, and from the animals that crawl on the ground *according to their kinds* -- will come to you so that you can keep them alive. Take with you every kind of food that is eaten; gather it as food for you and for them." - Genesis 6:19-21 CSB

- ***The Flood was universal, not local. The destruction was universal not local.***
"Understand that I am bringing a flood -- floodwaters on the earth to destroy every creature under heaven with the breath of life in it. *Everything on earth will perish.*" - Genesis 6:17 CSB

- ***God is a covenant God*—He provides for Noah and his family to survive the Flood.**
"But I will establish my covenant with you, and you will enter the ark with your sons, your wife, and your sons' wives." - Genesis 6:18 CSB

- ***Noah showed obedience despite never having seen rain. Previous to the Flood the earth had been watered by mist from the subsoil – sort of a "trickle-irrigation" method. Thus, the fact that Noah had never seen rain yet still obeyed is even more remarkable.***
"But mist would come up from the earth and water all the ground."- Genesis 2:6 CSB

"And Noah did this. He did everything that God had commanded him." - Genesis 6:22 CSB

Questions;

1. Why do we call the Flood of Genesis 6 a "universal flood"?

2. What does the fact that it had never rained tell us about the faith of Noah and his family?

3. What is the importance of "pairs" and "kinds" to Noah's instructions regarding the animals brought on the Ark?

4. Why is Noah a model for us today?

5. What does this verse tell us regarding the second part of the curse? "And the LORD said, 'My Spirit will not remain with mankind forever, because they are corrupt. Their days will be 120 years.'" - Genesis 6:3 CSB.

Questions with suggested answers:

1. Why do we call the Flood of Genesis 6 a "universal flood"?

Answer: In 2022 Ft Myers Beach endured the full force of Hurricane Ian. The flood surge caused extensive damage to the once-beautiful gulf side community. This was a devastating flood, but it was local. Other areas of Florida had some damage but not extensive. Minnesota where I lived was unscathed. The flood of Noah covered the whole earth thus it was a "universal flood" and God promised never to send another one. He shows us that promise with rainbows.

2. What does the fact that it had never rained tell us about the faith of Noah and his family?

Answer: This small fact makes us admire Noah even more. He spent years building a boat in preparation for this huge flood when no one could image that much water coming out of the sky.

3. What is the importance of "pairs" and "kinds" to Noah's instructions regarding the animals brought on the Ark? "You are also to bring into the ark two of all the living creatures, male and female, to keep them alive with you. Two of everything -- from the birds according to their kinds, from the livestock according to their kinds, and from the animals that crawl on the ground according to their kinds -- will come to you so that you can keep them alive." - Genesis 6:19-20 CSB

Answer: Pairs of male and female to enable post-Flood reproduction so the kind would not be lost forever. Kinds not species. This is critical to allow us to believe that the Ark story is credible. Not every species of animal we see today was on the ark. For example, Noah took one kind of cow. He did not have to take Holsteins (black and white spotted), Guernsey, Brown Swiss and all the other breeds of cows we see today. These species developed naturally and through breeding in the thousands of years since.

4. Why is Noah a model for us today?

Answer: Read Genesis 6:9 again –"These are the family records of Noah. Noah was a righteous man, blameless among his contemporaries; Noah walked with God." - Genesis 6:9 CSB. The key characteristics are righteous, blameless and he walked with God.

8: Genesis 1:11 Interpreting Current Issues with a Biblical Worldview

5. What does this verse tell us regarding the second part of the curse? "And the LORD said, 'My Spirit will not remain with mankind forever, because they are corrupt. Their days will be 120 years.'" - Genesis 6:3 CSB. Also read Psalm 90 by Moses and note "Our lives last seventy years or, if we are strong, eighty years. Even the best of them are struggle and sorrow; indeed, they pass quickly and we fly away." - Psalm 90:10 CSB.

Answer: People before the Flood lived over 900 years. That enabled many years of fertility and very large families. This shortens rapidly after the Flood. But by the time of Moses, he writes in Psalm 90 that we are likely to live into the 80's. Just think that in 2023 this is still the typical survival for a woman (slightly shorter for males). The science of Aging, Senescence, and telomere shortening are all important research areas today where investigators are studying mechanisms of aging. If you have the opportunity, do a research report on aging starting with the fact that the human body was "built to last" over 900 years. What happened that we are so limited?

Table 5: Age of selected Biblical Patriarchs from Adam to Abraham in relation to the universal flood. Psalm 90:10 still is true today.

Patriarch	Lifespan as Recorded (years)
Adam	930
Seth	912
Methusaleh	969
Noah	950
Shem	600
Eber	464
Terah	205
Abraham	175
Isaac	180
Jacob	175
Joseph	110

1950

Average US 68 years

Thomas Witzig

2023

Average US 79 years

Does God keep His promises? He did in the Flood—Genesis 7

The instructions to Noah were clear—take 7 pairs of clean animals and 7 days from now the rain will start and continue for 40 days and nights. The predictions were sobering - whatever is not in the Ark will be destroyed. Noah listened when God spoke. The instructions were clear and precise but hard to believe since Noah had never seen rain.

"Then the LORD said to Noah, 'Enter the ark, you and all your household, for I have seen that you alone are righteous before me in this generation.' You are to take with you seven pairs, a male and its female, of all the clean animals, and two of the animals that are not clean, a male and its female, and seven pairs, male and female, of the birds of the sky -- in order to keep offspring alive throughout the earth. Seven days from now I will make it rain on the earth forty days and forty nights, and every living thing I have made I will wipe off the face of the earth.'" - Genesis 7:1-4 CSB

- *Noah was 600 years old when the Flood came. Note it was a universal flood.*

"And Noah did everything that the LORD commanded him. Noah was six hundred years old when the flood came and water covered the earth." Genesis 7:5-6, CSB.

- *God does what He says (He still does today). God safely secured them in the Ark. Notice how God shut them in to protect them from the devastation outside.*

"On that same day Noah along with his sons Shem, Ham, and Japheth, Noah's wife, and his three sons' wives entered the ark with him. They entered it with all the wildlife according to their kinds, all livestock according to their kinds, all the creatures that crawl on the earth according to their kinds, every flying creature -- all the birds and every winged creature -- according to their kinds. Two of every creature that has the breath of life in it came to Noah and entered the ark. Those that entered, male and female of every creature, entered just as God had commanded him. *Then the LORD shut him in.*" - Genesis 7:13-16 CSB

- *The Flood was universal not local.*

"The flood continued for forty days on the earth; the water increased and lifted up the ark *so that it rose above the earth*. The water surged and increased greatly on the earth, and the ark floated on the surface of the water. Then the water surged even higher on the earth, and all the high mountains under the whole sky were covered. The mountains were covered as the water surged above them more than twenty feet." - Genesis 7:17-20 CSB

- ***All flesh outside the Ark dies.***

"Every creature perished -- those that crawl on the earth, birds, livestock, wildlife, and those that swarm on the earth, as well as all mankind. Everything with the breath of the spirit of life in its nostrils -- everything on dry land died. He wiped out every living thing that was on the face of the earth, from mankind to livestock, to creatures that crawl, to the birds of the sky, and they were wiped off the earth. Only Noah was left, and those that were with him in the ark." - Genesis 7:21-23 CSB

- ***It rained for 40 days, and the floodwaters remained for 150 days.***

"And the water surged on the earth 150 days." - Genesis 7:24 CSB

Questions:

1. Is there any evidence that Noah questioned God?

2. How old was Noah at the time of the Flood?

3. How many people entered the Ark?

4. What characteristics of God does this story of Noah and the Ark demonstrate?

5. Did Noah preach to others about upcoming judgement?

Questions with suggested answers:

1. Is there any evidence that Noah questioned God?

Answer: No, Noah obeyed exactly because the instructions were precise. He was also apparently able to convince his family too. What is God telling you to do in your current situation? Are you obedient like Noah? Remember, you can question God to a point but in the end, obedience is necessary despite not getting a complete understanding at the time.

2. How old was Noah at the time of the Flood?

Answer: 600 years old and making very good decisions. This tells us a lot about the ability of the human body. Just what has gone wrong that we only live 80-100 years now?

3. How many people entered the Ark?

Answer: 8 – all adults and all pairs. Noah and his wife and his 3 sons Shem, Ham and Japheth and their respective unnamed wives. No children.

4. What characteristics of God does this story of Noah and the Ark demonstrate?

Answer: God keeps His word; He is merciful yet will judge sin. Once the door was closed it was not re-opened. We are told judgement is coming again to this world and everyone in it. We need to make sure that we, like Noah, are prepared.

5. Did Noah preach to others about upcoming judgement?

Answer: It appears so based on this verse in Peter, "and if he didn't spare the ancient world, but protected *Noah, a preacher of righteousness*, and seven others, when he brought the flood on the world of the ungodly; ... then the Lord knows how to rescue the godly from trials and to keep the unrighteous under punishment for the day of judgment." - 2 Peter 2:5, 9 CSB

The end of the Flood – Genesis 8.

"God remembered Noah, as well as all the wildlife and all the livestock that were with him in the ark. *God caused a wind to pass over the earth, and the water began to subside.* The sources of the watery depths and the floodgates of the sky were closed, and the rain from the sky stopped. The water steadily receded from the earth, and by the end of 150 days the water had decreased significantly. The ark came to rest in the seventh month, on the seventeenth day of the month, on the mountains of Ararat. The water continued to recede until the tenth month; in the tenth month, on the first day of the month, the tops of the mountains were visible. After forty days, Noah opened the window of the ark that he had made, and he sent out a raven. It went back and forth until the water had dried up from the earth. Then he sent out a dove to see whether the water on the earth's surface had gone down, but the dove found no resting place for its foot. It returned to him in the ark because water covered the surface of the whole earth. He reached out and brought it into the ark to himself. So Noah waited seven more days and sent out the dove from the ark again. When the dove came to him at evening, there was a plucked olive leaf in its beak. So Noah knew that the water on the earth's surface had gone down. After he had waited another seven days, he sent out the dove, but it did not return to him again. In the six hundred and first year, in the first month, on the first day of the month, the water that had covered the earth was dried up. Then Noah removed the ark's cover and saw that the surface of the ground was drying. By the twenty-seventh day of the second month, the earth was dry." Genesis 8:1-14, CSB.

- ***The order was to re-populate the earth.***

"Then God spoke to Noah, 'Come out of the ark, you, your wife, your sons, and your sons' wives with you. Bring out all the living creatures that are with you -- birds, livestock, those that crawl on the earth -- and they will spread over the earth and be fruitful and multiply on the earth.' So Noah, along with his sons, his wife, and his sons' wives, came out. All the animals, all the creatures that crawl, and all the flying creatures -- everything that moves on the earth -- came out of the ark by their families." - Genesis 8:15-19 CSB

- ***Noah sacrifices clean animals to God in thanksgiving for escaping from the Flood.***

"Then Noah built an altar to the LORD. He took some of every kind of clean animal and every kind of clean bird and offered burnt offerings on the altar." Genesis 8:20, CSB.

- ***God is pleased with the sacrifice and makes important promises to humans. He understands the inclination of man is to sin; but He promises no more universal destruction. The promise also includes continuance of seasons and daily variation.***

"When the LORD smelled the pleasing aroma, he said to himself, I will never again curse the ground because of human beings, even though the inclination of the human heart is evil from youth onward. And I will never again strike down every living thing as I have done. As long as the earth endures, seedtime and harvest, cold and heat, summer and winter, and day and night will not cease." Genesis 8:21-22, CSB.

Questions:

1. Are there other places in the Bible that support the Flood as described in Genesis 6-9?

2. We understand what the Bible says about the universal flood; however, what is the evidence for it in geology?

3. How did the animals from all over the world get on the Ark?

Questions with suggested answers:

1. Are there other places in the Bible that support the Flood as described in Genesis 6-9?

Answer: Yes, there are numerous other references to the universal Flood.

• *Jesus* - Jesus used the Flood as an example of how the end of the world will come to an end. An understanding of the times of Noah help us to understand what is going on today.

Matthew 24:36-39 CSB

•*Peter in both his letters.*
In the first passage in 1 Peter 3:18-20 he refers to God's patience while the ark was built. In 2 Peter 3:5-7 CSB he emphasizes that indeed future judgement will come and provides several cases to back up that prediction - 2 Peter 2:4-5 CSB – God did act on the disobedience of the angels, He did judge through the universal flood, and he cites the case of Sodom and Gomorrah.

• *The prophet Isaiah* (Isaiah 54:9 CSB)

2. We understand what the Bible says about the universal flood; however, what is the evidence for it in geology?

Answer: In contrast to the rather brief description of the Creation in Genesis 1-2, we have ample precise data on Noah, the construction of the Ark, and the universal Flood. For this reason, the Flood is important in the field of apologetics. There are two camps of thought on this topic. The "creation geologists" or "young earth geologists" believe the that the fossil layers were in large part formed during the universal Flood. For example, this group would point to the geology of the Grand Canyon. The other group, the "secular geologists", believe that the fossil layers formed over millions of years. This is what is described in most public museums. A full discussion of the arguments is beyond the scope of this book but can be accessed at the Answers in Genesis (https://answersingenesis.org/) and the Institute for Creation Research websites (https://www.icr.org/). They have substantive articles that are well-researched and written The study of fossils and geology has been and will be important to understanding the flood. I will summarize a few points:

A. If the flood was local to the area of Iraq and not universal, we would not observe much of what we observe today. In addition, the only people who would have died would have been locals and they could have simply moved during the 40 days of rain. The Bible says that the height of the water rose to 20 feet (15 cubits) above the mountains – "Then the water surged even higher on the earth, and all the high mountains under the whole sky were covered. The mountains were covered as the water surged above them more than twenty feet." - Genesis 7:19-20 CSB. A flood of that height in the area of Mesopotamia would have been high enough to cover the whole world." Bible-believing geologists typically hold the view that most mountain ranges were "pushed up" during the final stages of the Flood (see Genesis 8-9 and Psalm 104:5-9). This means that the Flood did not need to cover today's tall peaks. Currently the total volume of water on the planet is estimated at 1.386 billion cubic kilometers. If we layer it on a smooth sphere it would be a layer with a radius of about 6,500 kilometers, subtracting from here and you get a depth of 2.61 km average. Without today's high mountain ranges that were created during the Flood, plenty of water (now in the oceans) could cover the world's land. That's why 75% of the continents are filled with sedimentary layers that average about 1 mile deep." (https://genesisapologetics.com/faqs/noahs-flood-where-did-all-the-water-come-from/ accessed November 5, 2022)

B. God promised with a rainbow that He would never again send a universal flood. He has kept that promise. Yes, we have many local floods, and they are often followed by a rainbow in the sky as a reminder that "this is local and not going to be universal".

C. God's commands to Noah's family to repopulate the earth (Genesis 8:15–17 and 9:1) are only necessary if it were a global flood, since animals and birds outside the flood zone could naturally repopulate the area otherwise.

D. Geology can change rapidly. Two recent case studies are the Mount St Helens volcano eruption[1] in May 1980 (https://www.usgs.gov/news/featured-story/mount-st-helens-1980-eruption-changed-future-volcanology) and the June 2022 flood of Yellowstone National Park. "The landscape literally and figuratively has changed dramatically in the last 36 hours," said Bill Berg, a commissioner in nearby Park County. "A little bit ironic that this spectacular landscape was created by violent geologic and hydrologic events, and it's just not very handy when it happens while we're all here settled on it." https://www.cnbc.com/2022/06/15/floods-leave-yellowstone-landscape-dramatically-changed.html

3. How did the animals from all over the world get on the Ark?

Answer: The animals came to Noah. "Two of everything -- from the birds according to their kinds, from the livestock according to their kinds, and from the animals that crawl on the ground according to their kinds -- will come to you so that you can keep them alive." - Genesis 6:20 CSB. The Bible does not give us details on this topic but science does. The evidence comes from three areas – land bridges, tectonic plates[2], and the fossil record. I refer you to Roger Patterson's excellent article on the fossil record (https://answersingenesis.org/fossils/fossil-record/the-fossil-record-1/). In brief he says, "…the fossil evidence is shared by everyone. There are not creationist fossils and evolutionist fossils, but there are creationist and evolutionist interpretations of the fossils. When we observe fossils in the present we can take measurements and determine composition, but the real interest in fossils is interpreting where they came from. Once we start attempting to explain how the organisms came to be fossilized or how and where they lived before they died, we must remember that we are using presuppositions in that explanation – we have gone from operational to historical science."

What did God say to Noah after the universal flood was over? What is the post-Flood diet? Genesis 9

In Genesis 9 we learn about God's command to the 8 humans to multiply, the origin of animal fear of humans, human responsibility for managing creation, a change in diet from the original recipe, why we need to avoid eating blood, and the difference between killing and murder.

• *God said, "I won't do this again; there will be seasons and the day/night schedule will continue". He also said to "repopulate the earth" and "spread out". There are 4 families, 8 people, and Noah is 601 years old. What a time to "start over"!*
"God blessed Noah and his sons and said to them, 'Be fruitful and multiply and fill the earth.'" Genesis 9:1, CSB.

• *After the Flood we see the beginning of animal's fear of humans as a result of the curse on creation due to sin. This natural fear is built into their DNA by God's design. Again, clear instructions from God that humans are to take good care of animals.*
"The fear and terror of you will be in every living creature on the earth, every bird of the sky, every creature that crawls on the ground, and all the fish of the sea. They are placed under your authority." Genesis 9:2, CSB.

8: Genesis 1:11 Interpreting Current Issues with a Biblical Worldview

• ***After the Flood, the diet was meat and plants.*** Although the original design in Genesis 1 was for diet to be plant-based, now post-Flood, meat was permitted. There was no mention as to which diet was better; both are allowed, and we see that the rest of the way in the Bible. The lifespan will also radically shorten post-Flood. Thus, this is a key change in instructions. Humans are to take care of the animals, but the animals are also edible. God does not explain why.

"Every creature that lives and moves will be food for you; as I gave the green plants, I have given you everything." Genesis 9:3, CSB.

• ***Blood should be drained from the animal prior to cooking.***
"However, you must not eat meat with its lifeblood in it." Genesis 9:4, CSB.

• ***No murder—notice that an animal killing a human was also considered wrong. This is why we euthanize animals if they behave out of character and are dangerous to people. God also allows for capital punishment post-Flood. He says that is necessary when murder occurs to maintain the sanctity of a human life.***
"And I will require a penalty for your lifeblood; I will require it from any animal and from any human; if someone murders a fellow human, I will require that person's life. Whoever sheds human blood, by humans his blood will be shed, for God made humans in his image." Genesis 9:5-6, CSB.

• ***God urges us to be productive.***
"But you, be fruitful and multiply; spread out over the earth and multiply on it." Genesis 9:7, CSB.

Questions:

1. What is Noah commended for?

2. If you are a member of the Armed Forces and a war breaks out and the enemy attacks and you shoot and kill that enemy is that considered to be a breach of the Ten Commandment number 5 "Do not murder." - Exodus 20:13 CSB?

3. Is an abortion performed for no medical reason (NMR) considered murder?

4. Why do governments (state and federal) put limits (or sometimes totally ban) on how many animals can be harvested each year?

5. Why did God change the dietary allowance?

6. In some states in the US a criminal can get the death penalty. Typically, this is for intentional murder. Is there any Biblical support for this?

7. On July 31, 2021, an engineer working in a remote forest in Alberta, Canada was mauled to death by a black bear. The attack was unprovoked. The bear was euthanized. In the summer of 2022, a buffalo in Yellowstone Park gored a woman tourist who was trying to get a close-up picture. The buffalo was not killed by rangers. What is the difference between these two stories?

Questions with suggested answers:

1. What is Noah commended for?

Answer: His faith. "By faith Noah, after he was warned about what was not yet seen and motivated by godly fear, built an ark to deliver his family. By faith he condemned the world and became an heir of the righteousness that comes by faith." - Hebrews 11:7 CSB. I am sure that this command to build the Ark for an upcoming flood when it had never rained was difficult for Noah to understand. But he trusted God and did as he as told. It worked out well for him and the other 7.

2. If you are a member of the Armed Forces and a war breaks out and the enemy attacks and you shoot and kill that enemy is that considered to be a breach of the Ten Commandment number 5 "Do not murder." - Exodus 20:13 CSB?

Answer: Murder is different than killing. The commandment in Hebrew is best translated murder in English. Some translations such as the King James Version of 1612 translate it "Thou shalt not kill." - Exodus 20:13 KJV but the better term is murder or homicide or premeditated killing of someone. In Romans 13 Paul talks about the role of governments to do this work rather than people individually or the Church. Here is the passage – "Let everyone submit to *the governing authorities*, since there is no authority except from God, and the authorities that exist are instituted by God. So then, the one who resists the authority is opposing God's command, and those who oppose it will bring judgment on themselves. For rulers are not a terror to good conduct, but to bad. Do you want to be unafraid of the authority? Do what is good, and you will have its approval. For it is God's servant for your good. But if you do wrong, be afraid, because it does not carry the sword for no reason. For it is God's servant, an avenger that brings wrath on the one who does wrong." - Romans 13:1-4 CSB. What this means is that when war breaks out and the President orders the Armed Forces into battle you are following governments orders. Now, if you still feel guilty and your conscience bothers you the government will allow you to serve in a capacity where you will not need to bear arms or kill. Examples would be a medic or other support staff. A good movie about this topic is "Hacksaw Ridge" which tells the WWII story of the noncombatant Desmond Doss.

3. Is an abortion performed for no medical reason (NMR) considered murder?

Answer: Decisions about abortion should be made with careful counseling considering the mother, the baby, and the father. There are abortions for medical reasons and those without a medical reason. There are vast differences and that is why a team approach is ideal. Abortions for medical conditions in the woman and/or the child are complex and need to be handled with care by the medical team. This team would include specialists in neonatology, pediatrics, high-risk obstetrics, and those informed about the mother or child's medical condition. Also on the team are genetic, spiritual, and social counselors if desired. The decision to abort is decided on a case-by-case basis in the privacy of the medical office. These decisions are serious and should be protected.

The situation of a woman seeking an abortion *without a medical reason* in the woman or baby is the more common situation. We call these NMR abortions (abortions for *no medical reason*) to clearly articulate the situation and how it is different. NMR abortion is a complex subject because it always has a moral aspect and in many states there is a legal aspect. Even in a state or country where there are no laws on abortion, every abortion still involves 4 people – the man who got the woman pregnant; the woman who is pregnant; the baby whose rights are linked to the other 3 people; and the health care team (doctors, nurses, pharmacists etc.) that participate in an NMR abortion. From the Bible we understand the concept that God recognizes personhood and purpose while the fetal human is in utero. This is specifically mentioned in 7 cases - Ishmael (Gen 16:11), Jeremiah (Jeremiah 1:4-5), Samson (Judges 13:5), King David (Psalm 139:15-16), John the Baptist (Luke 1), Jesus (Isaiah 49:1, 5; Luke 1), and the Apostle Paul (Galatians 1:15). Although the unborn child is the subject of this debate, it's survival rests with the mother. As of 2023, current law in my state of residence (Minnesota) allows abortion and considers it legal; so, from a legal standpoint, an NMR abortion would not be considered murder. From a moral standpoint it is considered taking a human life by many people.

We as a society remain very conflicted about NMR abortion. For example, in some states if a woman purposely injures her baby while pregnant with drugs or alcohol, she can be charged with child abuse. A woman who delivers the baby live then immediately disposes of it in a river is charged with murder. If a person injures a woman and the unborn baby suffers damage or dies the perpetrator can be charged with murder or manslaughter. The health care team also has a "right of conscience" in these cases. What is meant by this law (Right of Conscience law (https://www.hhs.gov/conscience/conscience-protections/index.html) is that although a woman many want an NMR abortion, she may find it difficult to find a pharmacist to give the pills for a chemical abortion or find a doctor and nurse team to do the abortion. Many doctors and nurses and hospitals want no part of NMR abortions because of the moral aspects thus most abortions are outsourced to a few outpatient clinics. As of January 2023, as the criteria for an abortion are being revamped state by state, the national opinion is that most people *feel* it should be legal for all but most personally feel for them it is immoral. Thus, they do not want to impose their morals on others. That is why people vote to permit abortion, but when it comes to themselves, they would not want to be the person conducting the abortion nor would they necessarily want an NMR abortion themselves. Physicians and nurses and pharmacists do not want to be required or ordered to perform NMR abortions. This battle will never go away because it involves death. So, what should we do? As a physician I feel that abortion counseling for medical issues must remain within the confines of the doctor/patient relationship and private. Each case is complex, and the health of the mother and her opinion is vital. I also think that we must now accept that because of the legal (or lack thereof) and moral aspects of NMR abortion, that it will remain with us forever. The rights of patients and the health care team should be respected, and no one forced to facilitate a NMR abortion. It is also time to shift the conversation to prevention. We need to raise the value of the baby and increase our prevention efforts on both men and women to avoid unwanted pregnancies. This will require efforts in the area of prevention. We also must respect right of conscience in our health care workers and hospitals.

4. Why do governments (state and federal) put limits (or sometimes totally ban) on how many animals (such as fish and deer) can be harvested each year?

Answer: Let's use the example of deer. In Minnesota where I live the Department of Natural Resources divides the state into hunting zones. Each year they set limits on how many deer can be harvested by hunters. They do this to manage the herd. If the herd becomes too large, then the deer wander onto roads and are killed by vehicles. Overcrowding also breeds disease. This is sound practice and complies with God's commands in Genesis 9:2 "The fear and terror of you will be in every living creature on the earth, every bird of the sky, every creature that crawls on the ground, and all the fish of the sea. They are placed under your authority." - Genesis 9:2 CSB Can you give other examples? Perhaps discuss management of the gray wolf population on Isle Royale – it is a good example of how humans are managing animals (see https://www.nps.gov/isro/learn/nature/wolves.htm).

5. Why did God change the dietary allowance?

Answer: Compare Genesis 1:29-30 with Genesis 9:3. When sin entered the Garden of Eden a blood sacrifice was required to make animal skins to clothe Adam and Eve. Why God chose blood as a sacrifice is unclear, but blood shed became the sacrifice required in the Old Testament. Jesus became the ultimate blood sacrifice when He died on the cross for all of our sins. At that time, animal sacrifice merely for sin thankfully ended. God also allowed animals to be used for meat. However, God is not picky about what you eat – it's your choice and you should obey your conscience. We are to accept people no matter what they eat and not argue about it. "Accept anyone who is weak in faith, but don't argue about disputed matters. One person believes he may eat anything, while one who is weak eats only vegetables. One who eats must not look down on one who does not eat, and one who does not eat must not judge one who does, because God has accepted him." - Romans 14:1-3 CSB.

6. In some states in the US a criminal can get the death penalty. Typically, this is for intentional murder. Is there any Biblical support for this?

Answer: Yes, this law or idea of capital punishment comes from "And I will require a penalty for your lifeblood; I will require it from any animal and from any human; if someone murders a fellow human, I will require that person's life." - Genesis 9:5 CSB. Capital punishment by lethal injection, firing squad, hanging or electricity is quite controversial in the US. In February 2018 Nikolis Cruz murdered 17 people at Florida's Marjory Stoneman Douglas High School. He was convicted and the jury had to decide whether to give him life in prison without parole or the death penalty. The state of Florida does allow the death penalty. In October 2022 the jury decided on life imprisonment. These are difficult decisions, and one must obey their conscience. In fact, this is a good example of the "right of conscience". Even if he had been given the death penalty many pharmaceutical companies will not sell the drugs for lethal injection to prisons out of a "conscience objection" and many doctors will not participate. It somewhat depends on the situation. Few had compassion on the Nazi war criminals who murdered millions of Jews in WWII. After the Nuremberg trials they were hanged.

7. On July 31, 2021, an engineer working in a remote forest in Alberta, Canada was mauled to death by a black bear. The attack was unprovoked. The bear was euthanized. In the summer of 2022, a buffalo in Yellowstone Park gored a woman tourist who was trying to get a close-up picture. The buffalo was not killed by rangers. What is the difference between these two stories?

Answer: "And I will require a penalty for your lifeblood; I will require it from any animal and from any human; if someone murders a fellow human, I will require that person's life." - Genesis 9:5 CSB. This verse applies to animals too. But we use our heads. In the first case, the woman was doing her job and not getting in the way of the bear when the bear instigated the attack. It was unprovoked. In the second case, a flock of tourists were basically in the "buffalo's territory" and getting in the way of their herd. In this case, the humans were the problem – they had disobeyed all posted warnings about getting too close to the buffalo. Thus, the humans were to blame, and the buffalo were appropriately spared any punishment. This is key – God gives humans responsibility to manage wildlife – we need to take that responsibility seriously.

What covenant (agreement) did God make with Noah and what does it mean for us today? Genesis 9.

• ***The Covenant was with Noah and with the animal kingdom— "never again will there be a universal flood"; God cares a lot about the animal world.***
"Then God said to Noah and his sons with him, 'Understand that I am establishing my covenant with you and your descendants after you, and with every living creature that is with you -- birds, livestock, and all wildlife of the earth that are with you -- all the animals of the earth that came out of the ark. I establish my covenant with you that never again will every creature be wiped out by floodwaters; there will never again be a flood to destroy the earth.'" - Genesis 9:8-11 CSB

8: Genesis 1:11 Interpreting Current Issues with a Biblical Worldview

- ***The rainbow is a sign that this covenant is true and enduring.***

"And God said, 'This is the sign of the covenant I am making between me and you and every living creature with you, a covenant for all future generations: I have placed my bow in the clouds, and it will be a sign of the covenant between me and the earth. Whenever I form clouds over the earth and the bow appears in the clouds, I will remember my covenant between me and you and all the living creatures: water will never again become a flood to destroy every creature. The bow will be in the clouds, and I will look at it and remember the permanent covenant between God and all the living creatures on earth.' God said to Noah, 'This is the sign of the covenant that I have established between me and every creature on earth.'" Genesis 9:12-17, CSB.

- ***The earth's population was restored from the three sons of Noah.***

"Noah's sons who came out of the ark were Shem, Ham, and Japheth. Ham was the father of Canaan. *These three were Noah's sons, and from them the whole earth was populated.*" Genesis 9:18-19, CSB.

- ***Noah's occupation is agriculture.***

"Noah, as a man of the soil, began by planting a vineyard." Genesis 9:20, CSB.

Questions:

1. What should you think of when you see a rainbow?

2. How many colors in the rainbow?

3. Who did God make the covenant with?

Questions with suggested answers:

1. What should you think of when you see a rainbow?

Answer: Rainbows usually are seen after a storm. They are a lovely sight, often brief, but a beautiful reminder that God is still there reminding us that His covenant to never again send a universal flood. There will be local floods but never a universal flood.

2. How many colors in the rainbow?

Answer: 7 and this is easy to remember with the mnemonic "ROYGBIV" – red, orange, yellow, green, blue, indigo, and violet. The wavelength ranges from 780-622 nm for red to the shortest violet at 455-390 nm.

3. Who did God make the covenant with?

Answer: All people *and* animals. "Understand that I am establishing my covenant with you and your descendants after you, and with every living creature that is with you -- birds, livestock, and all wildlife of the earth that are with you -- all the animals of the earth that came out of the ark." - Genesis 9:9-10 CSB. This was an "unconditional covenant" in that it was one-sided – God with us and the animals and it did not require anything of us.

How to handle an embarrassing situation—Genesis 9.

• *Noah consumes the fruit of the vine and, likely innocently, becomes under the influence of the alcohol, and is unaware of his actions.*
"Noah, as a man of the soil, began by planting a vineyard. He drank some of the wine, became drunk, and uncovered himself inside his tent." Genesis 9:20-21, CSB.

• *Ham exposes the embarrassing situation. Shem and Japheth refuse to look and work to minimize the shameful situation.*
"Ham, the father of Canaan, saw the nakedness of his father, and told his two brothers outside. But Shem and Japheth took a garment and laid it on both their shoulders and walked backward and covered the nakedness of their father; and their faces were turned away, so that they did not see their father's nakedness." - Genesis 9:22-23 NASB20

• *Noah's reaction is strong against Ham, but he interestingly takes it out more on Ham's son Canaan. This is the first recorded curse on a human. Unfortunately, our offspring often pay for the sins of the father.*
"When Noah awoke from his wine, he knew what his youngest son had done to him. So he said, 'Cursed be Canaan; A servant of servants He shall be to his brothers.' He also said, 'Blessed be the LORD, The God of Shem; And may Canaan be his servant.' May God enlarge Japheth, And may he live in the tents of Shem; And may Canaan be his servant." - Genesis 9:24-27 NASB20

• *Noah still lives a total of 950 years, 350 which were after the universal Flood.*
"Noah lived 350 years after the flood. So all the days of Noah were 950 years, and he died." - Genesis 9:28-29 NASB20

Table 6: Summary of Genesis 9

Noah is told to be fruitful and multiply
Origin of animal fear; animals naturally fear humans for the most part
Diet can be meat (bloodless) and plants – it is personal choice
Sanctity of human life because humans are made in the image of God
Purpose and meaning of the rainbow
Implications of covering vs exposing sin
Mind altering drugs can cause unwanted behavior

Questions:

1. What is the lesson of the story of Noah and his intoxication?

2. What is the difference between covering up a sin and exposing it but not embellishing it?

3. When is it important to expose sin?

4. Note in the story how Shem and Japheth avoided viewing Noah's private body parts. Why was and still is viewing someone's private parts considered wrong? Compare this situation with Noah and what happened to Adam and Eve after they sinned.

5. The punishment for Ham's reaction to his father's drunkenness fell on his son Canaan (the Canaanites). What became of them?

Questions with suggested answers:

1. What is the lesson of the story of Noah and his intoxication?

Answer: This was an embarrassing situation for Noah. It is possible that he did not understand the potency of alcohol on the brain. In any event, while drunk he was not aware of his surroundings, something he would never do with a sound mind. We have all heard of situations like this when a child or even an adult will do something unusual and out of character when intoxicated. Sometimes these situations are merely embarrassing but do not actually hurt anyone. Other times they are deadly such as when someone drives while intoxicated and kills another person.

2. What is the difference between covering up a sin and exposing it but not embellishing it?

Answer: This story does illustrate how although we do not excuse the wrong, we should try to minimize the harm. Shem and Japheth minimized the embarrassment whereas Ham participated in it. What do we do when we hear of an embarrassing situation? Do we put it out on social media and perpetuate it? Or, like Shem and Japheth do we keep it quiet and help the person through it. There is an old saying, "public sin, public confession; private sin, private confession". The point is that we should not cover up a sin, especially if someone has been hurt or property damaged, or the law was involved. There are other sins where the problem was discovered and dealt with privately. There is not always a need to expose it on social media where the person is shamed. This was the point of this story.

3. When is it important to expose sin?

Answer: When you are observing people doing wrong, especially when that wrongdoing hurts other innocent people, we are to expose the wrong. A good recent example of this was the case of Theranos. This was a company started by Elizabeth Holmes to perform blood tests on a small drop of blood. It appeared to be an exciting advance, but it was built on false data. Employees Tyler Schultz and Erika Cheung working at the company first reported this to Ms. Holmes, but she declined to listen and went on with the deception. They then became "whistleblowers" and exposed the wrongdoing and she and her colleague were convicted. The bravery of the whistleblowers saved harm to patients. This wrongdoing needed to be exposed.

4. Note in the story how Shem and Japheth avoided viewing Noah's private body parts. Why was and still is viewing someone's private parts considered wrong? Compare this situation with Noah and what happened to Adam and Eve after they sinned.

"Then the eyes of both of them were opened, and they knew they were naked; so they sewed fig leaves together and made coverings for themselves." - Genesis 3:7 CSB

Answer: Exposing our private parts to people other than our spouse remains shameful. The sense of shame came with the curse following Adam and Eve's sin. Some people seem to have lost this sense of shame and dress provocatively in public. We need to consider the feelings of others when we decide how to dress in public. What types of photos do you share with others? What do you wear to the beach? We are never to take advantage of a person with photos or bodily harm when they are unconscious due to medical reasons.

5. The punishment for Ham's reaction to his father's drunkenness fell on his son Canaan (the Canaanites). What became of them?

Answer: The Canaanites were a people group that behaved in an evil way. Moses warned the Israelites about them. "The LORD spoke to Moses: 'Speak to the Israelites and tell them: I am the LORD your God. Do not follow the practices of the land of Egypt, where you used to live, or follow the practices of the land of Canaan, where I am bringing you. You must not follow their customs. You are to practice my ordinances and you are to keep my statutes by following them; I am the LORD your God. Keep my statutes and ordinances; a person will live if he does them. I am the LORD.'" - Leviticus 18:1-5 CSB. Recent genetic studies of skeletons have been conducted and compared with the genes of the current peoples of Lebanon. The study showed genetic similarity indicating that "present-day" Lebanese derive most of their ancestry from a Canaanite-related population, which therefore implies substantial genetic continuity in the Levant since at least the Bronze Age.[3]

The "Table of Nations"- where we all came from — Genesis 10.

Thomas Constable says in his commentary on Genesis 10 (https://www.planobiblechapel.org/tcon/notes/html/ot/genesis/genesis.htm accessed January 13, 2023) "This chapter contains one of the oldest, if not the oldest, ethnological table in the literature of the ancient world. It reveals a remarkable understanding of the ethnic and linguistic situation following the Flood. Almost all the names in this chapter have been found in archaeological discoveries in the last century and a half. Many of them appear in subsequent books of the Old Testament.... In contrast to the genealogy in chapter 5, this one lists no ages. It contains place and group names, which are spoken of as the antecedents of other places or groups, as well as the names of individuals. God built nations from families. Thus it is quite clearly a selective list, not comprehensive. The writer's choice of material shows that he had a particular interest in presenting Israel's neighbors. Israel would deal with, displace, or subjugate many of these peoples, as well as the Canaanites (ch. 9). They all had a common origin. Evidently 70 nations descended from Shem, Ham, and Japheth: 26 from Shem, 30 from Ham, and 14 from Japheth (cf. Deut. 32:8). Seventy became a traditional round number for a large group of descendants.[598] Jacob's family also comprised 70 people (46:27), which may indicate that Moses viewed Israel as a microcosm of humanity, as he presented it here. God set the microcosm (Israel) apart to bless the macrocosm (all of humanity)."

After the Flood, the families of Shem, Ham and Japheth spread out. "These are the clans of Noah's sons, according to their family records, in their nations. The nations on earth spread out from these after the flood." - Genesis 10:32 CSB Each developed a different culture, and language as described in Genesis 10. *All people groups today are descendants of one of these 3 families.* It is important to note that Chapter 10 events actually happened after Chapter 11 (the Tower of Babel judgement) when the people were scattered, and different languages developed. Not understanding this makes it difficult to reconcile Genesis 10:5 with 11:1 "The whole earth had the same language and vocabulary." - Genesis 11:1 CSB.

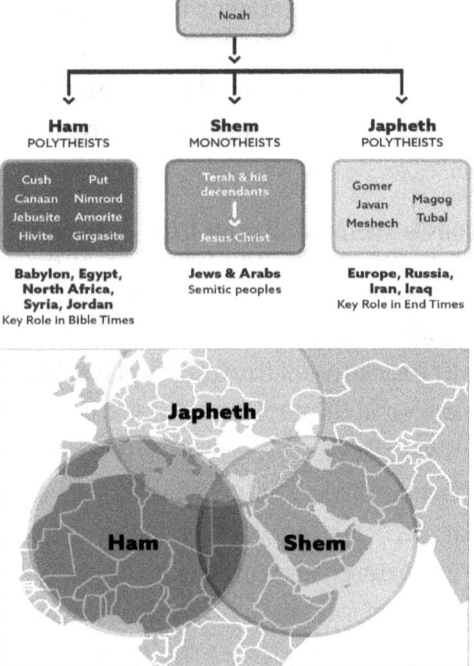

Figure 11: A. Descendants of Noah – from which of the three sons are you descended from? B. The general geographic location of where they each spread to.

8: Genesis 1:11 Interpreting Current Issues with a Biblical Worldview

"These are the family records of Noah's sons, Shem, Ham, and Japheth. They also had sons after the flood." - Genesis 10:1 CSB

• *Descendants of Japheth. Notice the beginning of languages here.*
"Japheth's sons: Gomer, Magog, Madai, Javan, Tubal, Meshech, and Tiras. Gomer's sons: Ashkenaz, Riphath, and Togarmah. And Javan's sons: Elishah, Tarshish, Kittim, and Dodanim. From these descendants, the peoples of the coasts and islands spread out into their lands according to their clans in their nations, *each with its own language.*" - Genesis 10:2-5 CSB

• *Descendants of Ham; Nimrod the powerful hunter; father of Babylon (Iraq). Notice the development of occupations. The descendants of Ham – the Egyptians and Philistines became enemies of the descendants of Shem and Japheth.*
Genesis 10:6-14 CSB

• *Canaanites.*
Genesis 10:15-20 CSB

• *Shem: note that in verse 25 the genealogy of Peleg stops here, and the story diverts to Joktan. It is left to the second lineage in Genesis 11 to trace out Peleg's role as ancestral father of Abraham (Constable page 153-54).*
Genesis 10:21-31 CSB

• *Where did we come from? All of us here today descended from this Table of Nations. We trace back to Noah and Noah carries the genes from Adam and Eve.*
"These are the clans of Noah's sons, according to their family records, in their nations. The nations on earth spread out from these after the flood." Genesis 10:32, CSB.

Questions:

1. Do you find chapter 10 boring? What is the key reason for including it and for our understanding people groups today?

2. What is the difference between race and cultural practices?

3. What does the Bible say about equality?

Thomas Witzig

Questions with suggested answers:

1. Do you find chapter 10 boring? What is the key reason for including it and for our understanding people groups today?

Answer: This chapter is referred to as the Table of Nations. It is solid data demonstrating our common ancestry from the three sons of Noah that emerged with their parents from the ark. Since we have a common ancestry, then there is no reason for discrimination by race – we are all related!! We have a common Creator and a common ancestry. Adam to Seth to Noah to Shem, Ham, and Japheth and to the rest of the world.

2. What is the difference between race and cultural practices?

Answer: All of us can trace our relatives back to Shem, Ham, or Japheth. The Apostle Paul in his great lecture in Athens at the Areopagus said, "From one man he has made every nationality to live over the whole earth and has determined their appointed times and the boundaries of where they live. He did this so that they might seek God, and perhaps they might reach out and find him, though he is not far from each one of us." - Acts 17:26-27 CSB.

Since many years have gone by, genetic analysis of our DNA will show bits of DNA from many different groups. You can find this out yourself by having your DNA analyzed. You may think of yourself as a Norwegian-American but when you look at your DNA you may be surprised where your ancestors were really from. This DNA will inform our phenotype – what we look like to others. Our phenotype is what often becomes a source of discrimination. As the relatives of Shem, Ham and Japheth spread out around the globe they acquired different languages, religions, and cultural practices such as music, art, food choices etc. These differences often enrich our lives and make them more colorful and interesting. If we try to always place people into categories, its becomes difficult. Do we classify by genetics (which we do not even know)? By skin color which is obvious? By where they are from or live? *That is why from a Biblical perspective God made it simple – we all have a common ancestry and are all equal in His eyes.* We indeed live in a diverse world and these differences are important to understand so that we can live and relate and enjoy each other. If we are to do business or missions or medicine on an international scale, we will leaders and employees that know the customs and language of those areas. Can you think of areas where diversity is important to team building? Think of forming a basketball team? How about recruiting people to work on a submarine.

3. What does the Bible say about equality?

Answer: It is very clear and quotable.

"In Christ there is not Greek and Jew, circumcision and uncircumcision, barbarian, Scythian, slave and free; but Christ is all and in all." - Colossians 3:11 CSB

"For there is no favoritism with God." - Romans 2:11 CSB Billy Graham a prominent evangelist of the 20th century once said: "Jesus was not a white man; He was not a black man. He came from that part of the world that touches Africa and Asia and Europe. Christianity is not a white man's religion and don't let anybody ever tell you that it's white or black. Christ belongs to all people; He belongs to the whole world." https://billygraham.org/story/5-responses-from-billy-graham-on-race-social-inequality/ accessed October 11, 2022.

In God's eyes we are equal with respect to our origins. This forms the basis for our US Constitution. We want to be treated as equals and be treated fairly when it comes to opportunities for jobs and college. This concept of equality with respect to race led to the Supreme Court decision on STUDENTS FOR FAIR ADMISSIONS, INC. v. PRESIDENT AND FELLOWS OF HARVARD COLLEGE. This case was argued October 31, 2022, and decided June 29, 2023. The Court ruled that the use of race in the decision to admit a student was wrong and violated the Equal Protection Clause of the Fourteenth Amendment. Pp. 6–40. You can read the entire opinion at https://www.supremecourt.gov › opinions › 22pdf 20-1199_hgdj.pdf

How did the different languages develop? Why is the development of languages at the Tower of Babel a major historical event? —Genesis 11:1-9.

Professor Thomas Constable provides important insight on Genesis 11:1-9 ((https://planobiblechapel.org/soniclight/ quoting page 428 of Mathews, Kenneth A. Genesis 1—11:26. New American Commentary series. N.C.: Broadman & Holman Publishers, 1996) "The Tower of Babel incident (11:1-9), though following the table in the present literary arrangement, actually precedes chronologically the dispersal of the nations. This interspersal of narrative (11:1-9) separates the two genealogies of Shem (10:21-31; 11:10-26), paving the way for the particular linkage between the Terah (Abraham) clan and the Shemite lineage (11:27). The story of the tower also looks ahead by anticipating the role that Abram (12:1-3) will play in restoring the blessing to the dispersed nations."

- ***The people post-Flood had one language up until this time.***
"The whole earth had the same language and vocabulary." - Genesis 11:1 CSB

- ***They then begin to sin by building this tower (ziggurat) which was actually an idol and thus an affront to God. Their goal was to be free from God.***
"As people migrated from the east, they found a valley in the land of Shinar and settled there. They said to each other, 'Come, let's make oven-fired bricks.' (They used brick for stone and asphalt for mortar.) And they said, 'Come, let's build ourselves a city and a tower with its top in the sky. Let's make a name for ourselves; otherwise, we will be scattered throughout the earth.'" - Genesis 11:2-4 CSB

- ***They were aiming to build upwards to God; He came down to them.***
Thomas Constable writes, "The sin of the builders was disobedience to God and probably idol worship or worship of gods. Sending judgment upon them for trying to establish a world state in opposition to divine rule (human government run amuck), God struck the thing that bound people together, namely, a common language."

"But the LORD came down to look at the city and the tower the people were building. 'Look!' he said. 'The people are united, and *they all speak the same language*. After this, nothing they set out to do will be impossible for them! Come, *let's go down and confuse the people with different languages*. Then they won't be able to understand each other.' In that way, the LORD scattered them all over the world, and they stopped building the city." - Genesis 11:5-8 NLT

- ***This multiplicity of languages was one of the three major judgements on humankind.***
The first was the Fall of Adam/Eve of Gen 3 and the resulting physical consequences to all Creation. The second was the universal Flood of Noah triggered by the extensive wickedness in the world. Then the third judgement was to scramble the languages leading to the dispersion of people groups and the development of different races and cultures that we observe today.

"That is why the city was called Babel, because that is where the LORD confused the people with different languages. In this way he scattered them all over the world." - Genesis 11:9 NLT

Question with Suggested Answer:

What are the implications of the Tower of Babel judgement (the scrambling of languages) for the issues of today?

Answer: When the people scattered, they naturally grouped themselves with other people who were speaking the same language. These people groups developed into the many people groups with their unique languages and customs (diet, dress etc.) that we see today. The variety of cultures makes travel interesting, and we enjoy the different cuisine. However, the multiplicity of languages remains a major issue today. I was referred a patient who had migrated to the US from Myanmar. She had cancer and spoke minimal English. My interview and exam were becoming impossible because of the communication issues. I then remembered that we had a physician in training from Myanmar. I paged him and asked him to come and help me with the patient. He came into the room and began to speak to the patient in the Burmese language. She and her family immediately brightened up and started chattering to him in a language completely unintelligible to me, but wonderfully clear to them. This problem of languages is due to a judgment on us from God that dates back to Genesis 11. What other problems or issues do you observe with these many languages? What does it mean for Bible translation?

The start of the Hebrew story - Genesis 11:10-32.

After the universal flood judgement, 8 people emerged from the Ark. We thus have a common race as defined by the gene pool of these 8 people. Since the purpose of the Bible is to tell the story of Jesus from start to finish, the story now narrows in its focus on Shem and his line of Semitic people that will eventually result in the birth of Jesus. The Bible is history, but it was never meant to be a comprehensive history of the world. That is why there are gaps in the story that skip over huge chunks of time. Moses focuses the story on getting us to Abraham and eventually Jesus. Why? Because God needed to show us that Jesus was the only way for us to be able to be saved from our sin. Humans, animals, and all creation bear the mark of sin and need redemption. That redemption was Jesus. Let's look at the last part of Genesis 11 as this is explained.

- ***Jesus, the Messiah, comes for all of us through the line of Shem, one of Noah's three sons that made it through the Flood. The first recorded lineage from Shem in Genesis 10 stopped at Joktan.***

Thomas Witzig

"And Shem, Japheth's older brother, also had sons. Shem was the father of all the sons of Eber." Genesis 10:21, CSB.

"Eber had two sons. One was named Peleg, for during his days the earth was divided; his brother was named Joktan." Genesis 10:25, CSB.

- *In Genesis Chapter 11, Moses again picks up this narrative after the Tower of Babel story and describes Shem to Abram.*

"These are the family records of Shem. Shem lived 100 years and fathered Arpachshad two years after the flood. After he fathered Arpachshad, Shem lived 500 years and fathered other sons and daughters." - Genesis 11:10-11 CSB

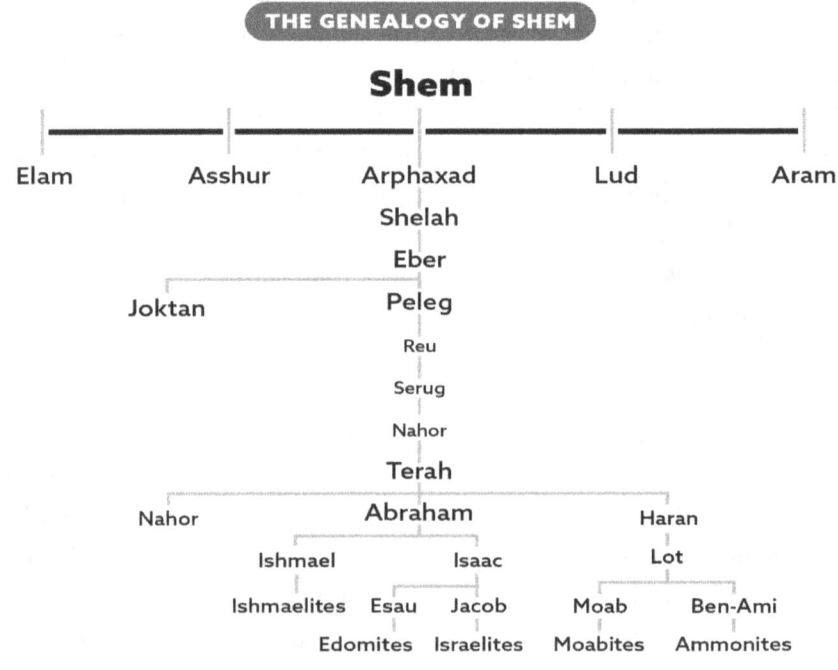

Figure 12: The genealogy of Shem from which Jesus will descend.

- *Eber means "the other side" and refers to people that came from the other side of the Euphrates River (Haran). Eber became Hebrew—the Jewish racial group. Israel today is that nation.*

"Arpachshad lived 35 years and fathered Shelah. After he fathered Shelah, Arpachshad lived 403 years and fathered other sons and daughters. Shelah lived 30 years and fathered

Eber. After he fathered Eber, Shelah lived 403 years and fathered other sons and daughters. Eber lived 34 years and fathered Peleg. After he fathered Peleg, Eber lived 430 years and fathered other sons and daughters. Peleg lived 30 years and fathered Reu. After he fathered Reu, Peleg lived 209 years and fathered other sons and daughters. Reu lived 32 years and fathered Serug. After he fathered Serug, Reu lived 207 years and fathered other sons and daughters. Serug lived 30 years and fathered Nahor. After he fathered Nahor, Serug lived 200 years and fathered other sons and daughters. Nahor lived 29 years and fathered Terah." - Genesis 11:12-24 CSB

- *Shem to Eber to Terah to Abram.*

"After he fathered Terah, Nahor lived 119 years and fathered other sons and daughters. Terah lived 70 years and fathered Abram, Nahor, and Haran." - Genesis 11:25-26 CSB

- *Abram migrates from Babylon (Iraq) to Haran (Turkey) to Shechem (Israel).*

"These are the family records of Terah. Terah fathered Abram, Nahor, and Haran, and Haran fathered Lot. Haran died in his native land, in Ur of the Chaldeans, during his father Terah's lifetime. Abram and Nahor took wives: Abram's wife was named Sarai, and Nahor's wife was named Milcah. She was the daughter of Haran, the father of both Milcah and Iscah. Sarai was unable to conceive; she did not have a child. Terah took his son Abram, his grandson Lot (Haran's son), and his daughter-in-law Sarai, his son Abram's wife, and they set out together from Ur of the Chaldeans to go to the land of Canaan. But when they came to Haran, they settled there. Terah lived 205 years and died in Haran." - Genesis 11:27-32 CSB

Summary: Genesis 1-11 happened in Babylonia (the country of Iraq today). Now, after this third judgment (confusion of peoples by different languages), God selects Abram and his family to birth two nations—Isaac (Israel) and Ishmael (Arabs). Thomas Constable says, "God now places his hope in a covenant with Abraham as a powerful solution to humanity's sinfulness. Thus problem (Ch. 11) and solution (Ch. 12) are brought into immediate juxtaposition". Genesis 12-36 will take place in the area of Palestine and Genesis 37-50 in Egypt.

These first 11 chapters are foundational to the rest of the Bible. After reading them, we now understand many key themes that are relevant to today. Having a solid understanding of Genesis 1-11 will help to understand the news and the issues people and nations are battling today.

• *So where do we go from here? In Genesis 12 God calls Abram to leave Haran and go to Canaan where the nations of Israel and Ismael are born.*

"The LORD said to Abram: Go out from your land, your relatives, and your father's house to the land that I will show you. I will make you into a great nation, I will bless you, I will make your name great, and you will be a blessing. I will bless those who bless you, I will curse anyone who treats you with contempt, and all the peoples on earth will be blessed through you. So Abram went, as the LORD had told him, and Lot went with him. Abram was seventy-five years old when he left Haran." - Genesis 12:1-4 CSB

Questions:

1. What are the three key judgements described in Genesis 1-11 and what are the implications for today?

2. What does your family tree look like? Where did your ancestors come from and where are they at today? Shem, Ham, or Japheth? Does it matter and why?

Questions with suggested answers:

1. What are the three key judgements described in Genesis 1-11 and what are the implications for today?

Answer: 1. Sin enters the world with Adam and Eve and this degrades all of creation – plants and animals and the environment. The result is disease, pain, pestilence, weeds, crime, pollution, polygamy, aging, climate change etc. "For the creation was subjected to futility -- not willingly, but because of him who subjected it -- in the hope that the creation itself will also be set free from the bondage to decay into the glorious freedom of God's children. For we know that the whole creation has been groaning together with labor pains until now." - Romans 8:20-22 CSB. 2. The universal flood and the death of all people except the family of Noah (n=8 people) in the Ark. 3. The Tower of Babel – the scrambling of languages which has left its mark on communication that exists today.

2. What does your family tree look like? Where did your ancestors come from and where are they at today? Shem, Ham, or Japheth? Does it matter and why?

Answer: Individualized

Epilogue

Now that you have finished the book look at **Figure 2** – have you grown spiritually? For sure you are physically older now, but are you also more mature spiritually? I trust that the Word of God has and is working in your life. If you continue to read His Word and follow it, you will make progress in your spiritual life up until you take your last breath on this earth and move to eternity to be with Jesus. I look forward to seeing you there! Remember when you close your eyes in death you will go through your "personal eternal passport control". The example of "your spiritual passport" **(Figure 13)** is a reminder that your entry to Heaven is based on your personal decision to accept Jesus' blood sacrifice for your sins.

You now have a Biblical foundation upon which to tackle the issues discussed in Volume 2. Review the Table of Contents and I trust you will "read on"!

College Prep Volume 2 -- *Key Strategies for Spiritual Growth*

Foreword

Chapter 1: Who am I? Why am I here? Does anybody love me? What is my ultimate hope?

Chapter 2: How to know the will of God.

Chapter 3: Temptation – where does it come from? How to handle it.

Chapter 4: What is a Biblical marriage and Biblical Sex?

Chapter 5: Does God allow freedom of choice?

Chapter 6: Career planning. What should I do with the rest of my life?

Chapter 7: How to have a quiet time in a very loud world.

Chapter 8: Why should I go to church?

Thomas Witzig

Appendix

How to become a Christ follower.

1. Admit we have a problem. We have a sin nature; we were born with it.

We all have at some time in our life committed a sin or sinned in general and thus have fallen short (missed the mark) of perfection.

"For all have sinned and fall short of the glory of God." - Romans 3:23 CSB

2. God requires a sacrifice for our sin, and it is Jesus. Each person must deal with the sin problem in their own lives. Entrance to Heaven requires us to be sinless (like Jesus) *or* have a sacrifice for the sin that we committed. Why? Very early in world history Adam and Eve sinned (Genesis 3) and God required an animal to be sacrificed to provide a covering for that sin. This was the beginning of blood sacrifice for sin. In the Old Testament this was the blood of an animal. God clearly showed us the need for blood in the story of Cain and Abel in Genesis 4. God did not accept Cain's sacrifice of vegetables but did accept Abel's sacrifice of blood. Why? We are not told – it's just the way God set it up. God wants us to go to Heaven, so He made it straightforward – He did not want the killing of animals all the time for sacrifice; so, He sent His own Son, Jesus to earth, Jesus has always been present with God the Father in Heaven. To be the ultimate blood sacrifice, Jesus was sent in the form of a human being to earth; lived a sinless life (so that He would be an acceptable sacrifice) and was crucified so that blood was shed and this blood appeased once for all the sin of all humans. There was an additional requirement - each person needs to *believe in and trust* in the blood sacrifice of Jesus as their *personal Savior* from eternal punishment. This is similar to the Old Testament when people *individually* had to bring the sacrificial animal to the Temple. Or in the case of the Israelites in Egypt they had to apply the blood of the animal on the doorpost of the house to avoid death of the firstborn. Each father had to do it – one household could not do it for the neighborhood. Thus, Jesus sacrificial death was for all people; however, all individually need to accept the gift. Since all of us have committed sin, we need to repent of that sin, accept Christ's sacrifice, and have the righteousness of God credited to our account so that we are considered "right in His sight". This is summarized in Paul's message to the Philippians "...I no longer count on my own righteousness through obeying the law; rather, I become righteous through faith in Christ. For God's way of making us right with himself depends on faith." - Philippians 3:9 NLT or as the CSB says "...not having a righteousness of my own from the law, but one that is through faith in Christ -- *the righteousness from God based on faith.*" - Philippians 3:9 CSB

3. Is there really an afterlife? The Bible says that there is eternity waiting for us after we die. At some point after we die, we are individually judged.

"For it is written, As I live, says the Lord, every knee will bow to me, and every tongue will give praise to God. So then, *each of us will give an account of himself to God.*" - Romans 14:11-12 CSB

Hebrews 4:12-13 CSB

Thus, the goal of having our sins forgiven is to spend eternity with God in Heaven rather than eternal separation from Him. In this earthly life things may not go well for us, and we may suffer greatly; but *eternity will be different.* Paul describes this as "our hope". This hope is based on the resurrection of Christ after He was crucified for our sins.

"If in this life only we have hope in Christ, we are of all men most miserable." - 1 Corinthians 15:19 KJV
1 Corinthians 15:20-22

4. We need to *believe* and *trust* that the blood of Christ will get us into eternity and that requires *faith*.

Jesus said, "Don't let your heart be troubled. *Believe in God; believe also in me.*" - John 14:1 CSB

Since Jesus is not currently on the earth where we can see or touch Him, we cannot definitively prove that believing on Him and trusting Him will get us into Heaven. So, some people struggle with this, and they try to work their way into Heaven. They keep some sort of mental scorecard or spreadsheet that has a column for good works and one for sins. They try to make sure the good outweighs the bad. God wants us to do good works *after* we believe in the sacrifice of Jesus for our sins. They do count for rewards, but they are not in of themselves sufficient for salvation.

Appendix

- ***Belief and trust must be mixed with faith – enough faith to believe in the unseen Jesus, to believe in the Bible's instructions.***

"After all, is God the God of the Jews only? Isn't he also the God of the Gentiles? Of course he is. There is only one God, and *he makes people right with himself only by faith*, whether they are Jews or Gentiles." - Romans 3:29-30 NLT

"Now *faith is the reality of what is hoped for, the proof of what is not seen*. For by it our ancestors won God's approval. By faith we understand that the universe was created by the word of God, so that what is seen was made from things that are not visible." - Hebrews 11:1-3 CSB.

You may say, "its really tough for me to believe that Jesus can get me into Heaven. That's a big slice of faith." But, when you think about it, you do a lot of things by faith without understanding the mechanism. You trust that when you get out of bed that gravity will keep your feet planted on the floor and you will not float up to the ceiling.

5, Grace, not works. Grace is undeserved. When a student gets an answer partially wrong on a test in school the law would say the student gets no credit. However, if the teacher gives the student grace, they will say, "I see that you understood the concept so I will be graceful and let you take credit." In the spiritual realm, grace is the *underserved gift of God* – undeserved because we are not perfect; a gift because it is given by God and must be received. We need God to be graceful to us. "For the wages of sin is death, but the *gift of God* is eternal life in Christ Jesus our Lord." - Romans 6:23 CSB. Good works are not sufficient in and of themselves to get us to heaven because they rely on our own power, and we just do not have enough power to live perfectly. Paul summarizes this in Romans 8 – "*The law of Moses was unable to save us because of the weakness of our sinful nature. So, God did what the law could not do. He sent his own Son in a body like the bodies we sinners have. And in that body God declared an end to sin's control over us by giving his Son as a sacrifice for our sins. He did this so that the just requirement of the law would be fully satisfied for us, who no longer follow our sinful nature but instead follow the Spirit.*" - Romans 8:3-4 NLT

6. Surrender. There is a great natural desire to achieve a goal on our own merits. We live in a merit-based society where are told that achievement comes from hard work and discipline. When it comes to spiritual things, indeed discipline and living a good life is very important but it is not sufficient to achieve Heaven because that requires perfection.

So, we must get the order right – trust Christ's sacrifice for our sin, become a Christian *then* the good works that follow are important.

7. Count the cost before committing to Jesus. Like any project or relationship, we enter into there is a cost and we need to be sure before we commit. There is a cost to following Jesus. The main "costs" are that we cannot do whatever we want, and we may be despised by others for our faith. Examine the words of Jesus as recorded Luke -

"If you want to be my disciple, you must hate everyone else by comparison--your father and mother, wife and children, brothers and sisters--yes, even your own life. Otherwise, you cannot be my disciple. And if you do not carry your own cross and follow me, you cannot be my disciple." *But don't begin until you count the cost. For who would begin construction of a building without first calculating the cost to see if there is enough money to finish it?* Otherwise, you might complete only the foundation before running out of money, and then everyone would laugh at you. They would say, 'There's the person who started that building and couldn't afford to finish it!' "Or what king would go to war against another king without first sitting down with his counselors to discuss whether his army of 10,000 could defeat the 20,000 soldiers marching against him? And if he can't, he will send a delegation to discuss terms of peace while the enemy is still far away. So you cannot become my disciple without giving up everything you own." - Luke 14:26-33 NLT

8. He leads we follow. Where to? We follow Him as He leads us through life's experiences to our Heavenly Home. "Then Jesus said to his disciples, 'If anyone wants to follow after me, let him deny himself, take up his cross, and follow me.'" - Matthew 16:24 CSB

9. Are there other ways to get to Heaven other than through Jesus? "*There is salvation in no one else*, for there is no other name under heaven given to people by which we must be saved." - Acts 4:12 CSB
Acts 15:11, John 10:1

"I am the gate. If anyone enters by me, he will be saved and will come in and go out and find pasture." - John 10:9 CSB

"I -- I am the LORD. Besides me, there is no Savior. 'I alone declared, saved, and proclaimed -- and not some foreign god among you. So you are my witnesses -- this is the LORD's declaration -- and I am God." - Isaiah 43:11-12 CSB
John 3:5

"I have been the LORD your God ever since the land of Egypt; you know no God but me, and no Savior exists besides me." - Hosea 13:4 CSB

10. Benefit package of being a follower of Jesus.

• *Eternal life is our inheritance after we become a Christ-follower.* Remember, we inherit, not earn, eternal life. Our righteousness comes by faith and is a remarkable gift from God. Our sins are erased because of Jesus, not because of a pile of good works. Our account with God is credited with Christ's righteousness and we are now able to inherit eternal life.

"Your reward for trusting him will be the salvation of your souls." 1 Peter 1:9, NLT.

"He declared us not guilty because of his great kindness. And now we know that we will inherit eternal life." Titus 3:7, NLT.
Philippians 3:9

• *We are no longer a slave to sin. We now have an eternal inheritance.*
"And because you are sons, God sent the Spirit of his Son into our hearts, crying, 'Abba, Father!' So you are *no longer a slave but a son*, and if a son, then God has made you an heir." - Galatians 4:6-7 CSB

• *Death has been conquered (destroyed; abolished); we no longer fear death.*
"This has now been made evident through the appearing of our Savior Christ Jesus, who has *abolished death and has brought life and immortality to light through the gospel*." - 2 Timothy 1:10 CSB

• *We are made "right in His sight"*. Claiming the sacrifice of Jesus as the bearer of our sin makes us appear perfect in God's sight.

"And he is entirely fair and just in this present time when he declares sinners to be right in his sight because they believe in Jesus." Romans 3:26, NLT.

- **We get a fresh start, so look forward not backward.**
"Therefore, if anyone is in Christ, *he is a new creation*; the old has passed away, and see, the new has come!" - 2 Corinthians 5:17 CSB

- **We are justified.** Justification is a one-time judicial act where God applies credit from Jesus. We then appear "just as if we never sinned". This is a free gift but not cheap—it cost Jesus much suffering and death.

"They are justified freely by his grace through the redemption that is in Christ Jesus." - Romans 3:24 CSB

- **We have peace with God.**
"Therefore, since we have been declared righteous by faith, *we have peace with God* through our Lord Jesus Christ." - Romans 5:1 CSB

- **We receive the Holy Spirit.** The Holy Spirit is a gift that comes only after conversion. Jesus and the Holy Spirit now help us live a life in accordance to the Scriptures and to do good works. We are justified once but achieving holy living is the ongoing process of sanctification (becoming holy) that is driven by the power of the Holy Spirit.

"Peter replied, 'Each of you must turn from your sins and turn to God, and be baptized in the name of Jesus Christ for the forgiveness of your sins. Then you will receive the gift of the Holy Spirit.'" Acts 2:38, NLT.

In summary, let's put this plan of salvation into the analogy of a passport.

The Spiritual Passport Analogy. When we travel outside of our home country, we need a passport. The passport has our personal information and our photo. It must be up to date and valid. When we enter the new country or return to our home country, we go through a checkpoint called passport control. Each person with passport in hand file one by one to the serious-looking officer in the booth who checks our passport to give permission to enter. They then stamp our passport for approval. When we go through this process, we do it alone; we don't go through with someone else or using someone else's passport. *There is no other way to get into the new country without our individual valid stamped passport*

Using this analogy, when we come to the Eternal Passport Control after we die there are two lines – one line is labeled "for perfect people" and the other is labeled "for sinners".

Appendix

If you ask the angel controlling the lines, "I was a really good person during my life with few sins, can I go to the 'perfect line?" They will say "No, even one sin makes you a 'sinner' and thus you need to go through the line for sinners. We have never seen a perfect person yet." So, the line for sinners is long but it moves fast.

One woman tries to go to the passport manager with her husband and go in under his passport, but she is sent back and told, "each person must come in on their own account". The passport control manager looks quickly through the pages of each person's passport. The officer is looking for a "blood stamp" a blot of blood that has engraved underneath, "the blood of Jesus Christ shed for you" that makes them perfect in God's sight. People that have the blood stamp pass quickly through the gate and move into a great hall with a large sign over it entitled "Heaven". As the door to the Great Hall opens, we get a glimpse of the large crowd of people who are rejoicing as they meet fellow believers and begin their eternity with Jesus. It looks beautiful and full of light.

A man steps to the line with a very thick passport with many pages. As the officer skims through the pages he comments, "I notice that you have been to many countries and have done many good works –feeding the poor, helping orphans and the sick. But I don't see a 'blood stamp'. Where is it?" The man replies, "well I never thought that I needed the blood stamp since I had so many good works." The manager says, "I'm really sorry but the blood stamp is needed." Can I go back and get one the man asks? "No, you have died, and we don't allow people to go back to earth. It's a one-way gate." You will now need to follow the black line to the Hallway marked "Eternal Punishment". In that Hallway there is darkness and no light as the people are separated from God. The exact nature of their punishment is not known but it will not be a happy place.

Someday all of us will die and go through eternal passport control. God has made it really easy to have the acceptable passport for Heaven because there is only One Way to get it. He said the requirement is to acknowledge that we have committed sin, trust in the blood sacrifice of Jesus for that sin; be truly sorry for what we did and turn from it to believe that the blood of Jesus will be enough and live our life for Jesus. That process of being genuinely sorry for our sin and being willing to turn from it is called "repentance". Once we have repented and have received the gift of Christ's sacrifice for our sin our eternal passport is stamped with the Blood Stamp. After that life-changing decision we go about living and working for Christ and adding good works to the other pages of the passport. These will determine our eternal rewards once inside Heaven.

Thomas Witzig

Appendix

Figure 13: This model of a passport is a reminder that to obtain entry into Heaven each person needs to show proof that we have accepted the sacrifice of Jesus, His shed blood on the cross, as the payment for our sin. He has already done this for us but like any gift, it must be opened and accepted by the recipient. Make sure your "spiritual passport" is signed and stamped so that you are ready for eternity.

Other books by Thomas Witzig:

Mostly Scripture Q.D. A Topical Study for Daily Living". Published by BookBaby

Thomas Witzig

www.ingramcontent.com/pod-product-compliance
Lightning Source LLC
Chambersburg PA
CBHW050135170426
43197CB00011B/1848